P9-CQA-562

SAMURAI

HEAVEN AND EARTH

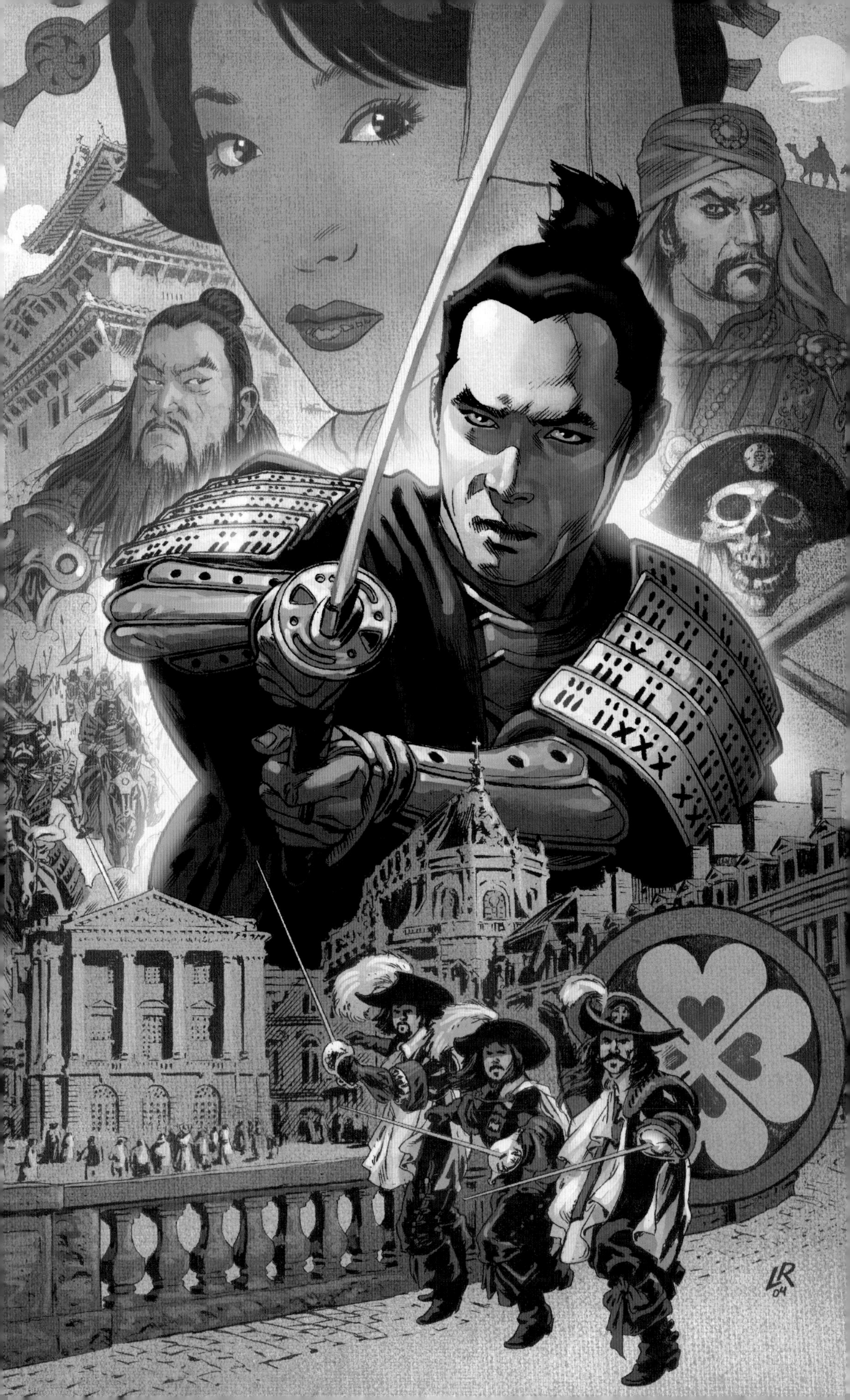

SAMURAI
HEAVEN AND EARTH

Script
RON MARZ

Art
LUKE ROSS

Colors
JASON KEITH

Letters
DAVE LANPHEAR

Cover
LUKE ROSS
and
JASON KEITH

Dark Horse Books™

Publisher
MIKE RICHARDSON

Editor
DAVE LAND

Assistant Editor
KATIE MOODY

Collection Designer
M. JOSHUA ELLIOTT

Art Director
LIA RIBACCHI

Published by
Dark Horse Books
A division of Dark Horse Comics, Inc.
10956 SE Main Street
Milwaukie, OR 97222

darkhorse.com

To find a comics shop in your area, call the Comic Shop Locator
Service toll-free at 1-888-266-4226.

First edition: April 2006
ISBN: 1-59307-388-7

1 3 5 7 9 10 8 6 4 2
Printed in China

SAMURAI: HEAVEN & EARTH™

This book collects issues one through five of the Dark Horse
comic-book series *Samurai: Heaven & Earth*.

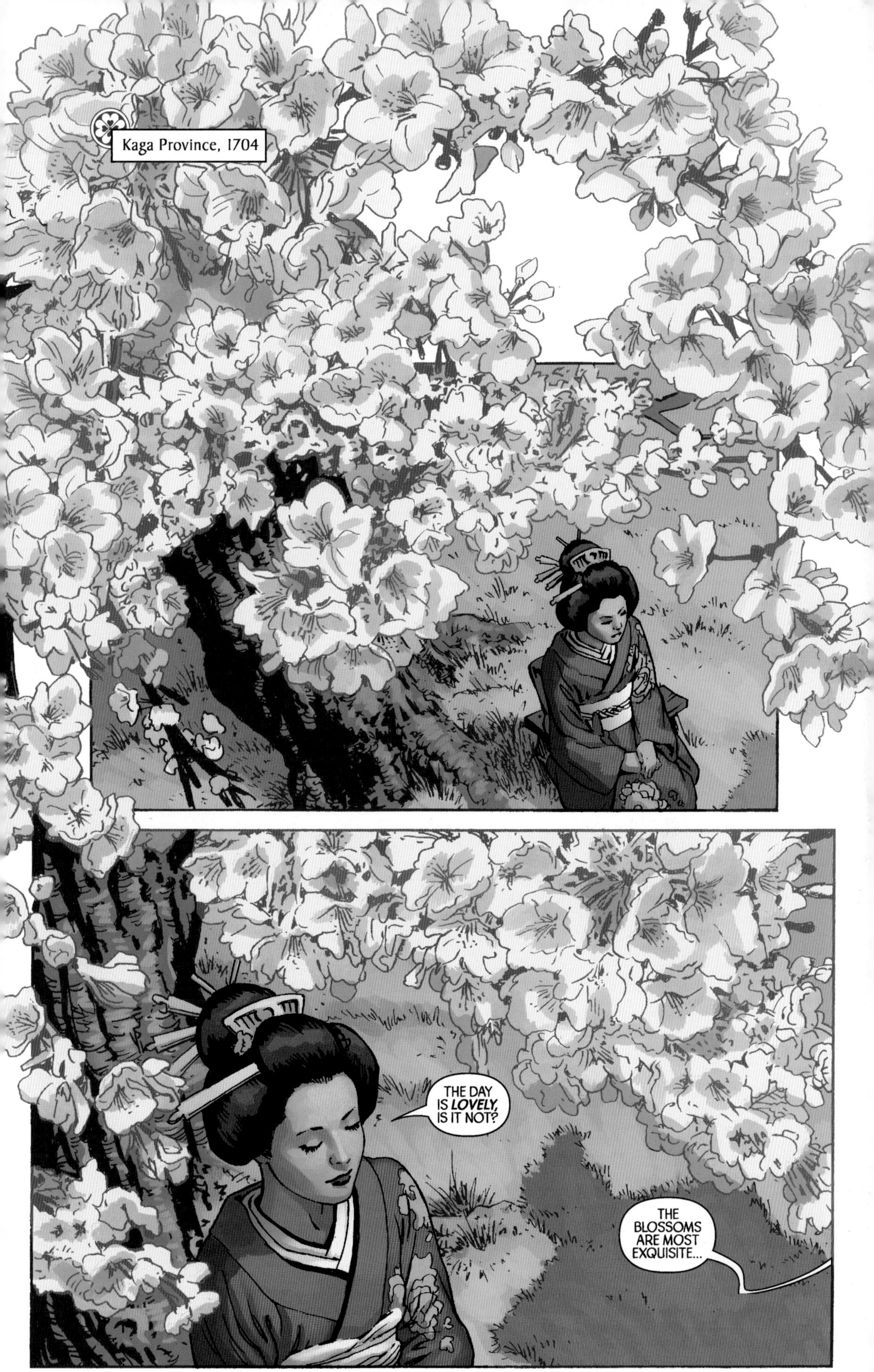

Kaga Province, 1704
THE DAY IS *LOVELY,* IS IT NOT?
THE BLOSSOMS ARE MOST EXQUISITE...

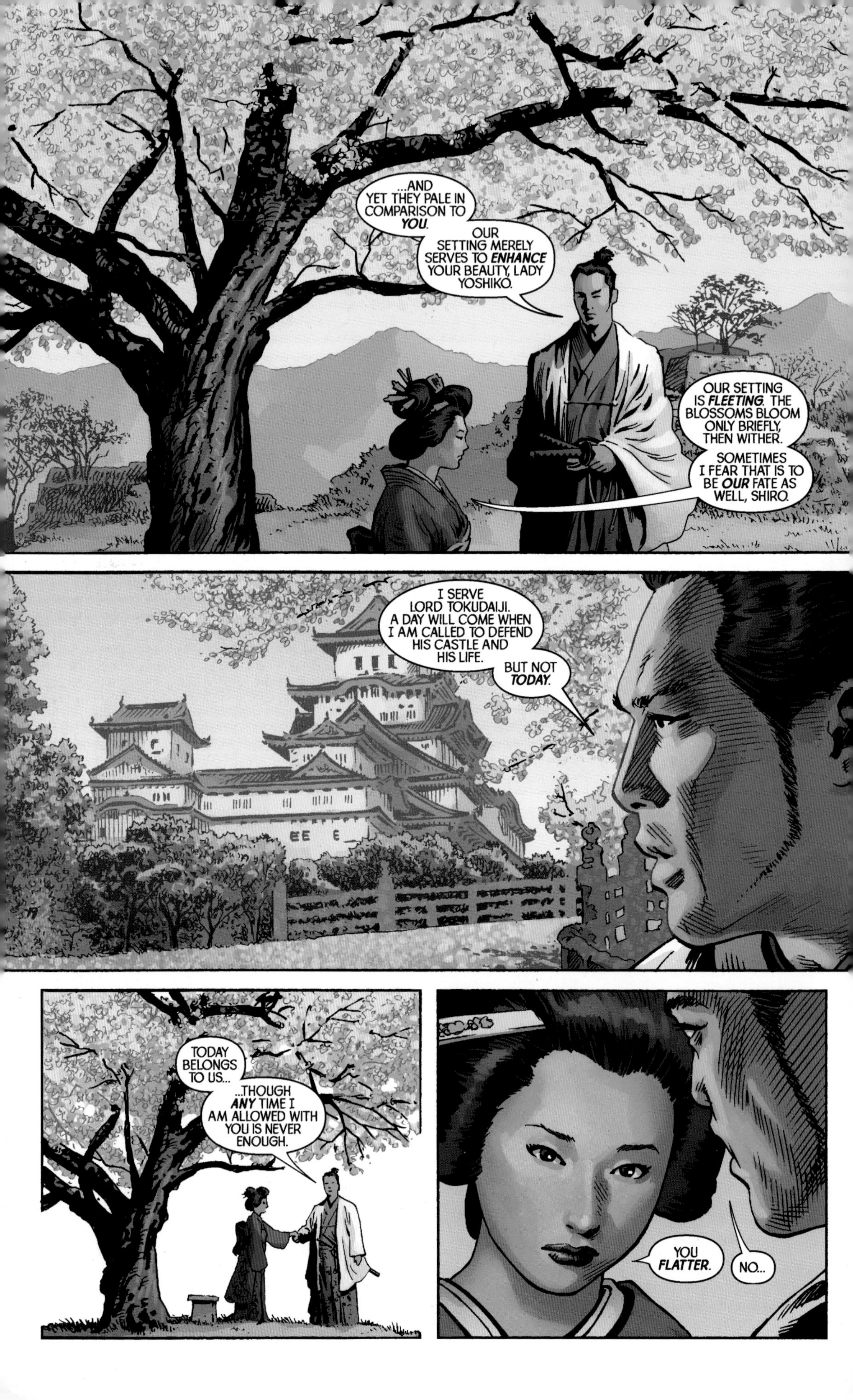
...AND YET THEY PALE IN COMPARISON TO YOU.
OUR SETTING MERELY SERVES TO ENHANCE YOUR BEAUTY, LADY YOSHIKO.
OUR SETTING IS FLEETING. THE BLOSSOMS BLOOM ONLY BRIEFLY, THEN WITHER.
SOMETIMES I FEAR THAT IS TO BE OUR FATE AS WELL, SHIRO.
I SERVE LORD TOKUDAIJI. A DAY WILL COME WHEN I AM CALLED TO DEFEND HIS CASTLE AND HIS LIFE.
BUT NOT TODAY.
TODAY BELONGS TO US...
...THOUGH ANY TIME I AM ALLOWED WITH YOU IS NEVER ENOUGH.
YOU FLATTER.
NO...

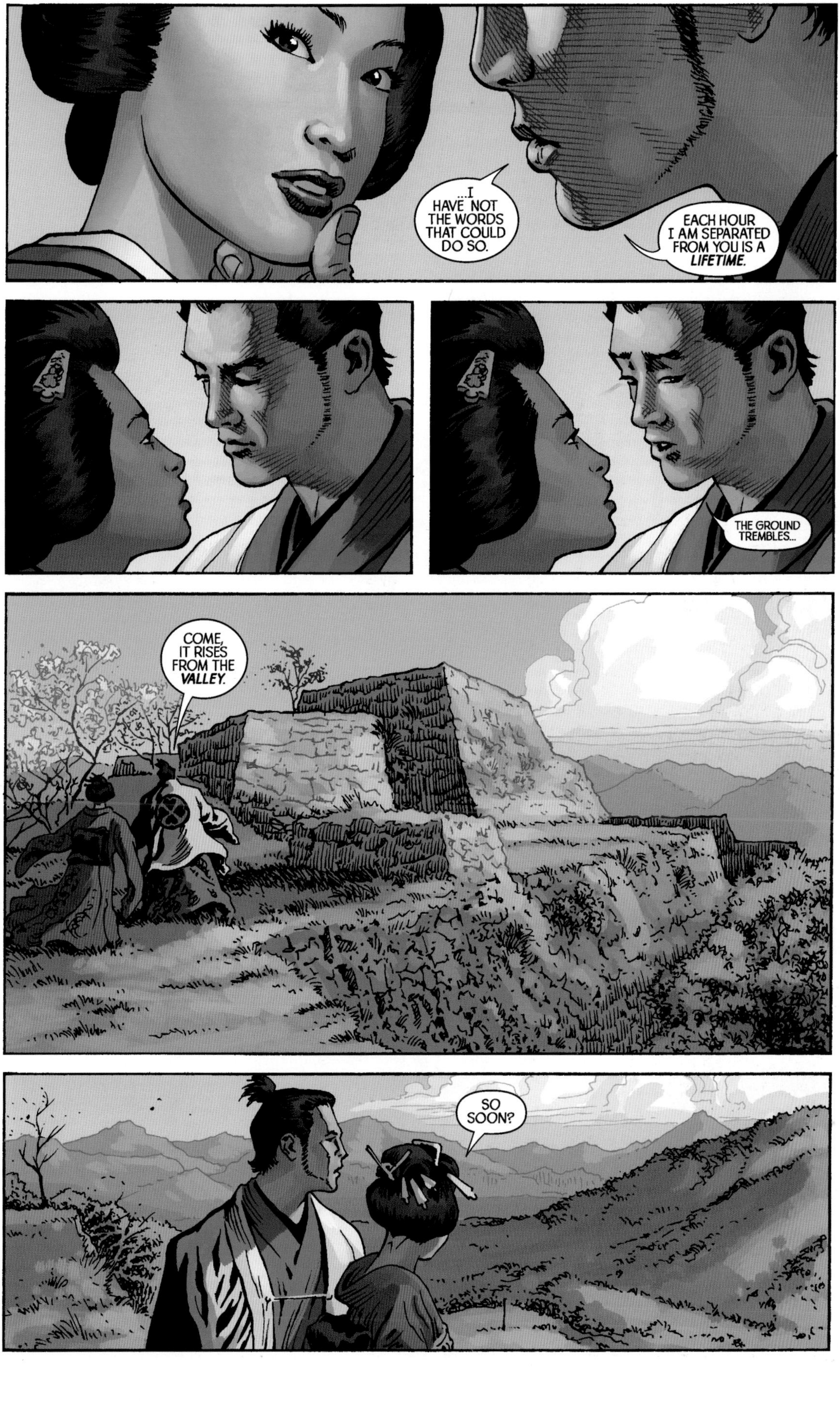
...I HAVE NOT THE WORDS THAT COULD DO SO.
EACH HOUR I AM SEPARATED FROM YOU IS A *LIFETIME*.
THE GROUND TREMBLES...
COME, IT RISES FROM THE *VALLEY*.
SO SOON?

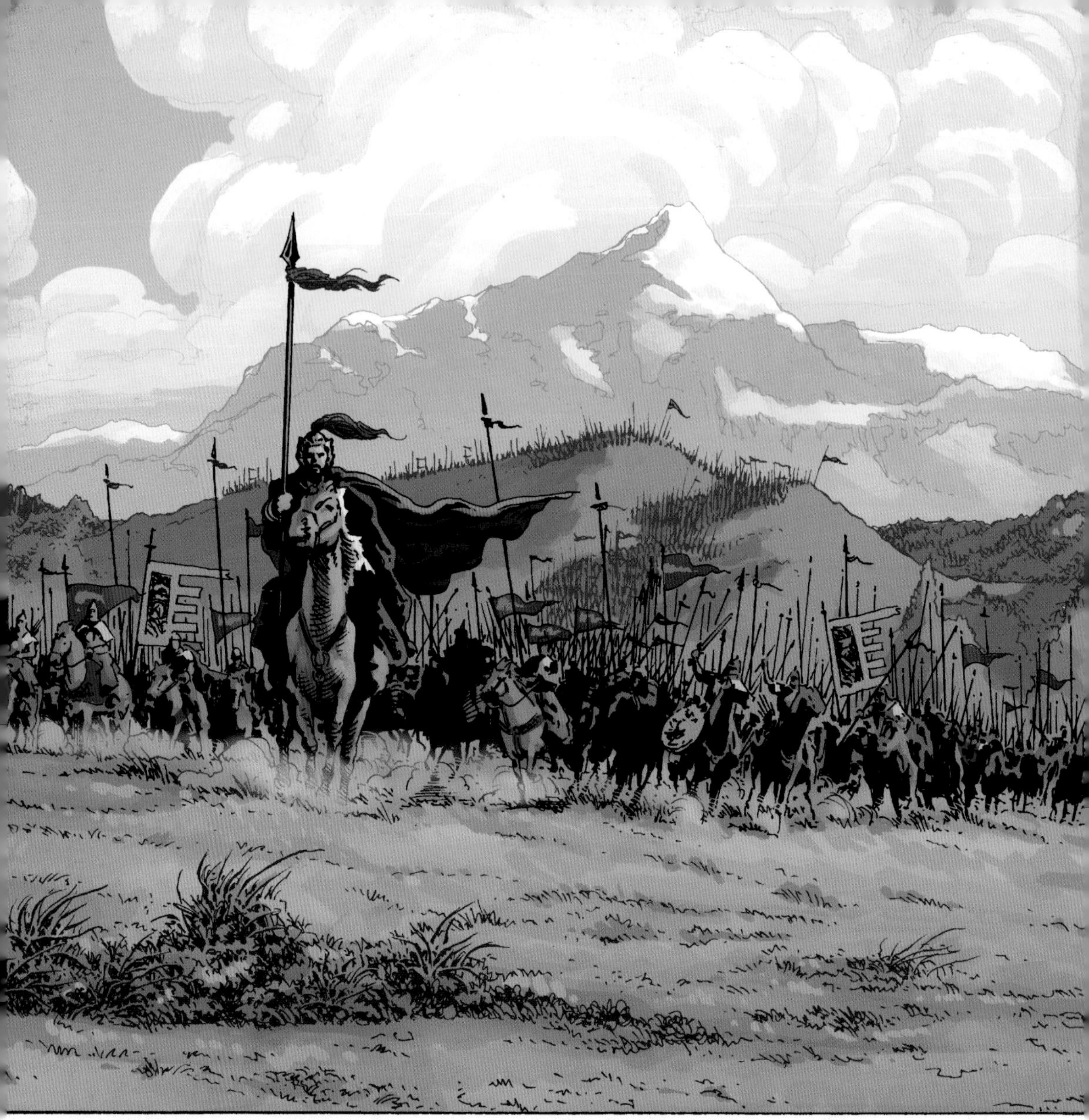

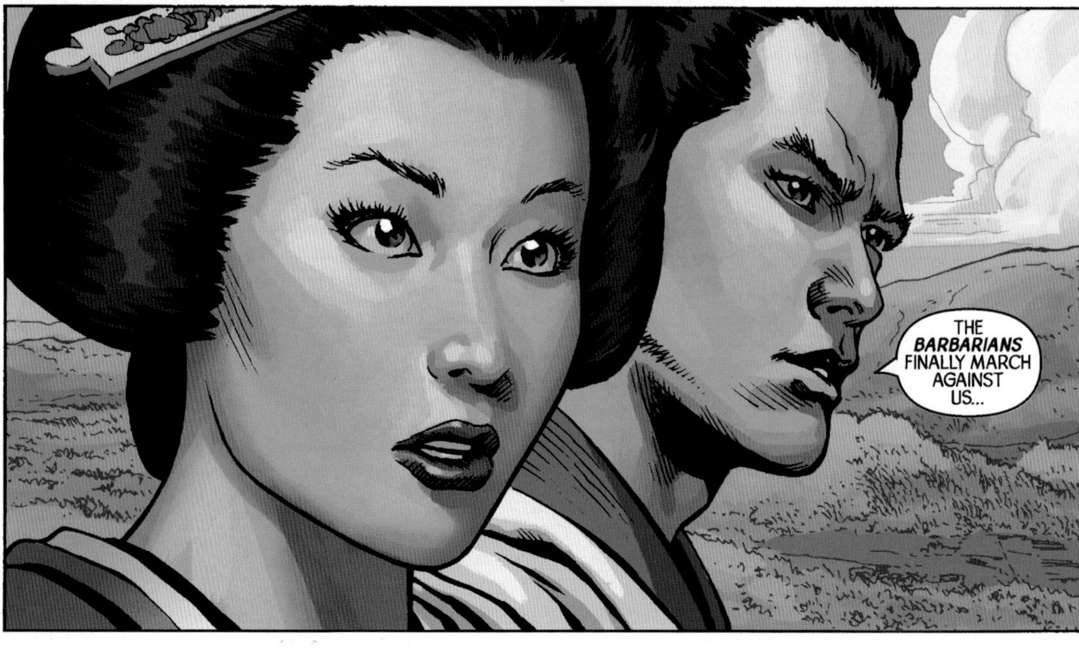
THE BARBARIANS FINALLY MARCH AGAINST US...

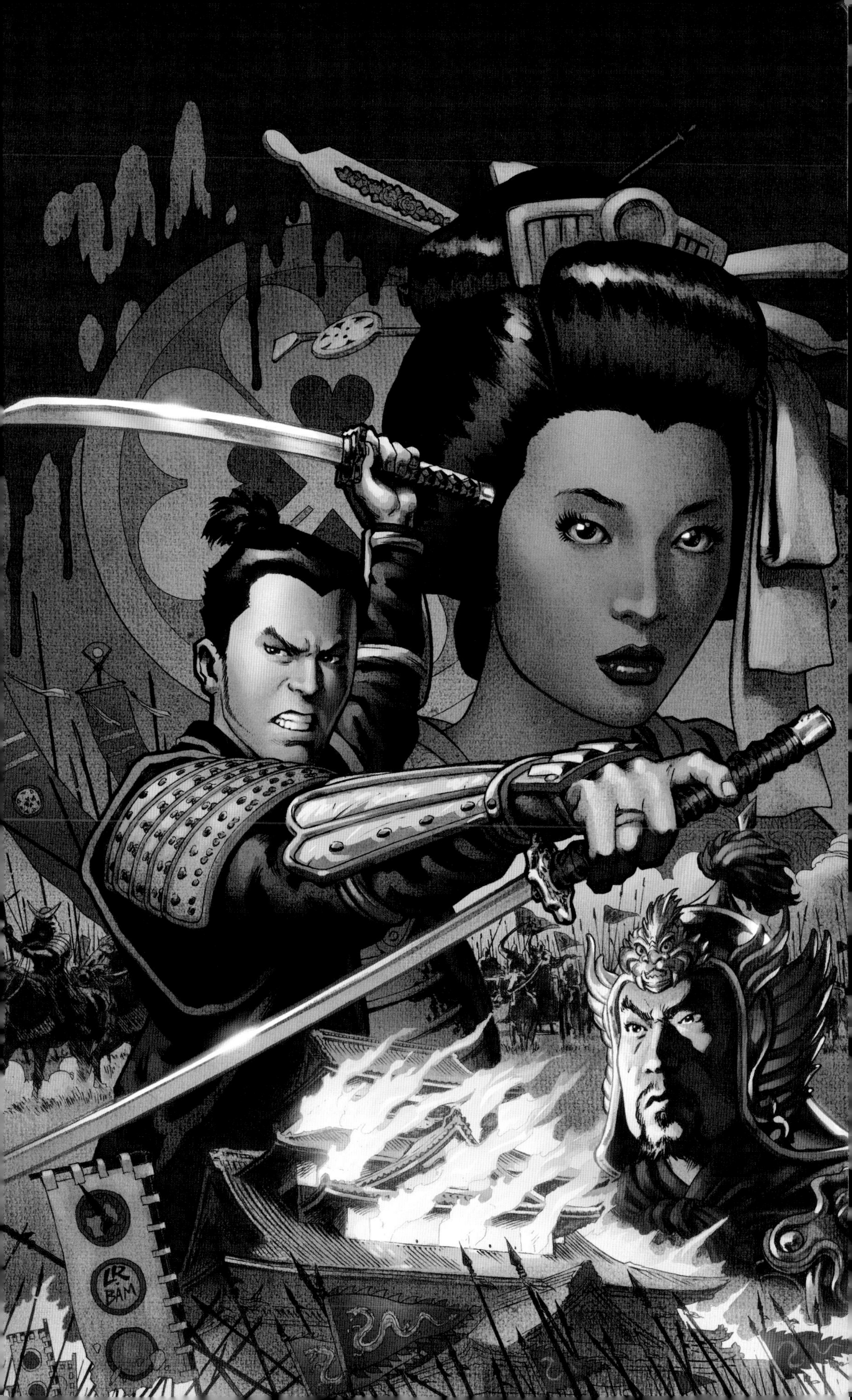
LR.
BAM

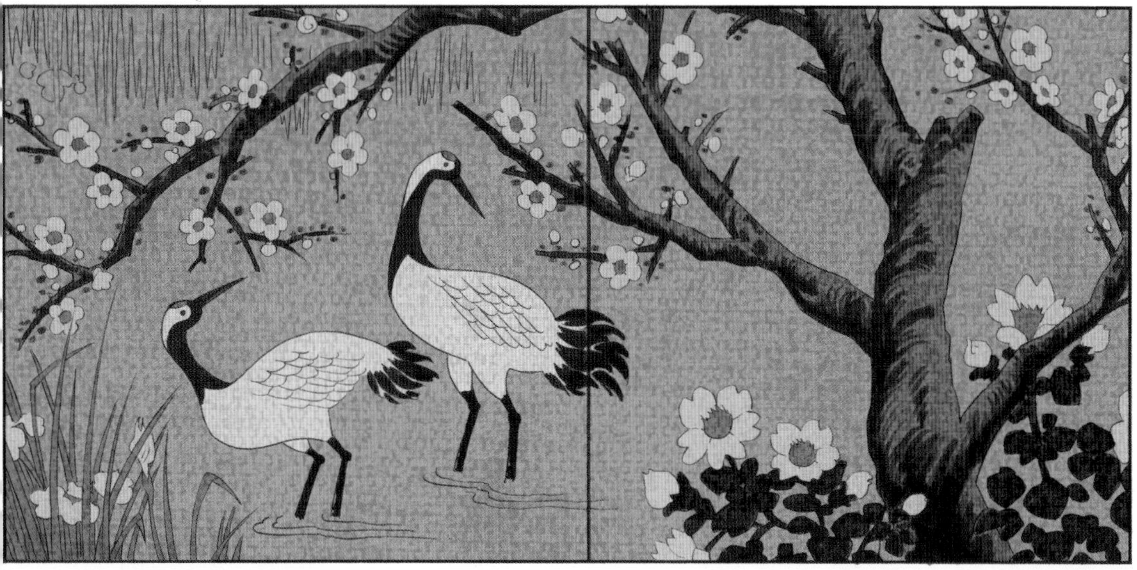

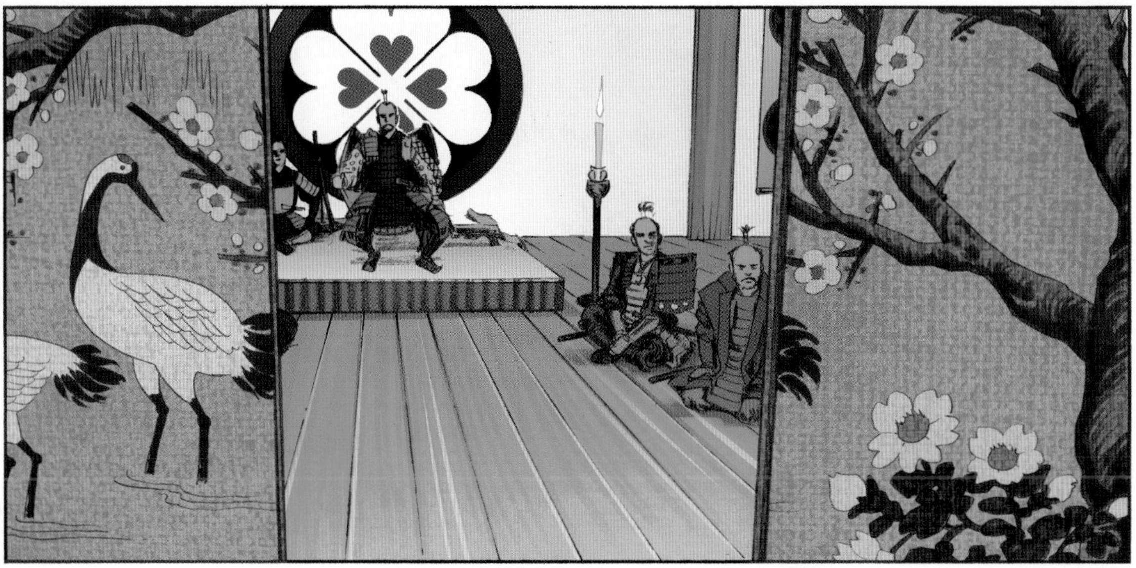

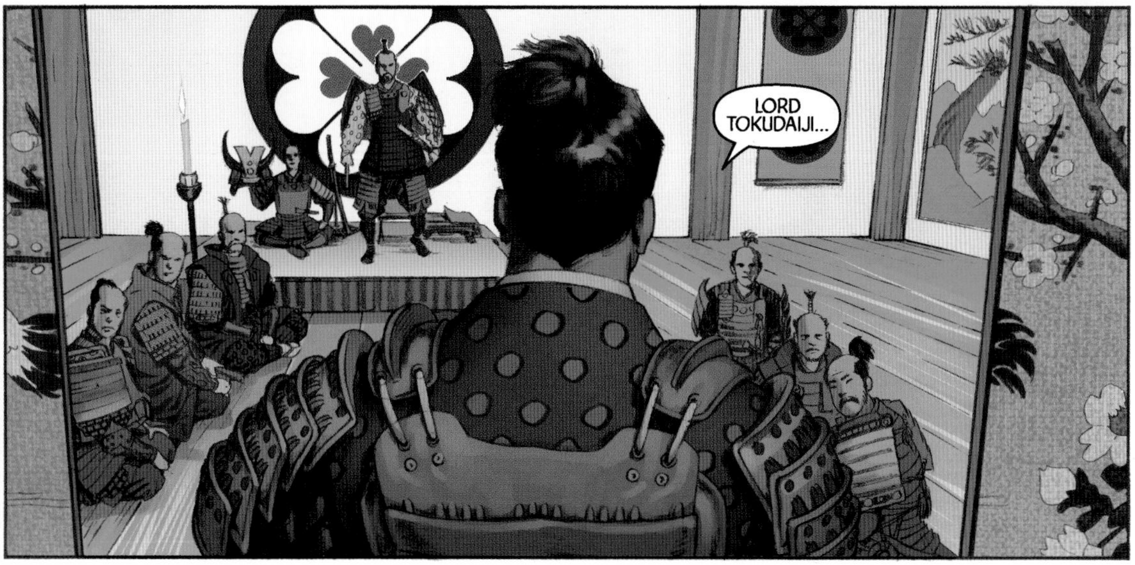
LORD TOKUDAIJI...

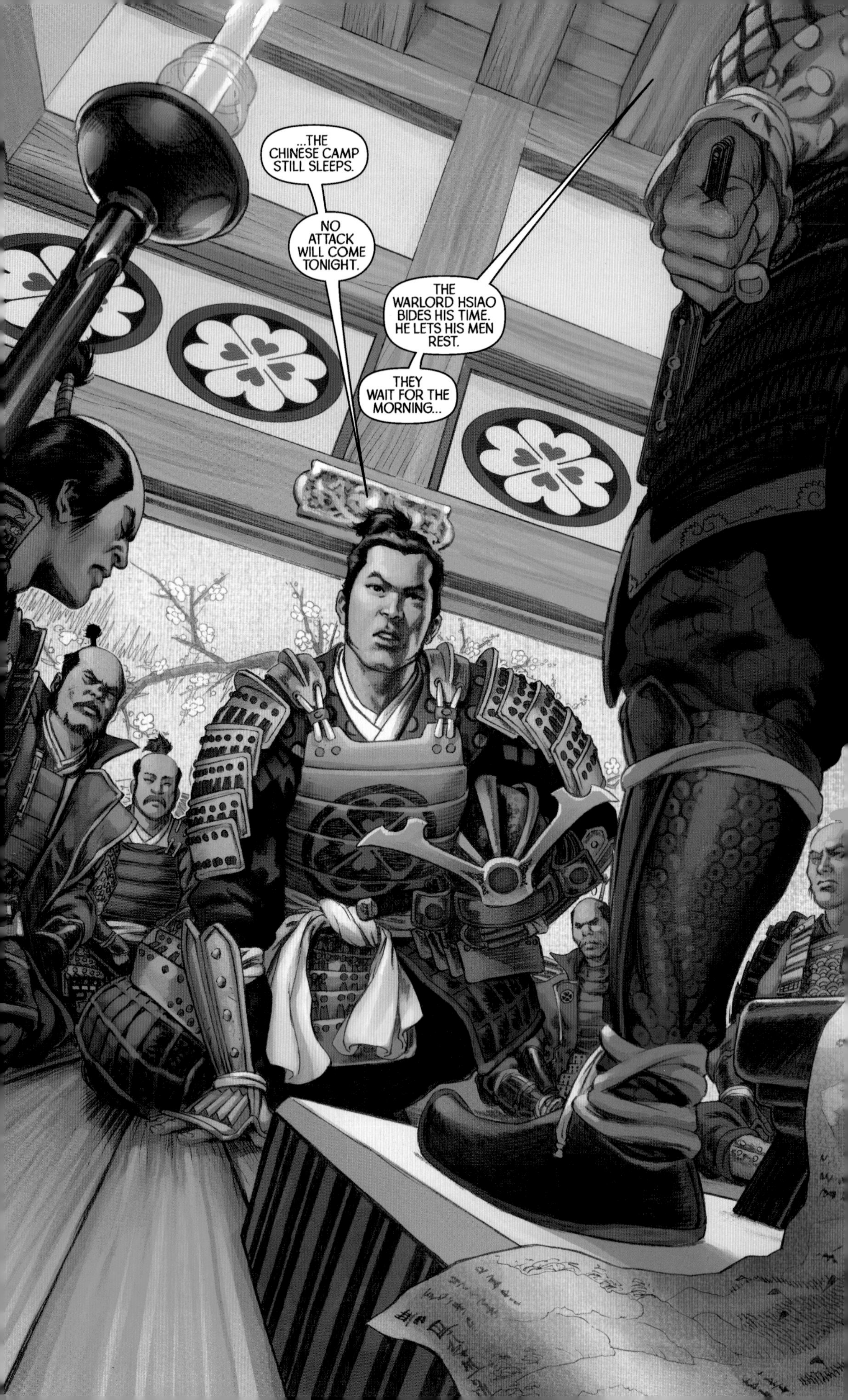
...THE CHINESE CAMP STILL SLEEPS.
NO ATTACK WILL COME TONIGHT.
THE WARLORD HSIAO BIDES HIS TIME. HE LETS HIS MEN REST.
THEY WAIT FOR THE MORNING...

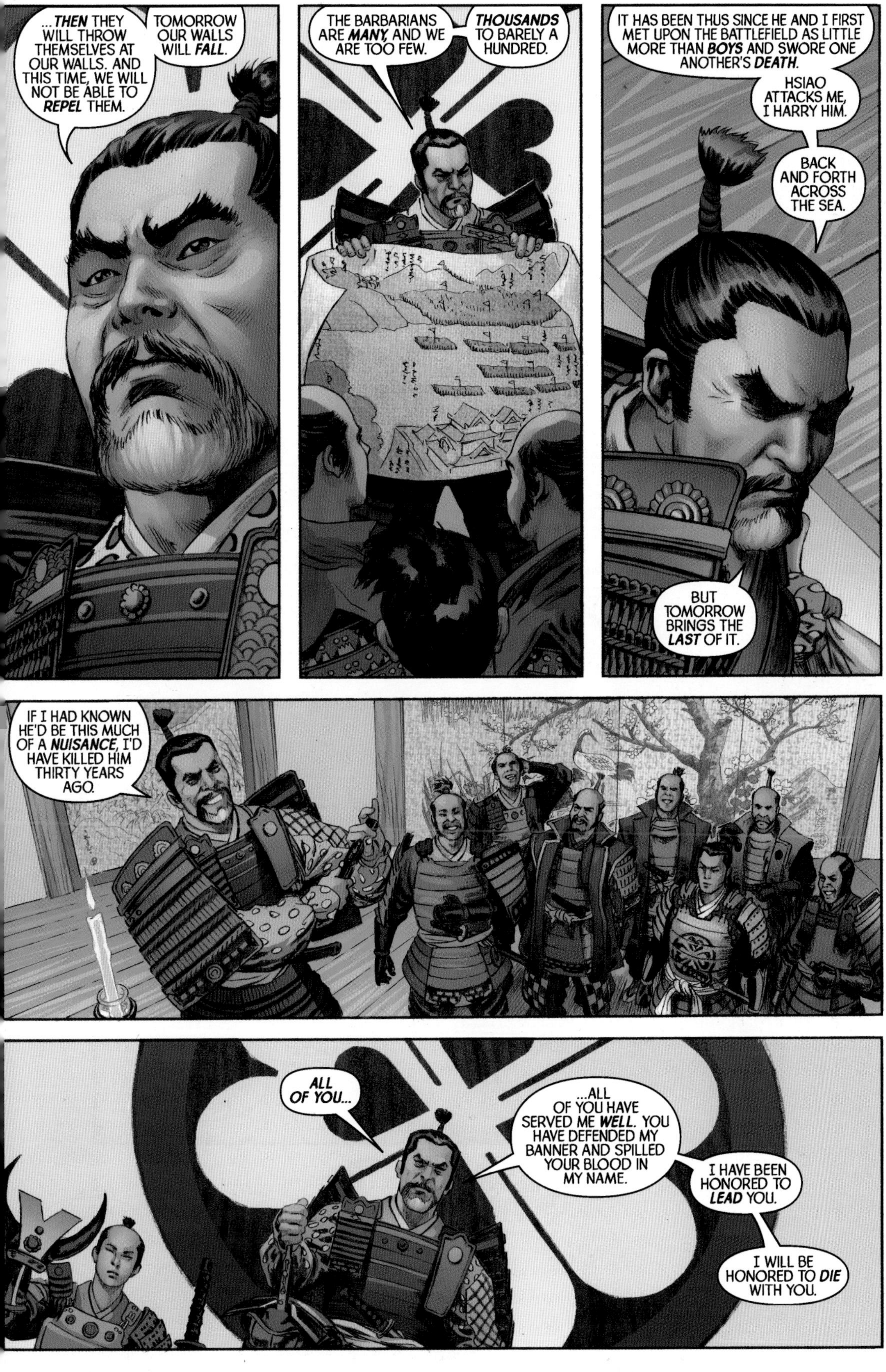

TOMORROW OUR WALLS WILL FALL.
...THEN THEY WILL THROW THEMSELVES AT OUR WALLS. AND THIS TIME, WE WILL NOT BE ABLE TO REPEL THEM.
THE BARBARIANS ARE MANY, AND WE ARE TOO FEW.
THOUSANDS TO BARELY A HUNDRED.
IT HAS BEEN THUS SINCE HE AND I FIRST MET UPON THE BATTLEFIELD AS LITTLE MORE THAN BOYS AND SWORE ONE ANOTHER'S DEATH.
HSIAO ATTACKS ME, I HARRY HIM.
BACK AND FORTH ACROSS THE SEA.
BUT TOMORROW BRINGS THE LAST OF IT.
IF I HAD KNOWN HE'D BE THIS MUCH OF A NUISANCE, I'D HAVE KILLED HIM THIRTY YEARS AGO.
ALL OF YOU...
...ALL OF YOU HAVE SERVED ME WELL. YOU HAVE DEFENDED MY BANNER AND SPILLED YOUR BLOOD IN MY NAME.
I HAVE BEEN HONORED TO LEAD YOU.
I WILL BE HONORED TO DIE WITH YOU.

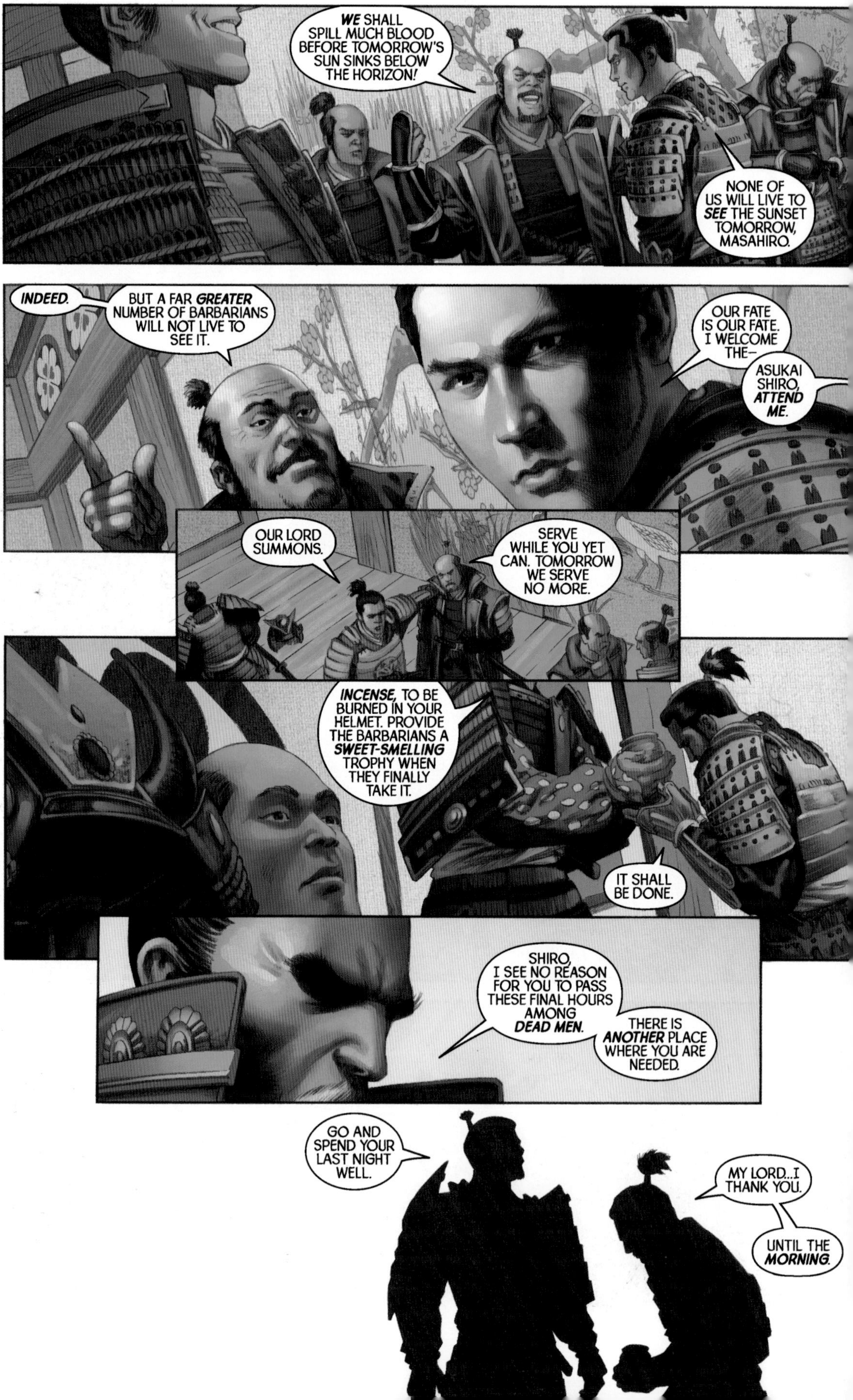
WE SHALL SPILL MUCH BLOOD BEFORE TOMORROW'S SUN SINKS BELOW THE HORIZON!
NONE OF US WILL LIVE TO SEE THE SUNSET TOMORROW, MASAHIRO.
INDEED.
BUT A FAR GREATER NUMBER OF BARBARIANS WILL NOT LIVE TO SEE IT.
OUR FATE IS OUR FATE. I WELCOME THE—
ASUKAI SHIRO, ATTEND ME.
OUR LORD SUMMONS.
SERVE WHILE YOU YET CAN. TOMORROW WE SERVE NO MORE.
INCENSE, TO BE BURNED IN YOUR HELMET. PROVIDE THE BARBARIANS A SWEET-SMELLING TROPHY WHEN THEY FINALLY TAKE IT.
IT SHALL BE DONE.
SHIRO, I SEE NO REASON FOR YOU TO PASS THESE FINAL HOURS AMONG DEAD MEN.
THERE IS ANOTHER PLACE WHERE YOU ARE NEEDED.
GO AND SPEND YOUR LAST NIGHT WELL.
MY LORD...I THANK YOU.
UNTIL THE MORNING.

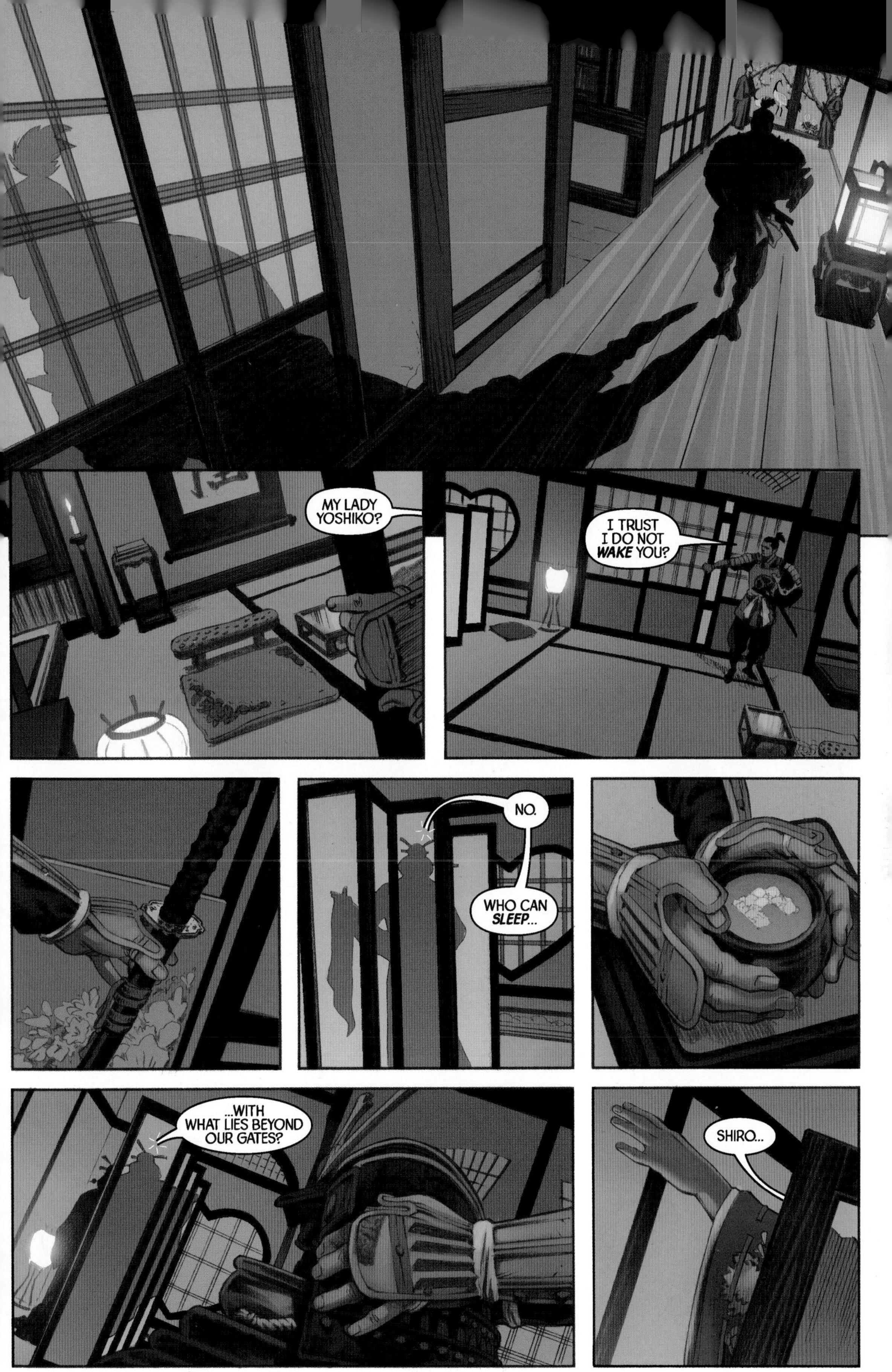
MY LADY YOSHIKO?
I TRUST I DO NOT WAKE YOU?
NO.
WHO CAN SLEEP...
...WITH WHAT LIES BEYOND OUR GATES?
SHIRO...

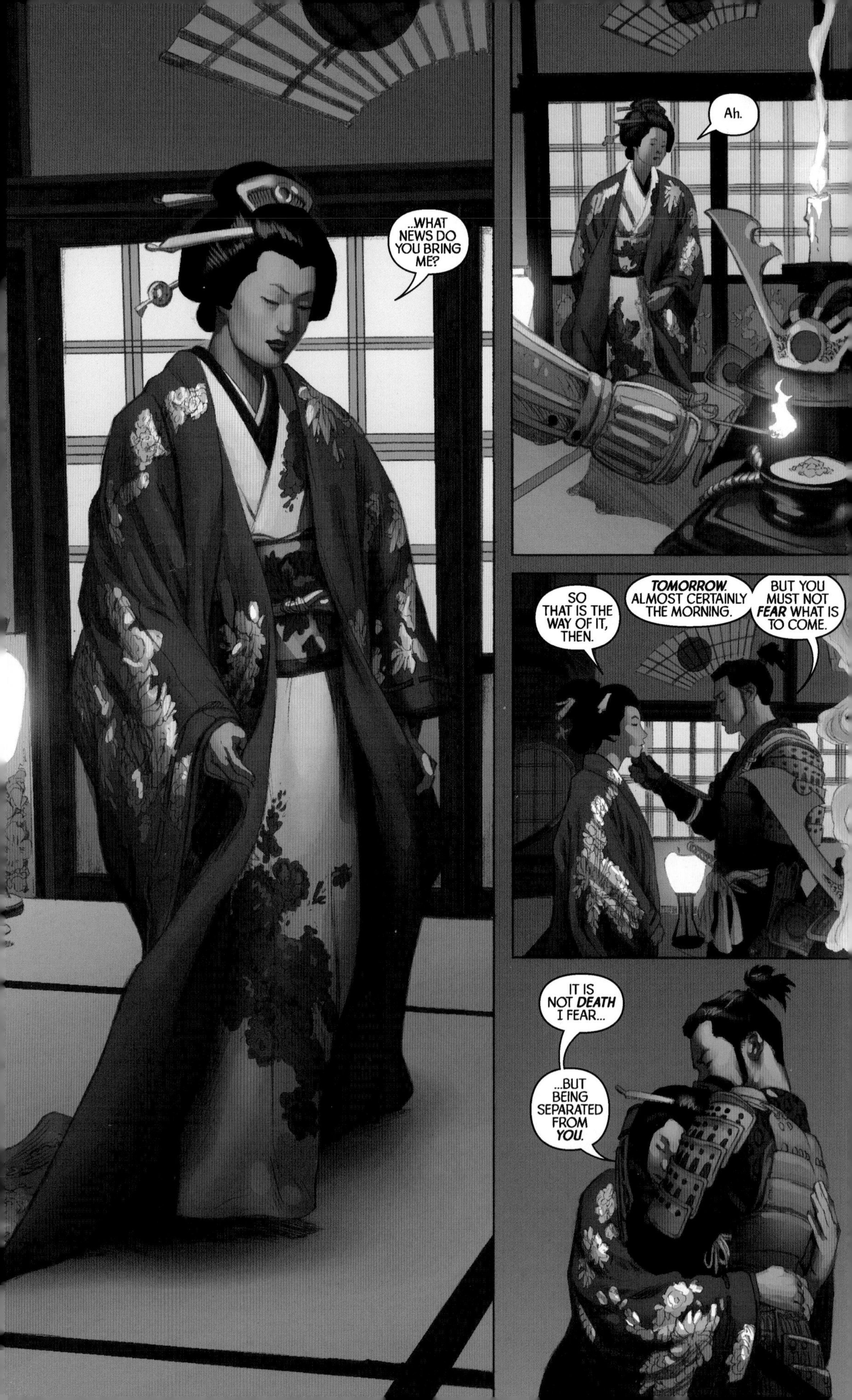

...WHAT NEWS DO YOU BRING ME?
Ah.
SO THAT IS THE WAY OF IT, THEN.
TOMORROW. ALMOST CERTAINLY THE MORNING.
BUT YOU MUST NOT FEAR WHAT IS TO COME.
IT IS NOT DEATH I FEAR...
...BUT BEING SEPARATED FROM YOU.

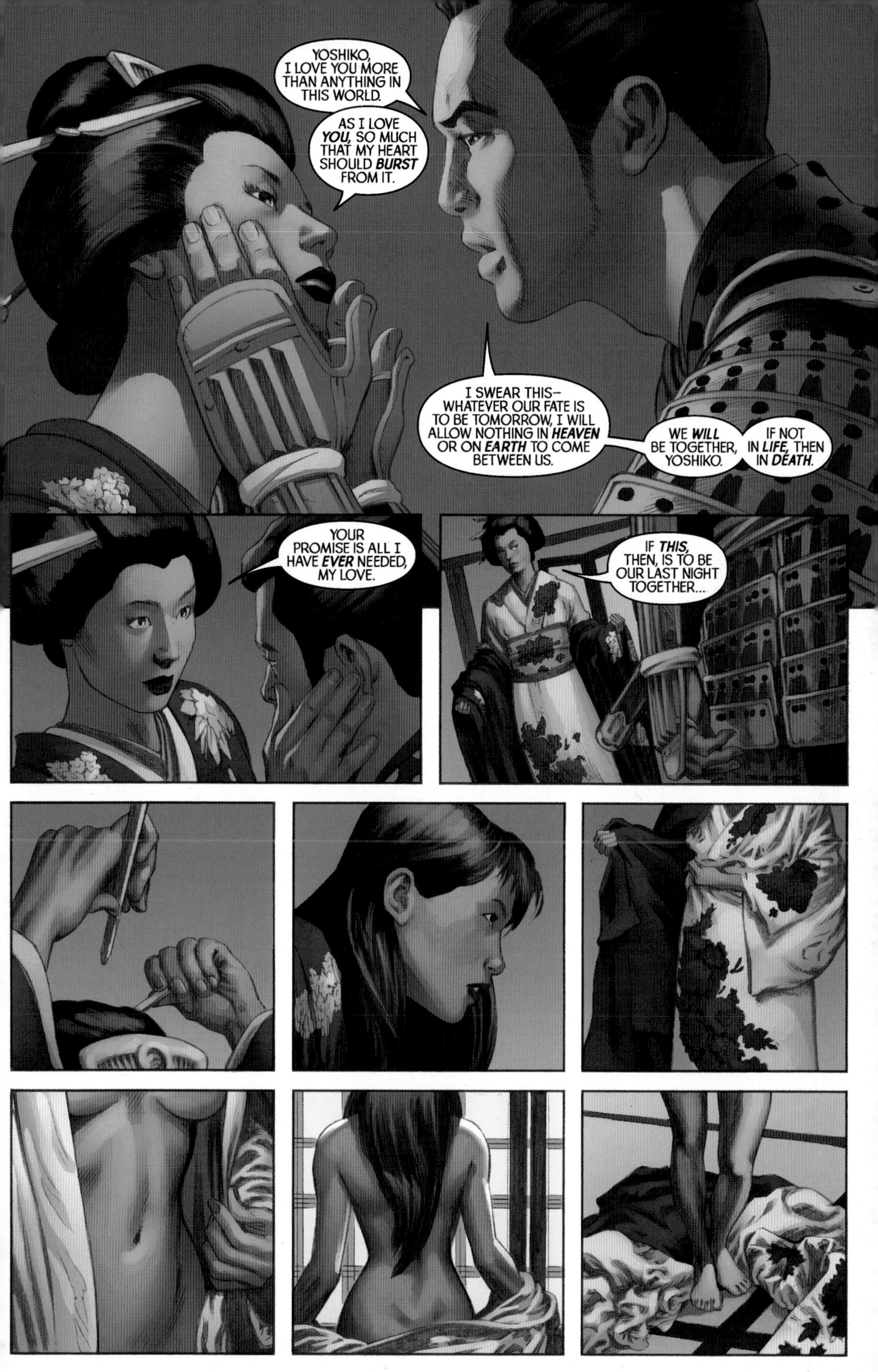
YOSHIKO, I LOVE YOU MORE THAN ANYTHING IN THIS WORLD.
AS I LOVE YOU, SO MUCH THAT MY HEART SHOULD BURST FROM IT.
I SWEAR THIS-- WHATEVER OUR FATE IS TO BE TOMORROW, I WILL ALLOW NOTHING IN HEAVEN OR ON EARTH TO COME BETWEEN US.
WE WILL BE TOGETHER, YOSHIKO.
IF NOT IN LIFE, THEN IN DEATH.
YOUR PROMISE IS ALL I HAVE EVER NEEDED, MY LOVE.
IF THIS, THEN, IS TO BE OUR LAST NIGHT TOGETHER...

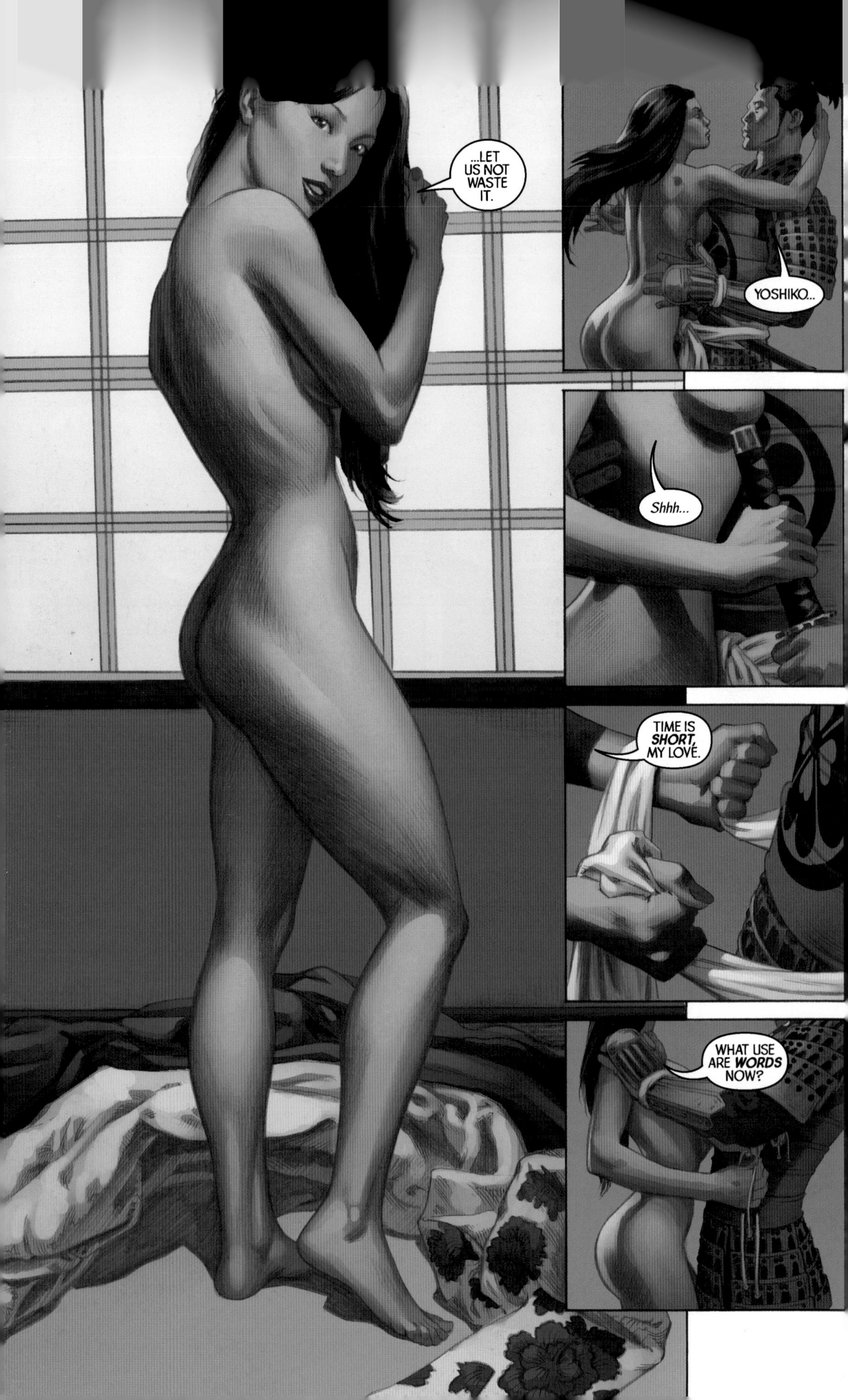
...LET US NOT WASTE IT.
YOSHIKO...
Shhh...
TIME IS SHORT, MY LOVE.
WHAT USE ARE WORDS NOW?

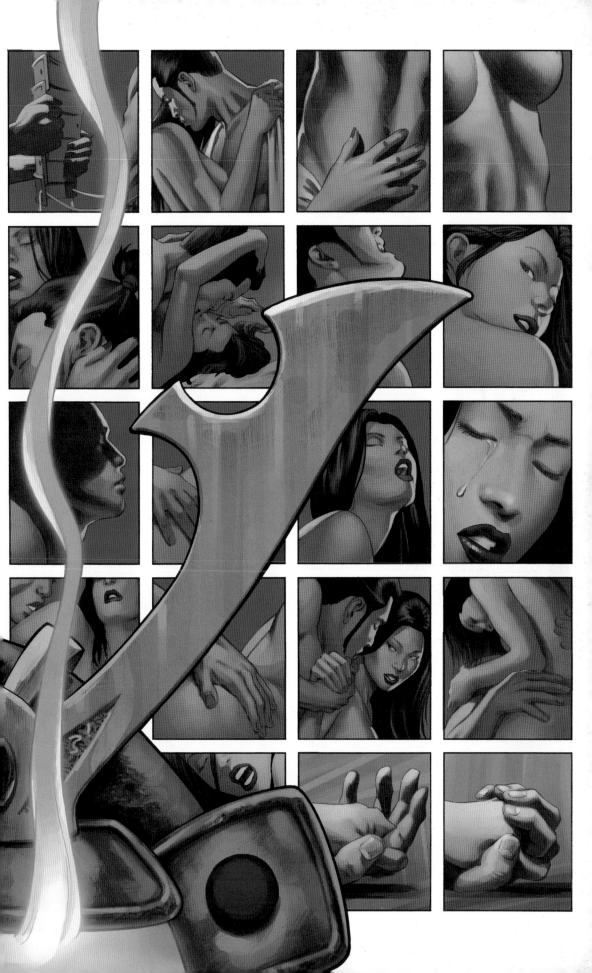

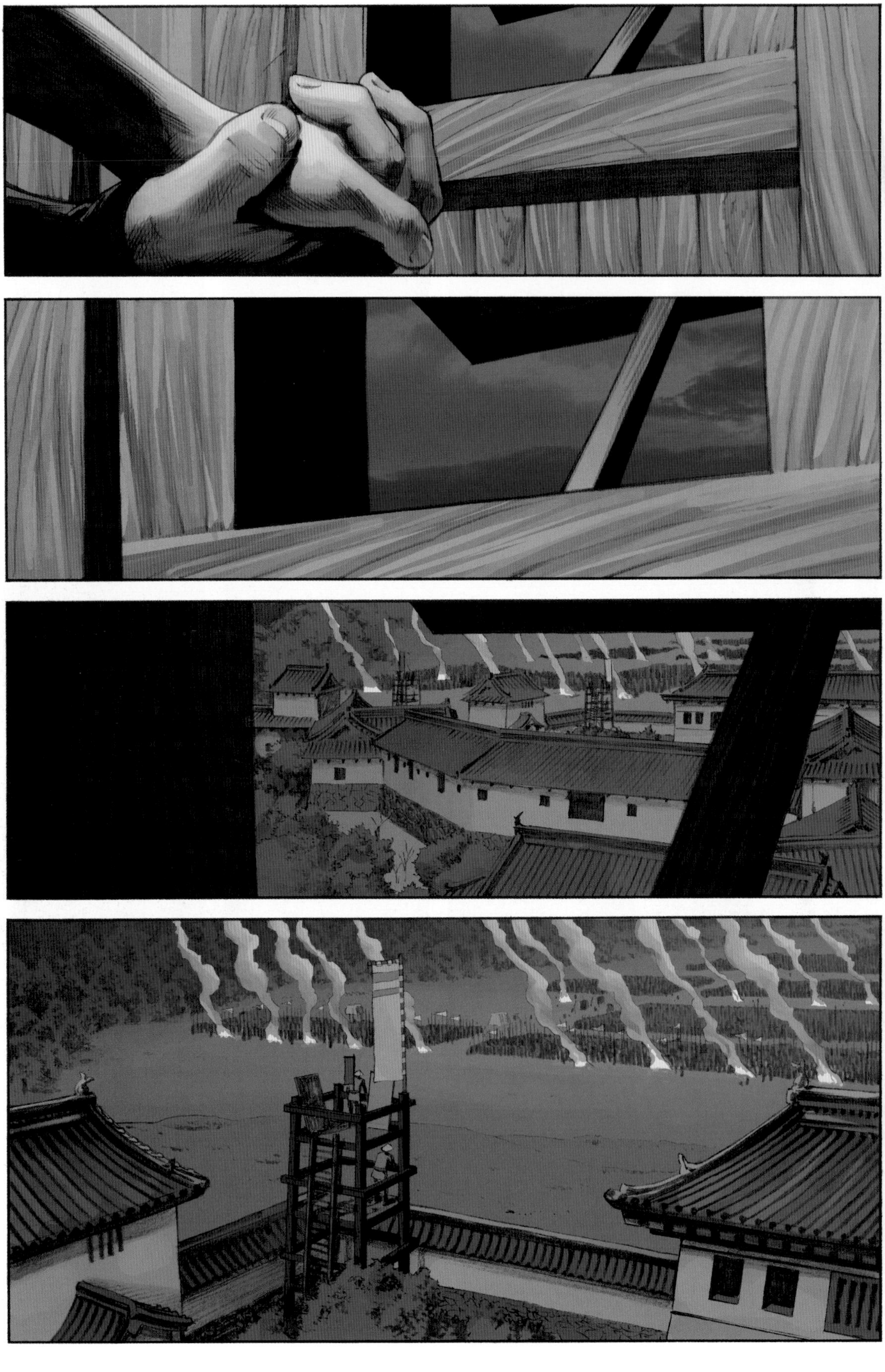

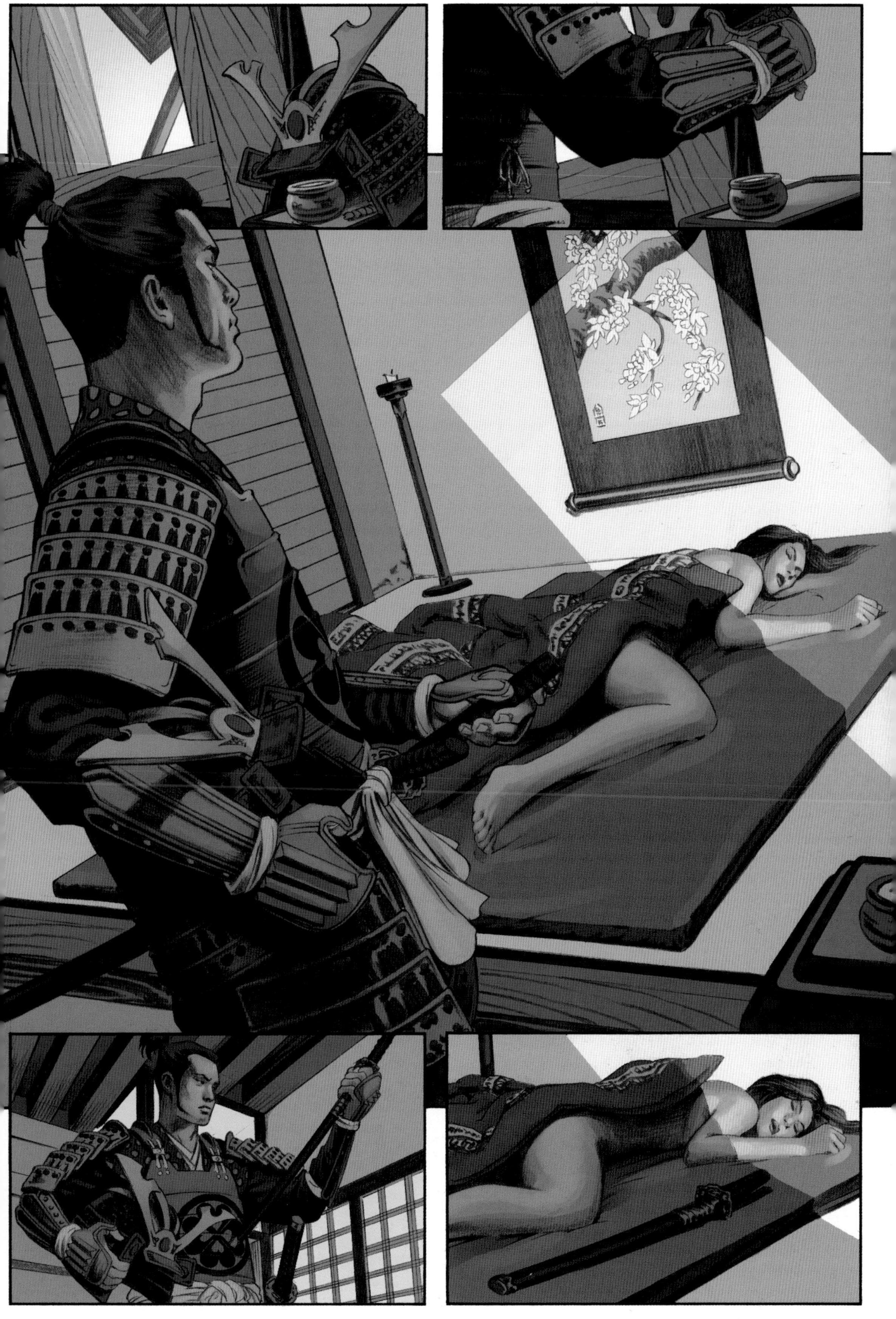

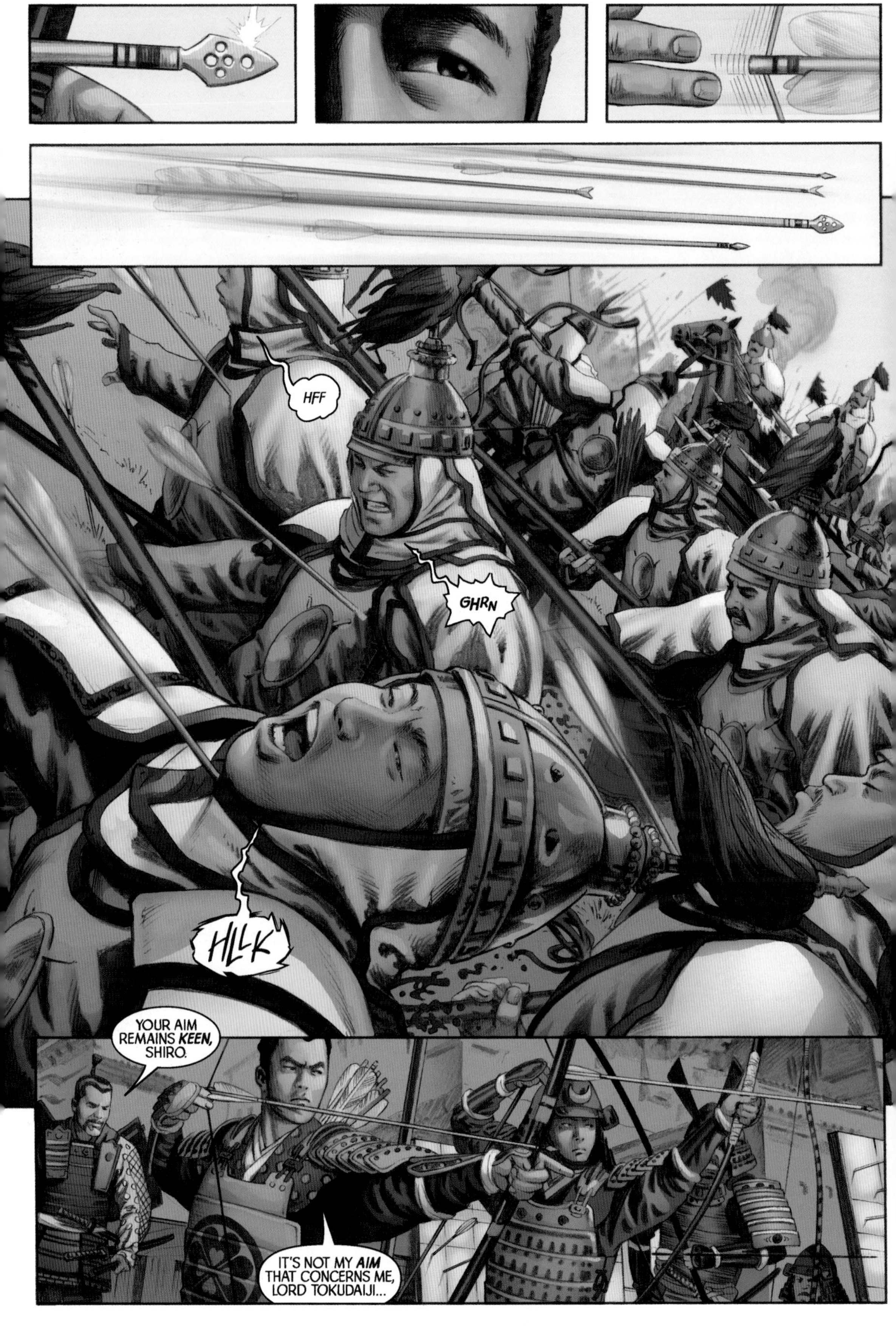
HFF
GHRN
HLLK
YOUR AIM REMAINS KEEN, SHIRO.
IT'S NOT MY AIM THAT CONCERNS ME, LORD TOKUDAIJI...

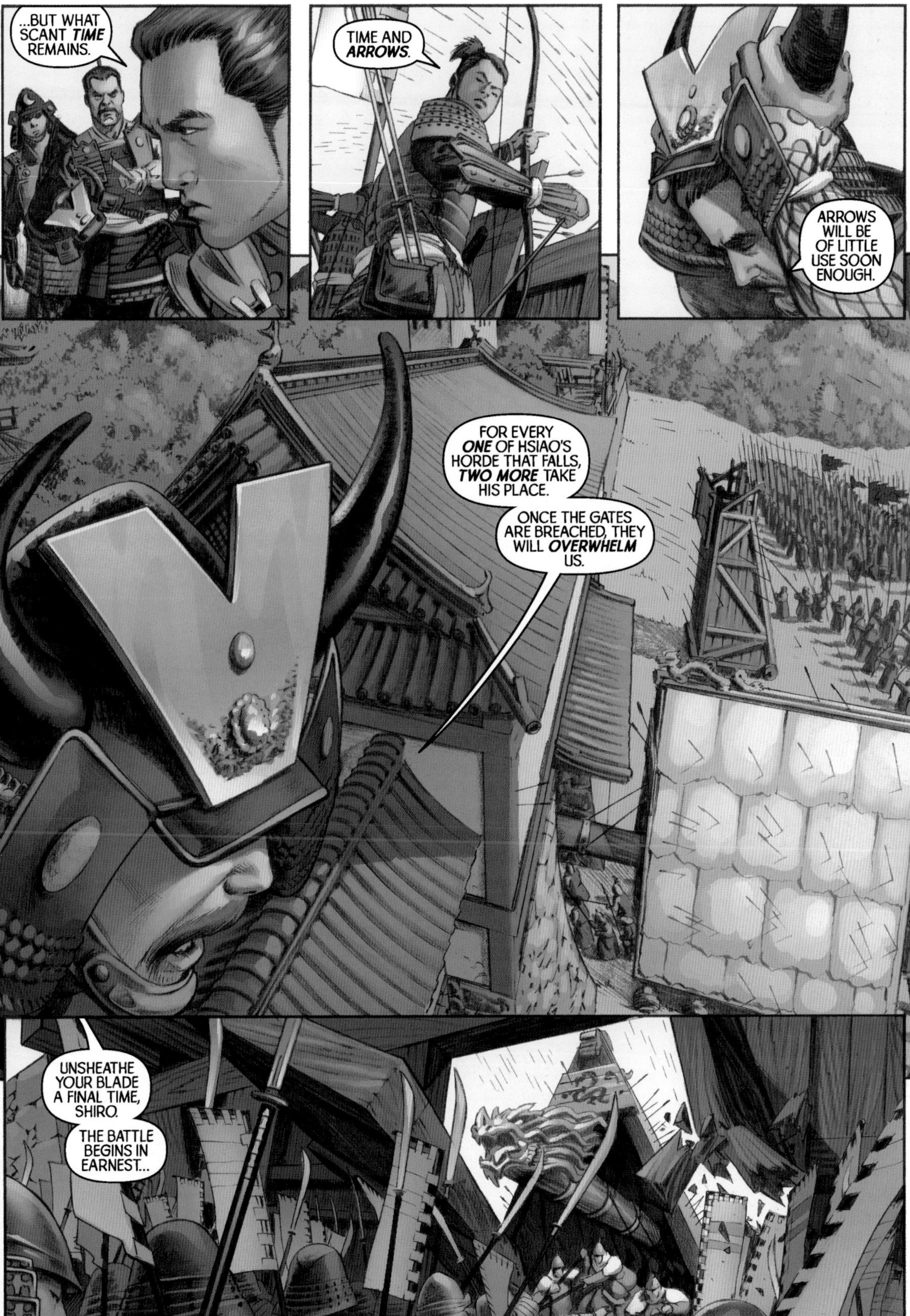
...BUT WHAT SCANT *TIME* REMAINS.
TIME AND *ARROWS*.
ARROWS WILL BE OF LITTLE USE SOON ENOUGH.
FOR EVERY *ONE* OF HSIAO'S HORDE THAT FALLS, *TWO MORE* TAKE HIS PLACE.
ONCE THE GATES ARE BREACHED, THEY WILL *OVERWHELM* US.
UNSHEATHE YOUR BLADE A FINAL TIME, SHIRO.
THE BATTLE BEGINS IN EARNEST...

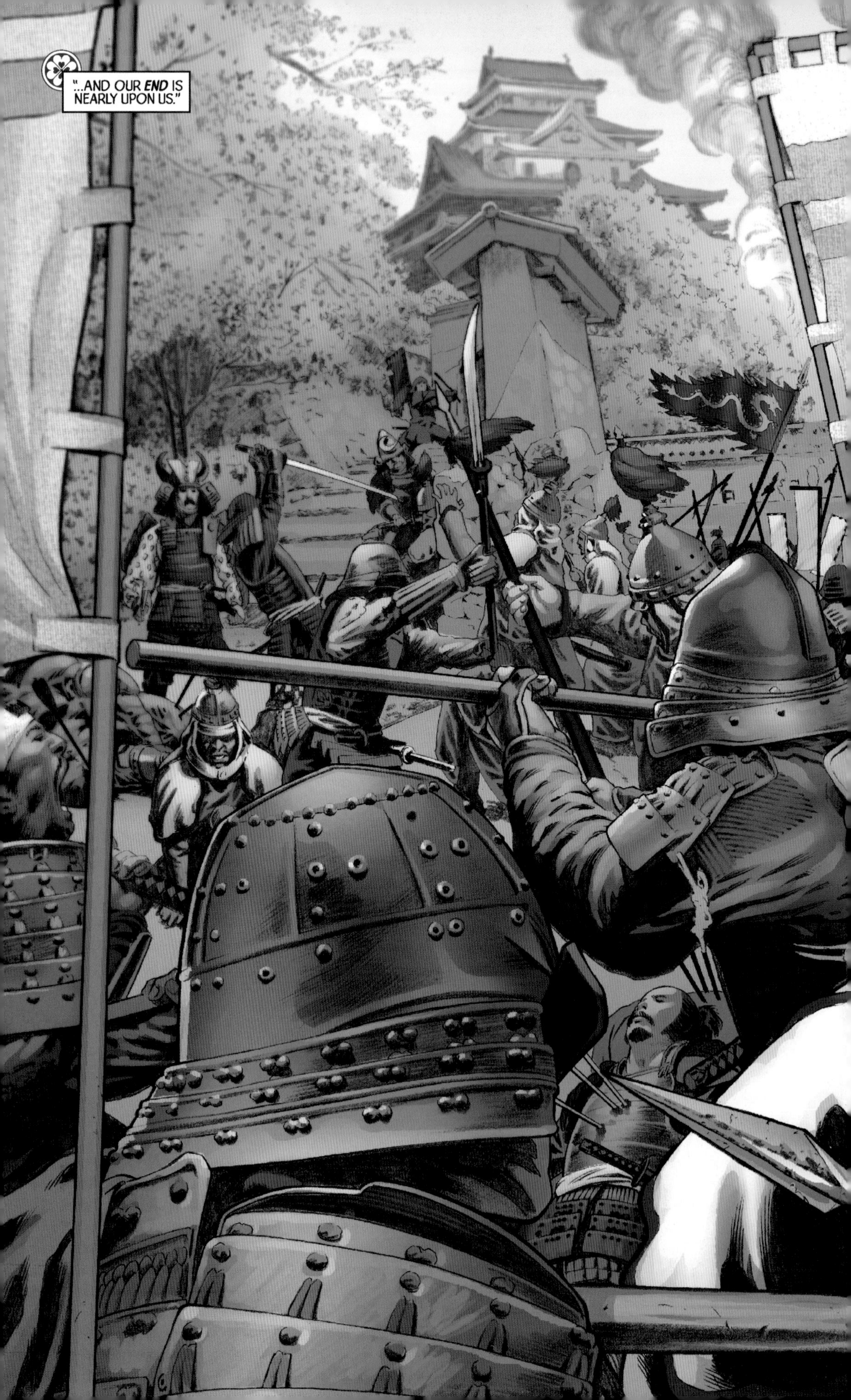
"...AND OUR END IS NEARLY UPON US."

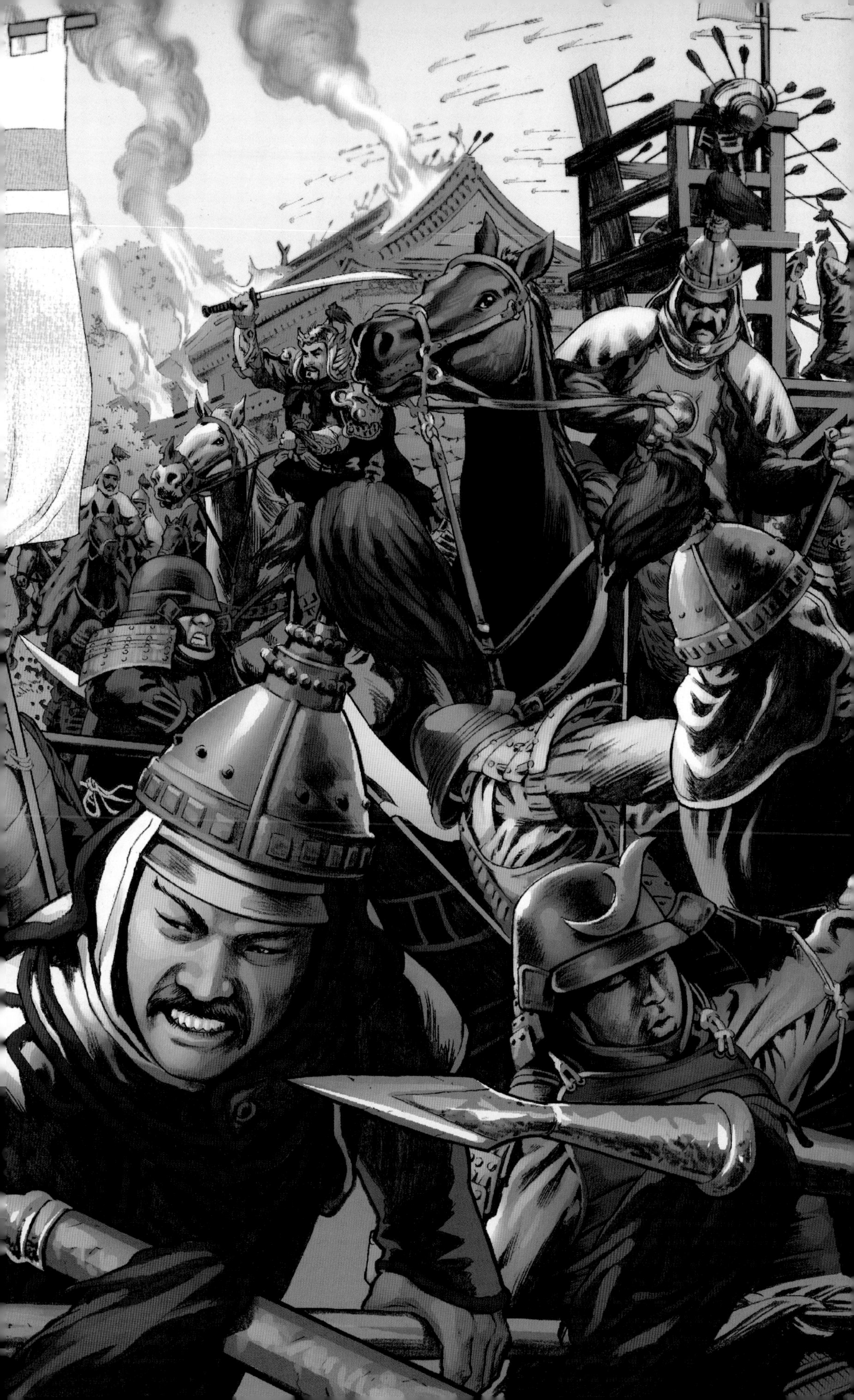

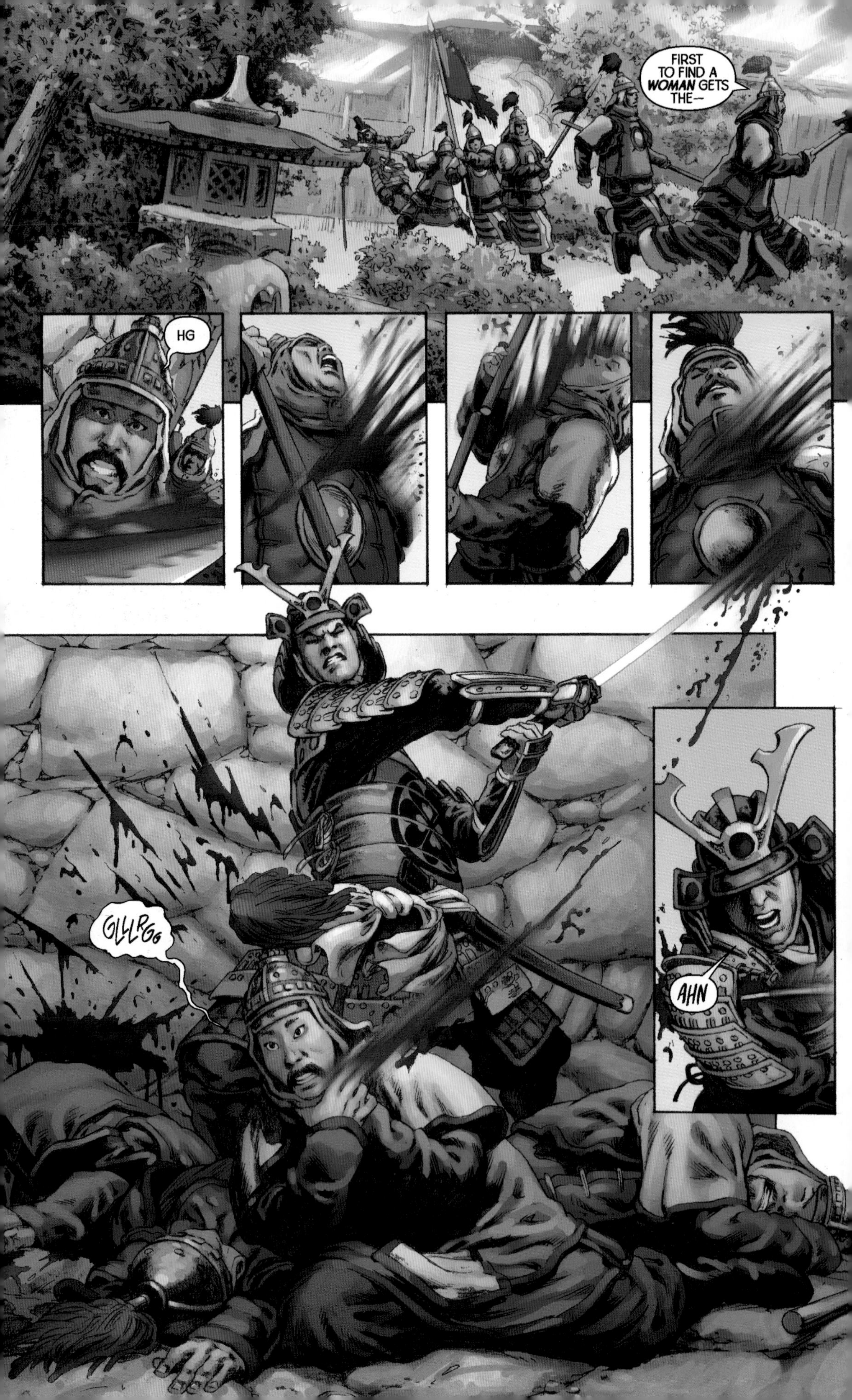
FIRST TO FIND A WOMAN GETS THE--
HG
GLLLRGG
AHN

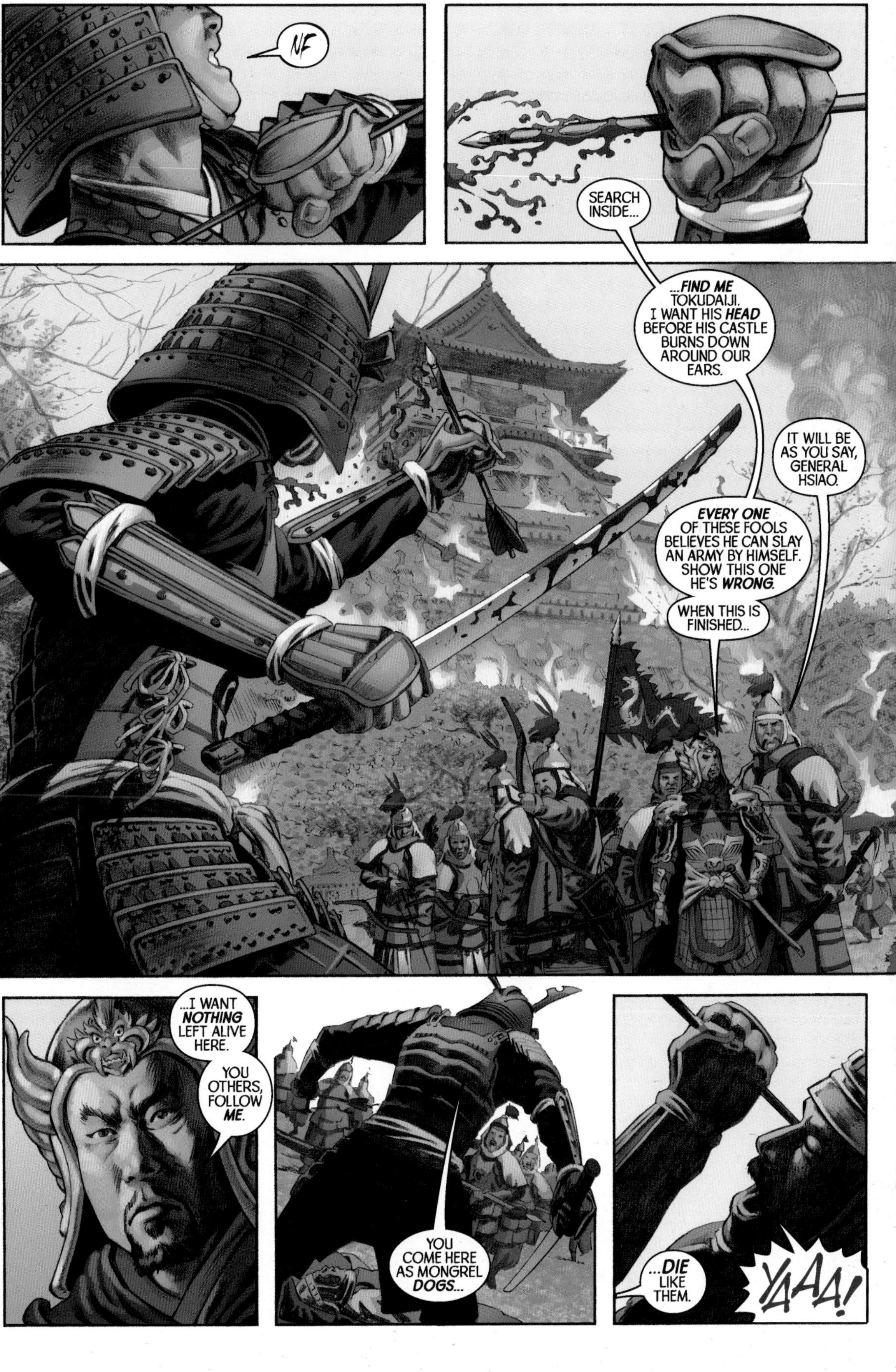
NF
SEARCH INSIDE...
...FIND ME TOKUDAIJI. I WANT HIS HEAD BEFORE HIS CASTLE BURNS DOWN AROUND OUR EARS.
EVERY ONE OF THESE FOOLS BELIEVES HE CAN SLAY AN ARMY BY HIMSELF. SHOW THIS ONE HE'S WRONG.
IT WILL BE AS YOU SAY, GENERAL HSIAO.
WHEN THIS IS FINISHED...
...I WANT NOTHING LEFT ALIVE HERE.
YOU OTHERS, FOLLOW ME.
YOU COME HERE AS MONGREL DOGS...
...DIE LIKE THEM.
YAAA!

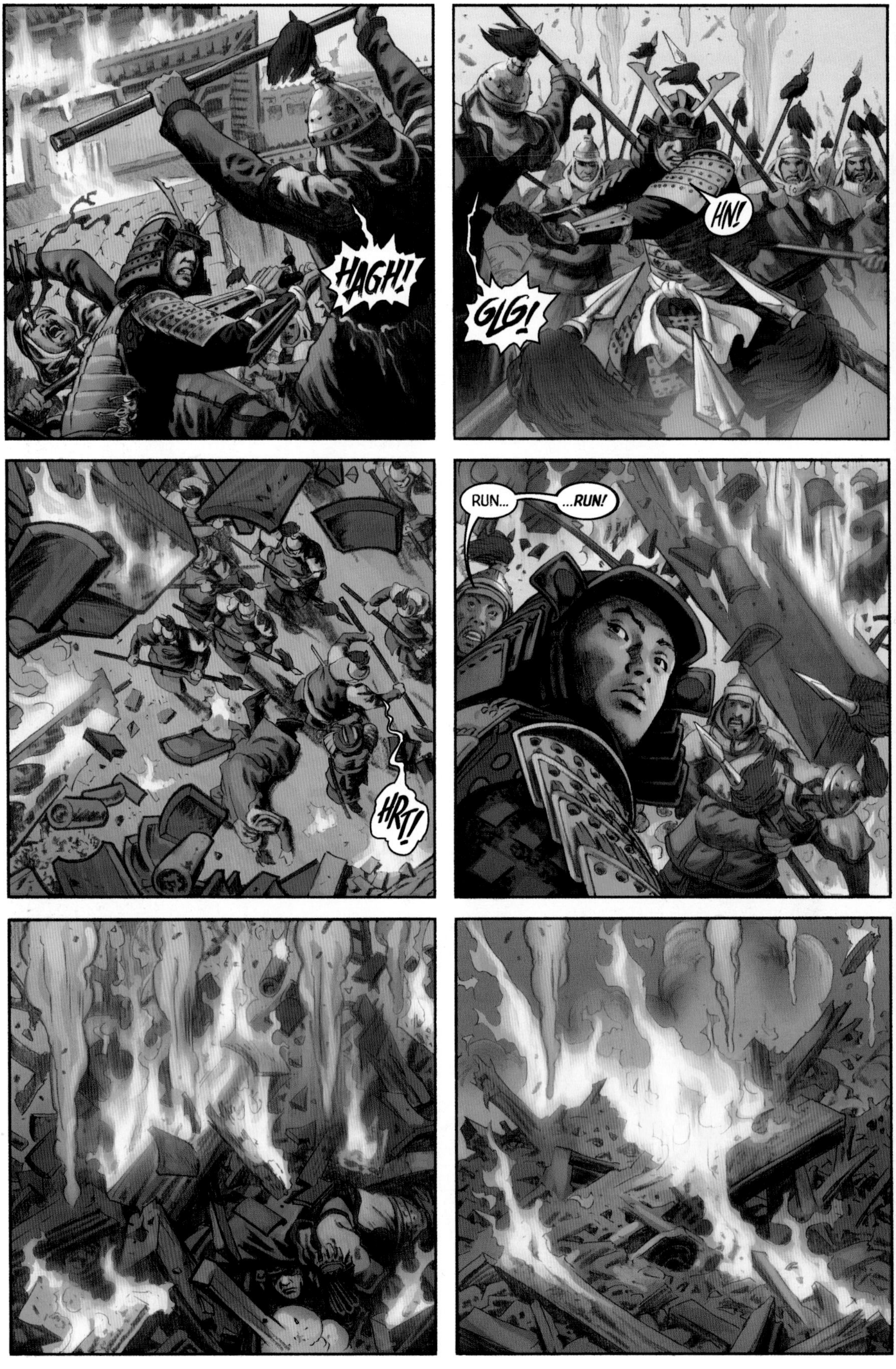
HAGH!
HN!
GLG!
HRT!
RUN...
...RUN!

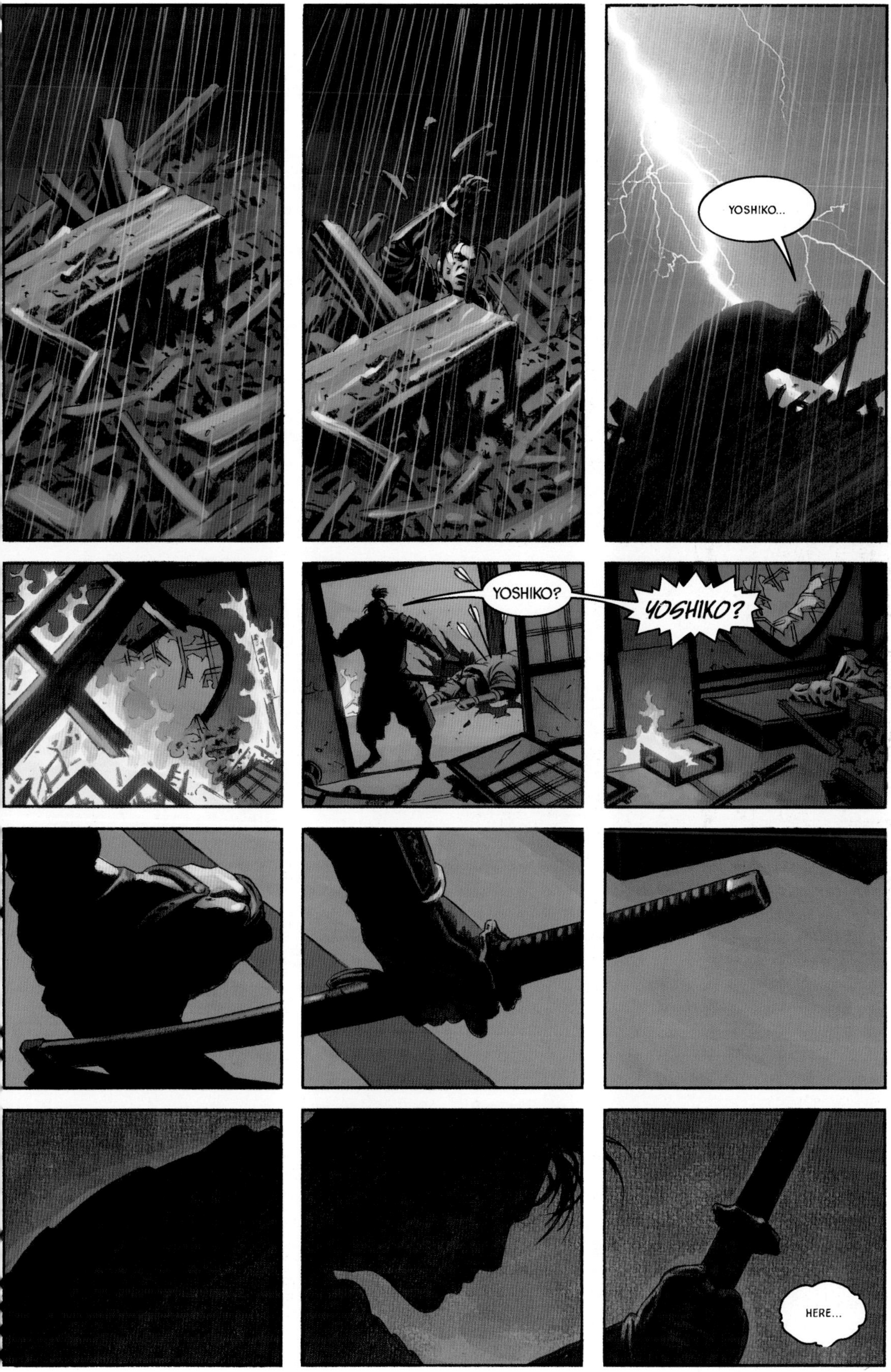
YOSHIKO...
YOSHIKO?
YOSHIKO?
HERE...

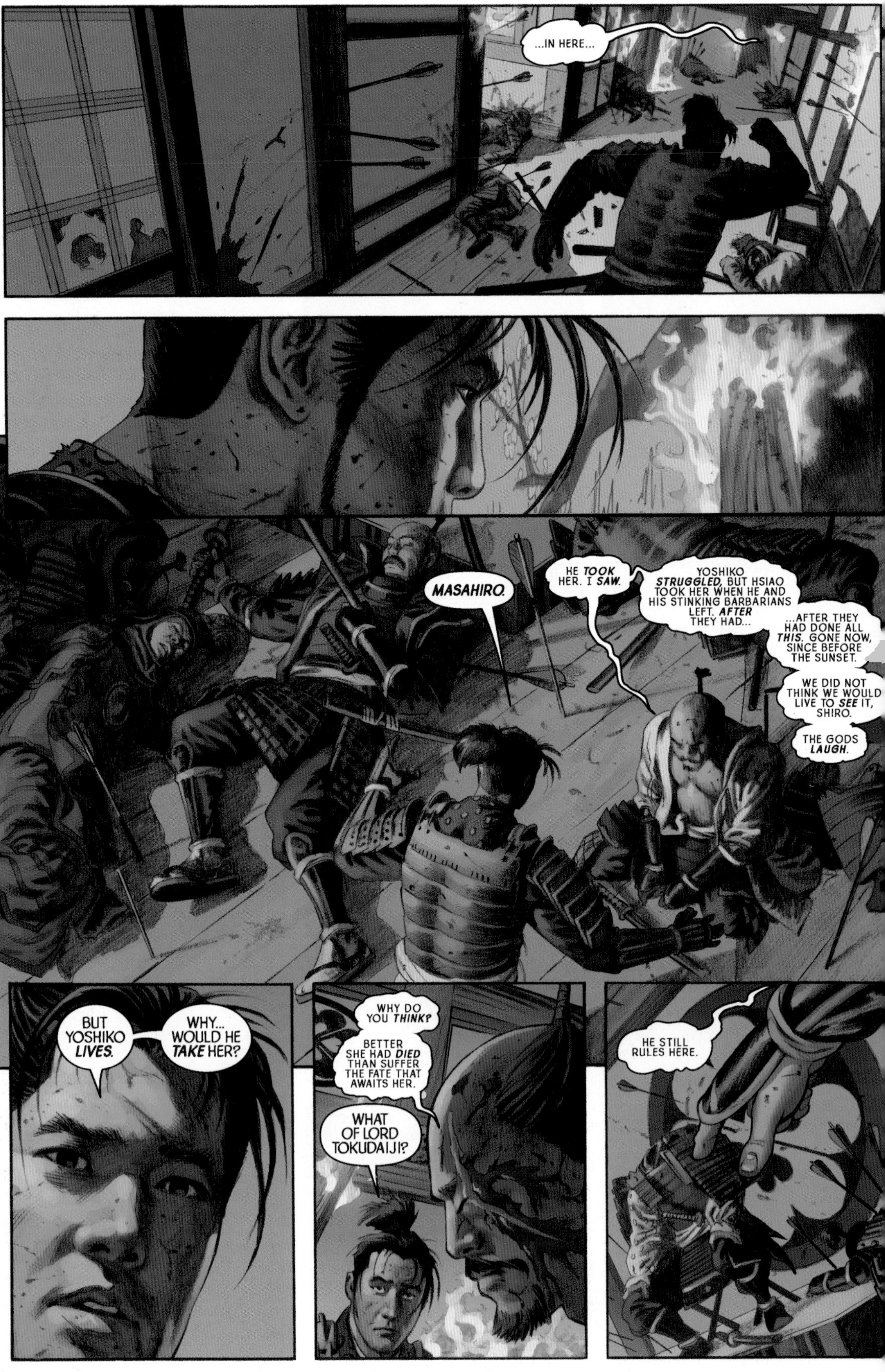
...IN HERE...
MASAHIRO.
HE TOOK HER. I SAW.
YOSHIKO STRUGGLED, BUT HSIAO TOOK HER WHEN HE AND HIS STINKING BARBARIANS LEFT. AFTER THEY HAD...
...AFTER THEY HAD DONE ALL THIS. GONE NOW, SINCE BEFORE THE SUNSET.
WE DID NOT THINK WE WOULD LIVE TO SEE IT, SHIRO.
THE GODS LAUGH.
BUT YOSHIKO LIVES.
WHY... WOULD HE TAKE HER?
WHY DO YOU THINK?
BETTER SHE HAD DIED THAN SUFFER THE FATE THAT AWAITS HER.
WHAT OF LORD TOKUDAIJI!?
HE STILL RULES HERE.

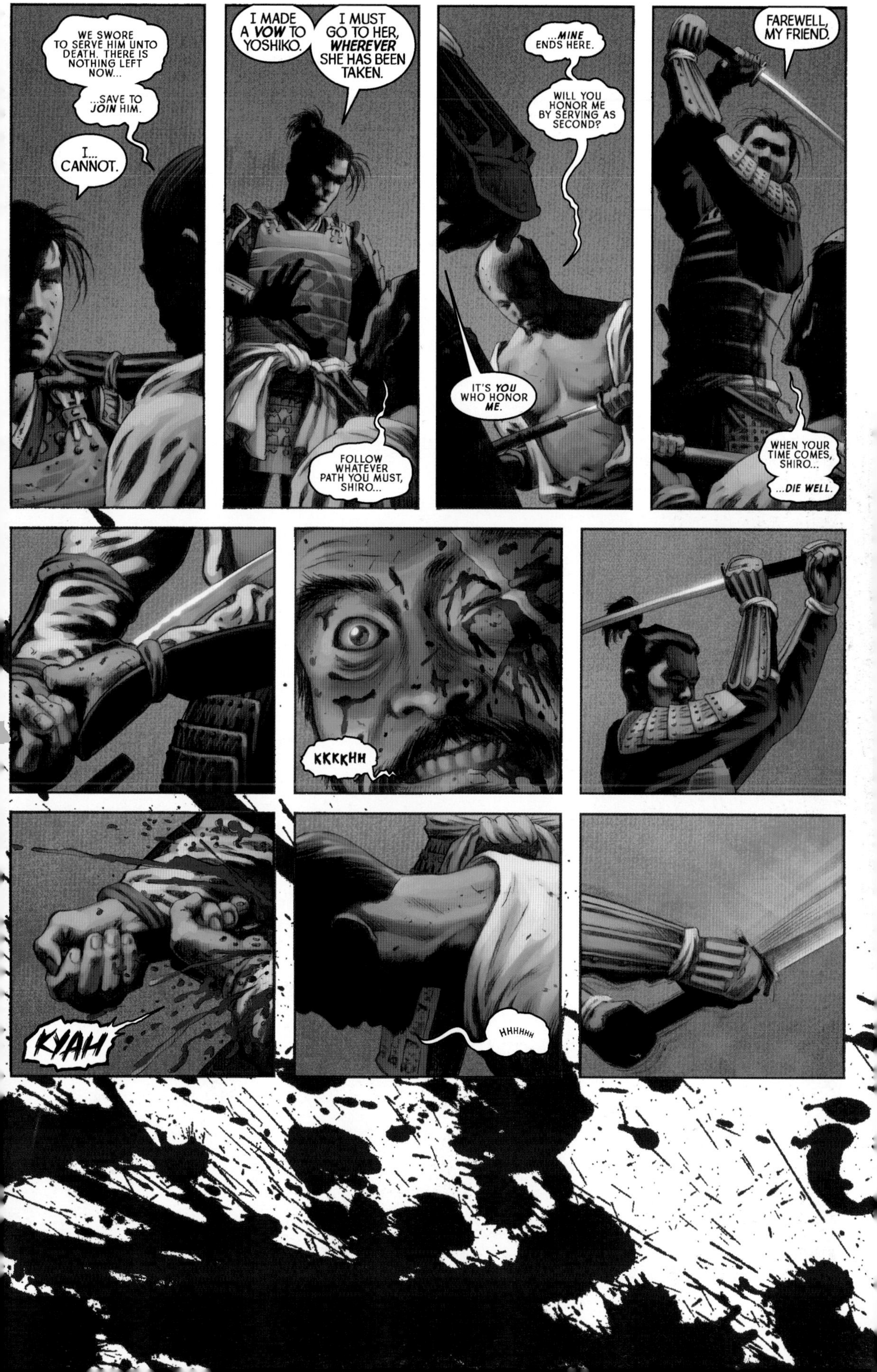

WE SWORE TO SERVE HIM UNTO DEATH. THERE IS NOTHING LEFT NOW...
...SAVE TO JOIN HIM.
I... CANNOT.
I MADE A VOW TO YOSHIKO.
I MUST GO TO HER, WHEREVER SHE HAS BEEN TAKEN.
FOLLOW WHATEVER PATH YOU MUST, SHIRO...
...MINE ENDS HERE.
WILL YOU HONOR ME BY SERVING AS SECOND?
IT'S YOU WHO HONOR ME.
FAREWELL, MY FRIEND.
WHEN YOUR TIME COMES, SHIRO...
...DIE WELL.
KKKKHH
KYAH
HHHHHH

YOSHIKO...

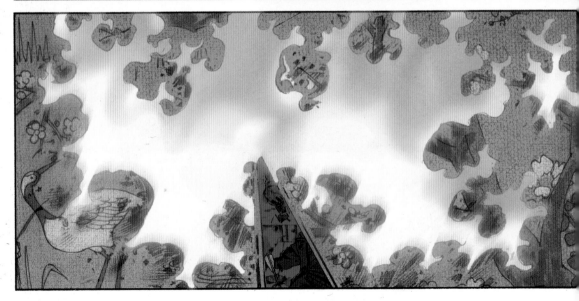

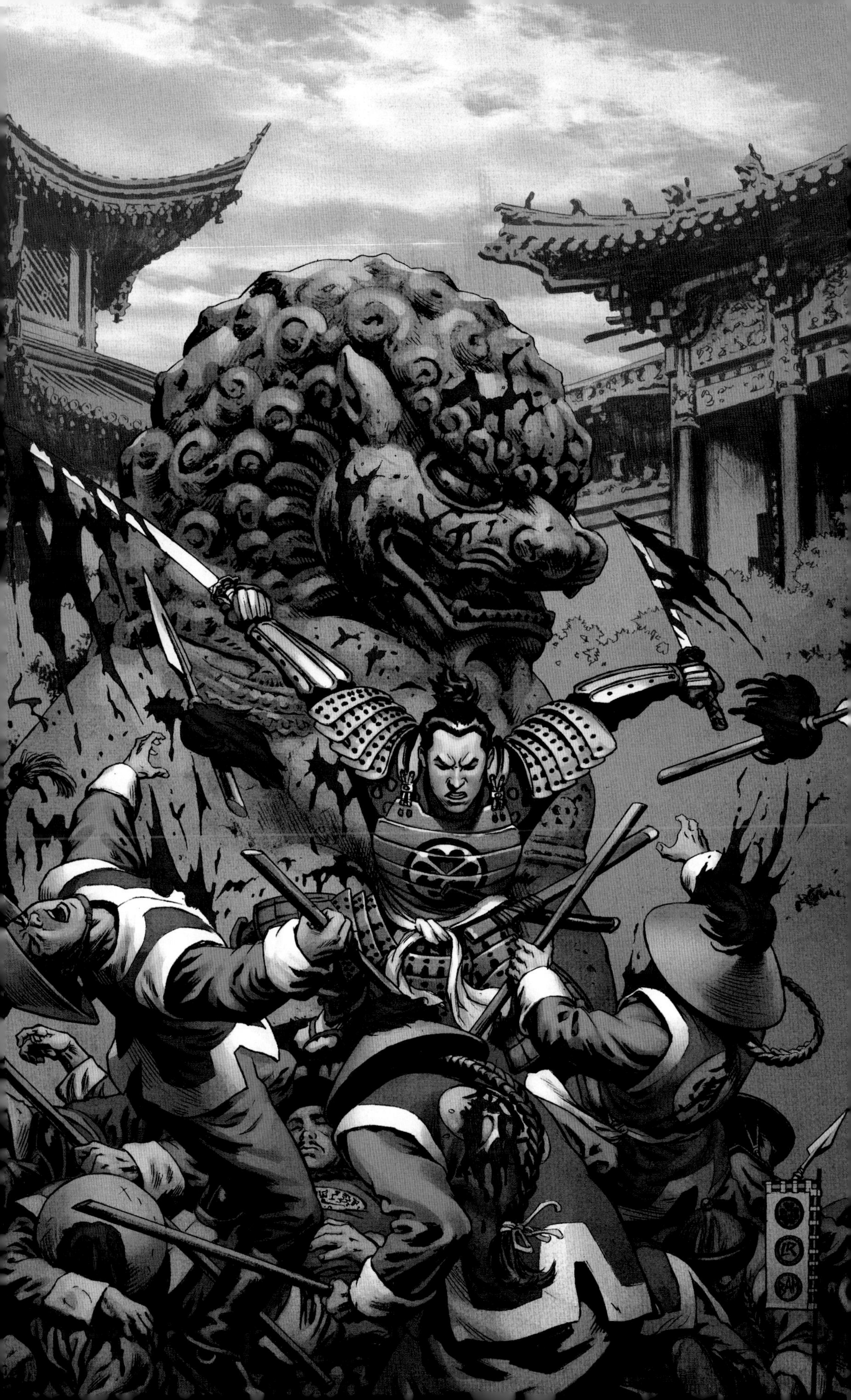

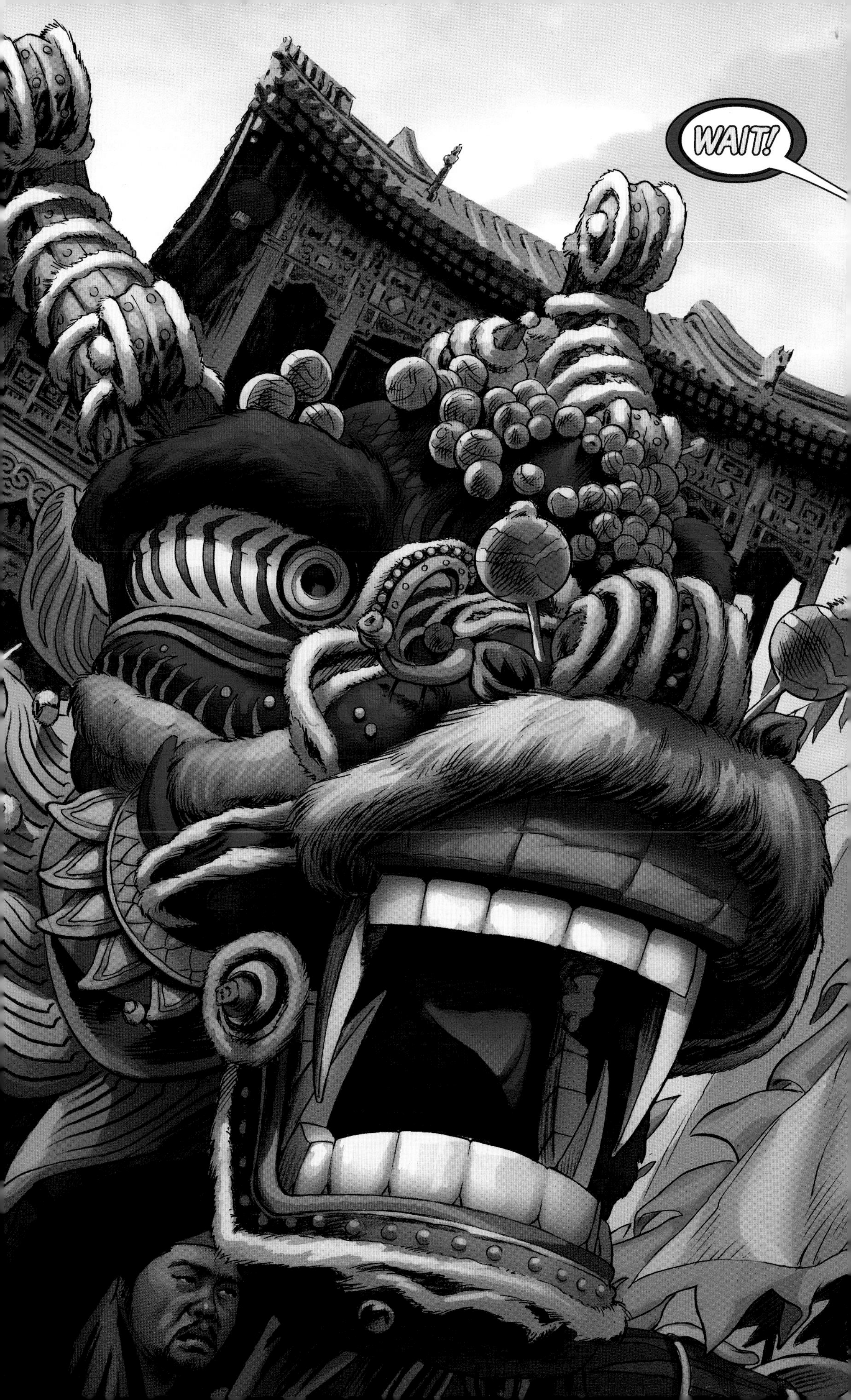
WAIT!

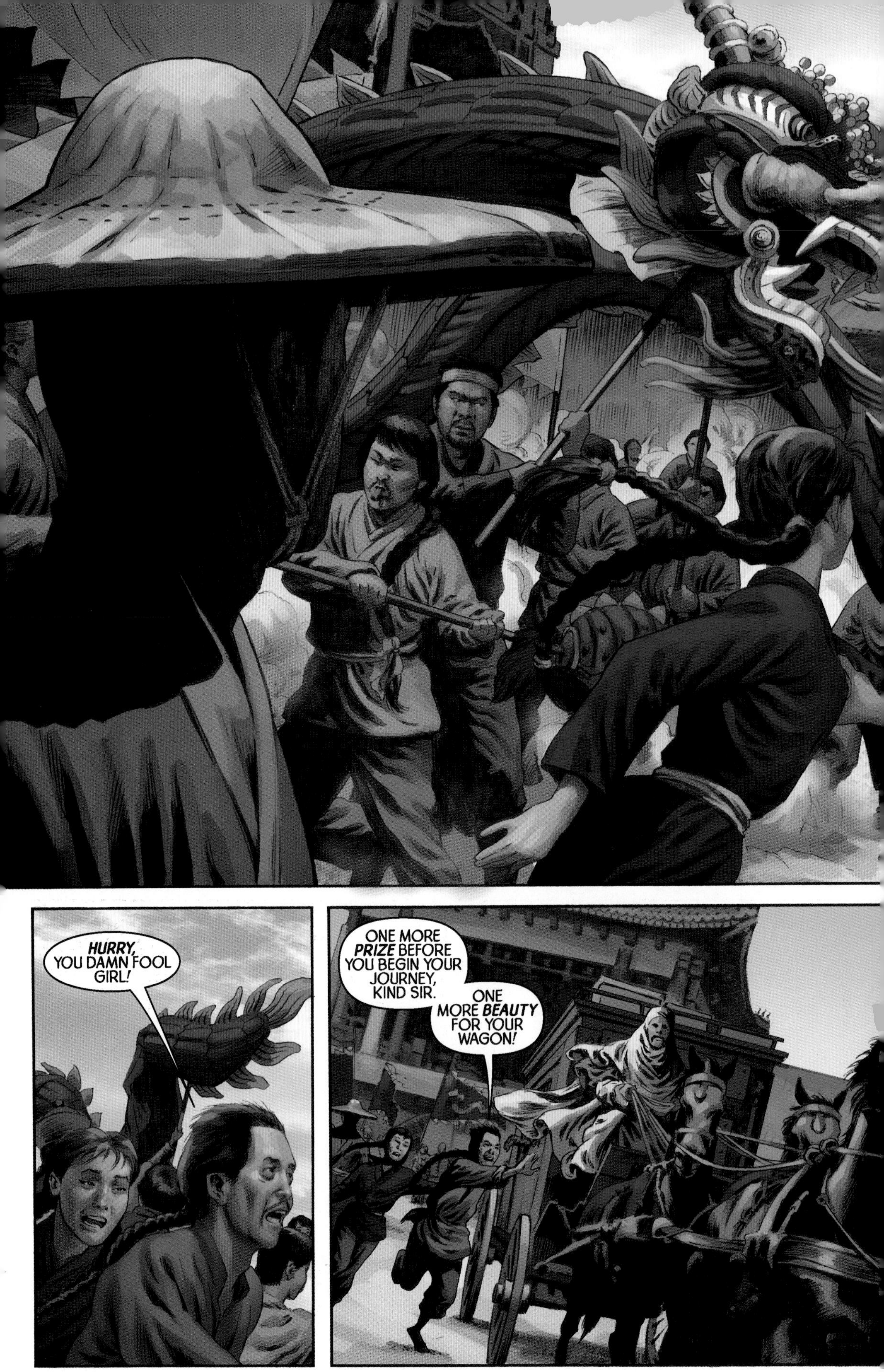
HURRY, YOU DAMN FOOL GIRL!
ONE MORE **PRIZE** BEFORE YOU BEGIN YOUR JOURNEY, KIND SIR.
ONE MORE **BEAUTY** FOR YOUR WAGON!

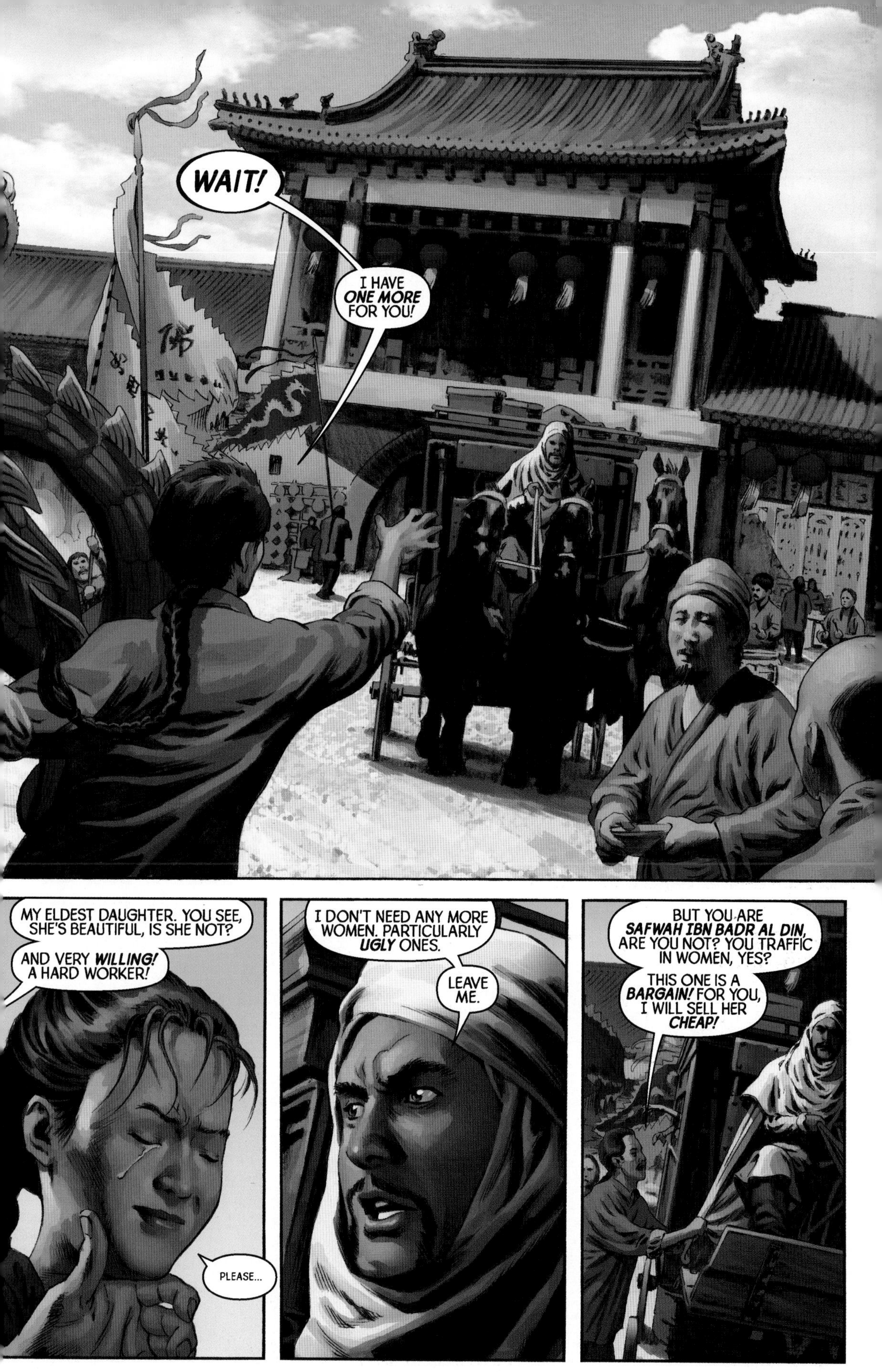
WAIT!
I HAVE ONE MORE FOR YOU!
MY ELDEST DAUGHTER. YOU SEE, SHE'S BEAUTIFUL, IS SHE NOT?
AND VERY WILLING! A HARD WORKER!
PLEASE...
I DON'T NEED ANY MORE WOMEN. PARTICULARLY UGLY ONES.
LEAVE ME.
BUT YOU ARE SAFWAH IBN BADR AL DIN, ARE YOU NOT? YOU TRAFFIC IN WOMEN, YES?
THIS ONE IS A BARGAIN! FOR YOU, I WILL SELL HER CHEAP!

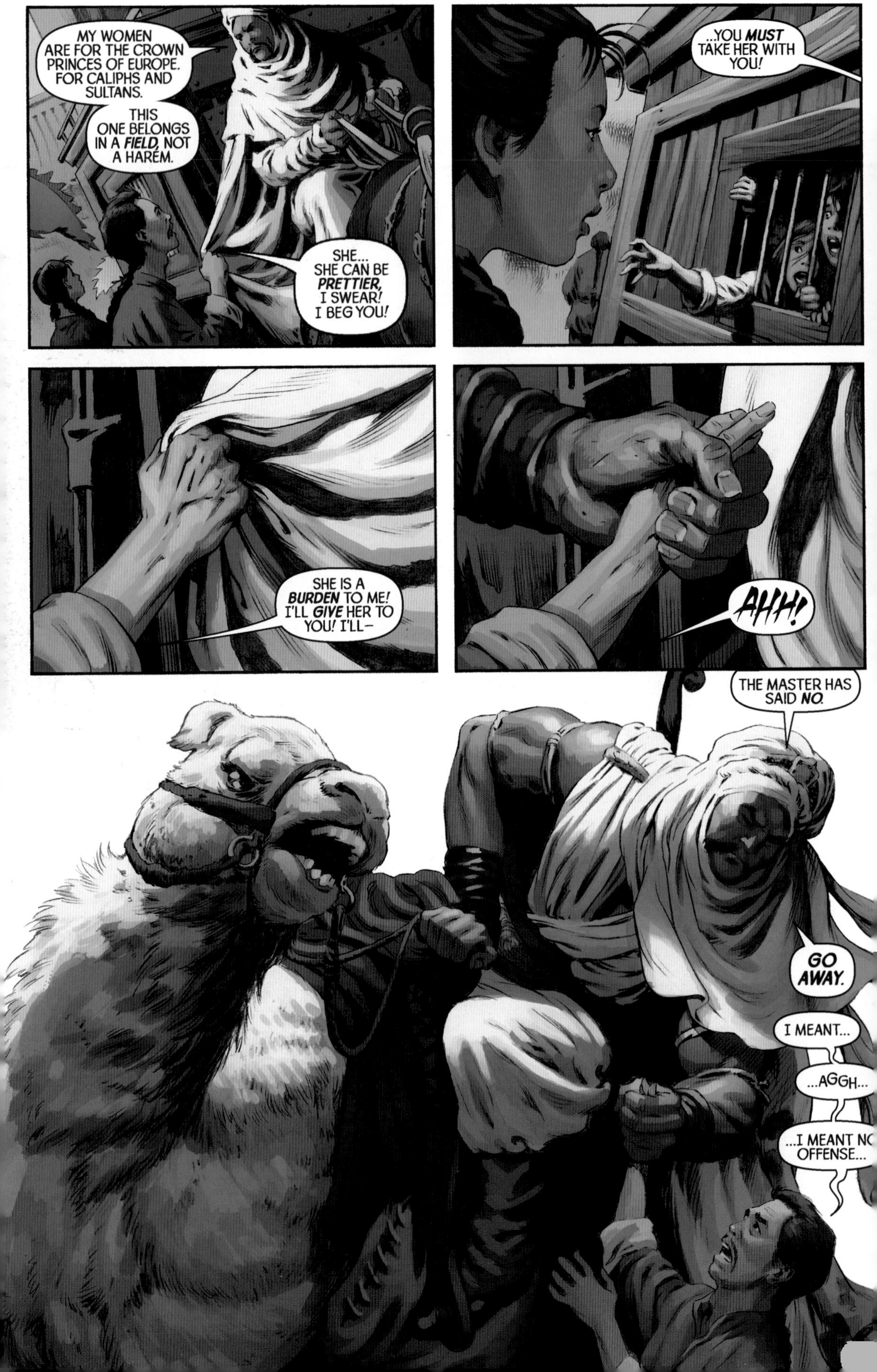
MY WOMEN ARE FOR THE CROWN PRINCES OF EUROPE. FOR CALIPHS AND SULTANS.
THIS ONE BELONGS IN A *FIELD,* NOT A HARÉM.
SHE... SHE CAN BE *PRETTIER,* I SWEAR! I BEG YOU!
...YOU *MUST* TAKE HER WITH YOU!
SHE IS A *BURDEN* TO ME! I'LL *GIVE* HER TO YOU! I'LL—
AHH!
THE MASTER HAS SAID *NO.*
GO AWAY.
I MEANT...
...AGGH...
...I MEANT NO OFFENSE...

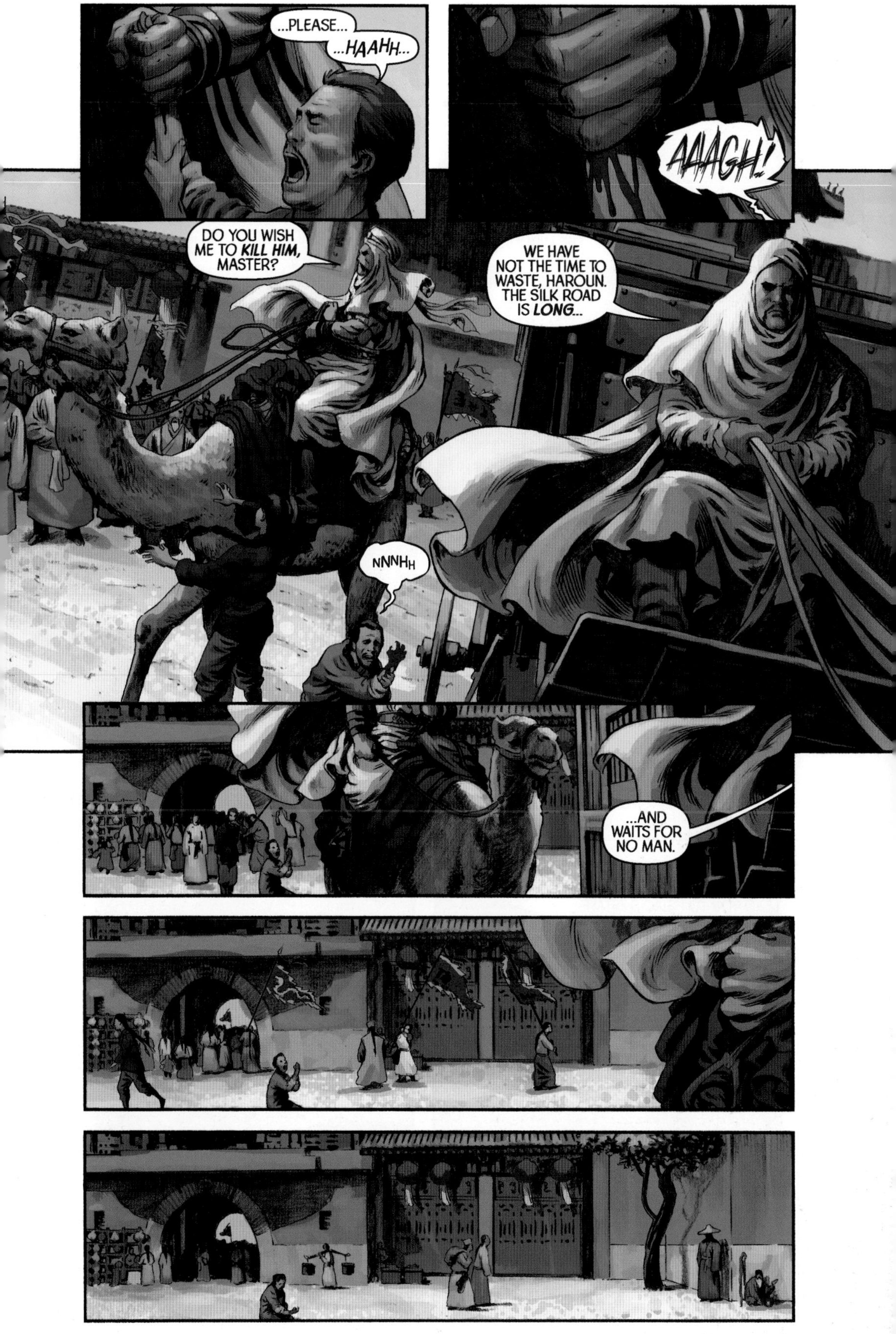

...PLEASE...
...HAAHH...
AAAGH!
DO YOU WISH ME TO *KILL HIM,* MASTER?
WE HAVE NOT THE TIME TO WASTE, HAROUN. THE SILK ROAD IS *LONG*...
NNNHH
...AND WAITS FOR NO MAN.

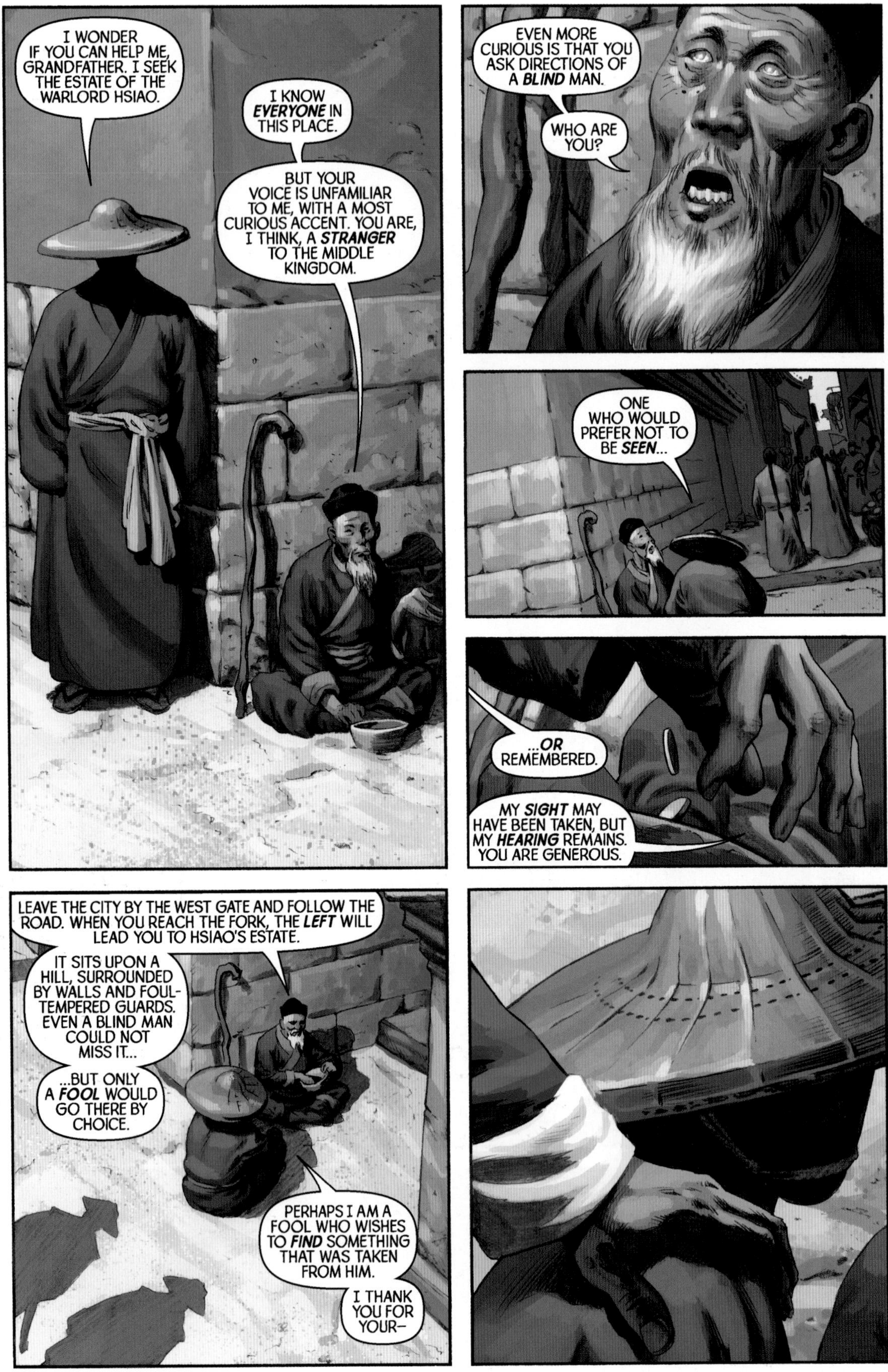
I WONDER IF YOU CAN HELP ME, GRANDFATHER. I SEEK THE ESTATE OF THE WARLORD HSIAO.
I KNOW *EVERYONE* IN THIS PLACE.
BUT YOUR VOICE IS UNFAMILIAR TO ME, WITH A MOST CURIOUS ACCENT. YOU ARE, I THINK, A *STRANGER* TO THE MIDDLE KINGDOM.
EVEN MORE CURIOUS IS THAT YOU ASK DIRECTIONS OF A *BLIND* MAN.
WHO ARE YOU?
ONE WHO WOULD PREFER NOT TO BE *SEEN*...
...*OR* REMEMBERED.
MY *SIGHT* MAY HAVE BEEN TAKEN, BUT MY *HEARING* REMAINS. YOU ARE GENEROUS.
LEAVE THE CITY BY THE WEST GATE AND FOLLOW THE ROAD. WHEN YOU REACH THE FORK, THE *LEFT* WILL LEAD YOU TO HSIAO'S ESTATE.
IT SITS UPON A HILL, SURROUNDED BY WALLS AND FOUL-TEMPERED GUARDS. EVEN A BLIND MAN COULD NOT MISS IT...
...BUT ONLY A *FOOL* WOULD GO THERE BY CHOICE.
PERHAPS I AM A FOOL WHO WISHES TO *FIND* SOMETHING THAT WAS TAKEN FROM HIM.
I THANK YOU FOR YOUR–

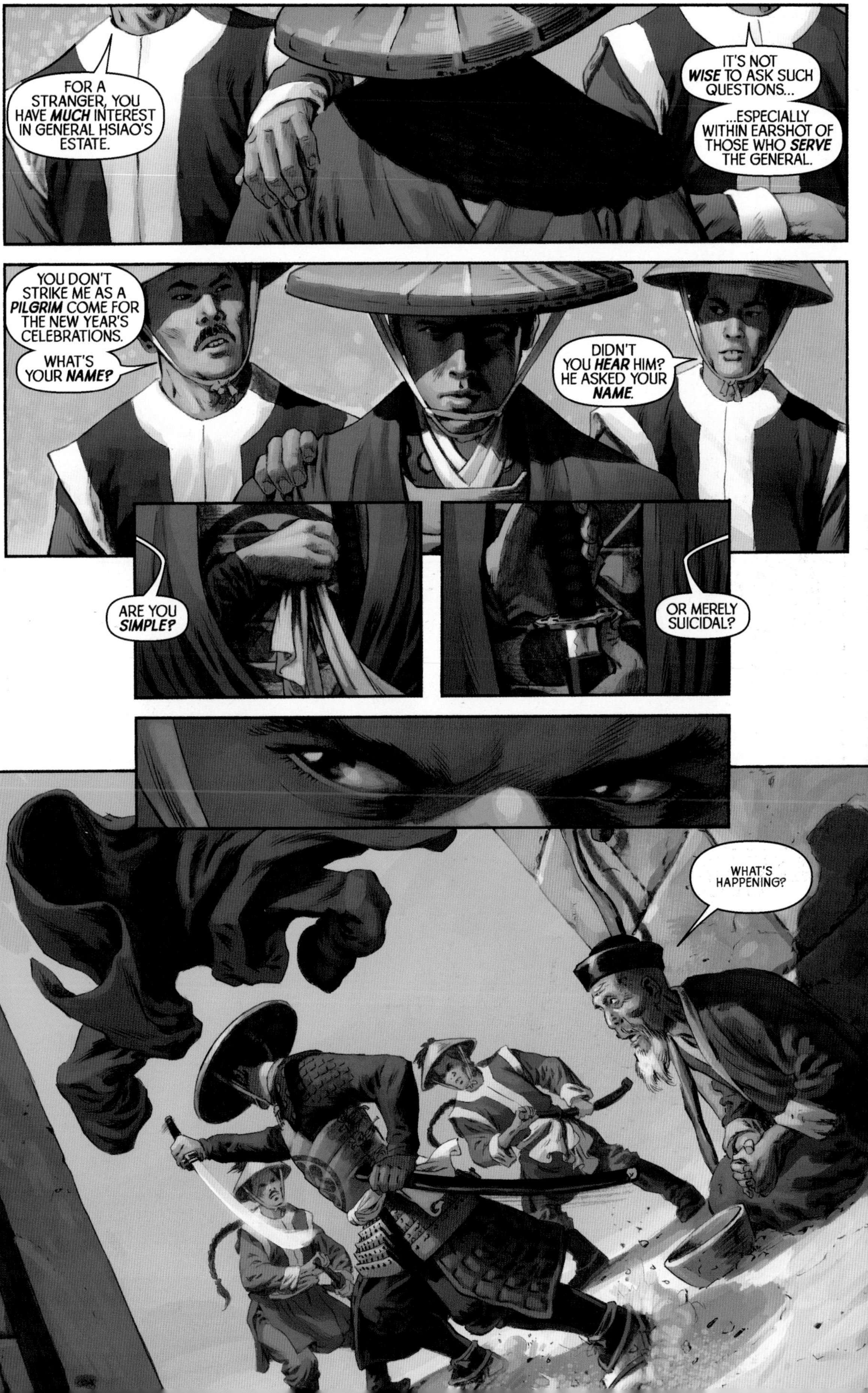
FOR A STRANGER, YOU HAVE MUCH INTEREST IN GENERAL HSIAO'S ESTATE.
IT'S NOT WISE TO ASK SUCH QUESTIONS...
...ESPECIALLY WITHIN EARSHOT OF THOSE WHO SERVE THE GENERAL.
YOU DON'T STRIKE ME AS A PILGRIM COME FOR THE NEW YEAR'S CELEBRATIONS.
WHAT'S YOUR NAME?
DIDN'T YOU HEAR HIM? HE ASKED YOUR NAME.
ARE YOU SIMPLE?
OR MERELY SUICIDAL?
WHAT'S HAPPENING?

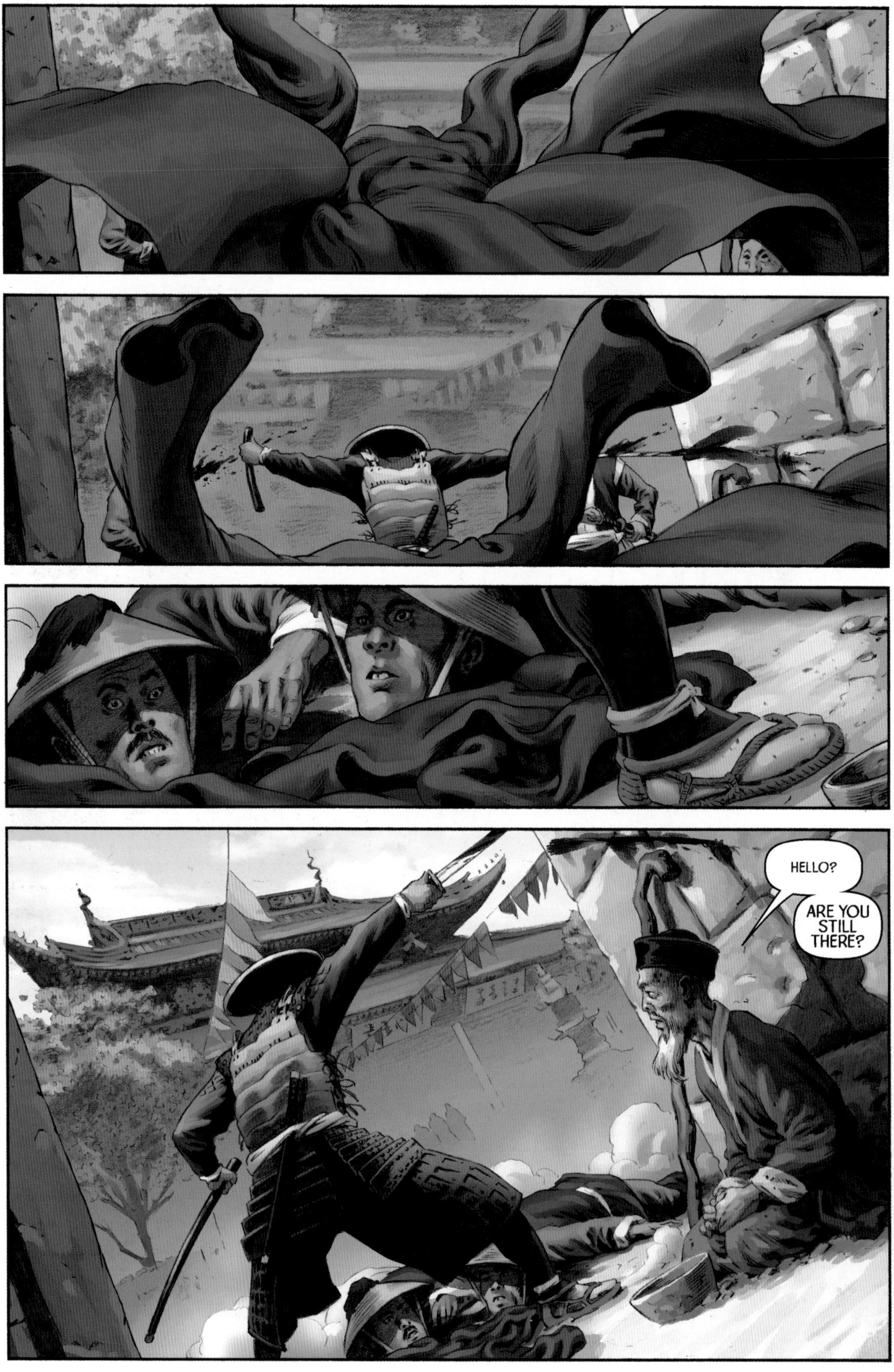
HELLO?
ARE YOU STILL THERE?

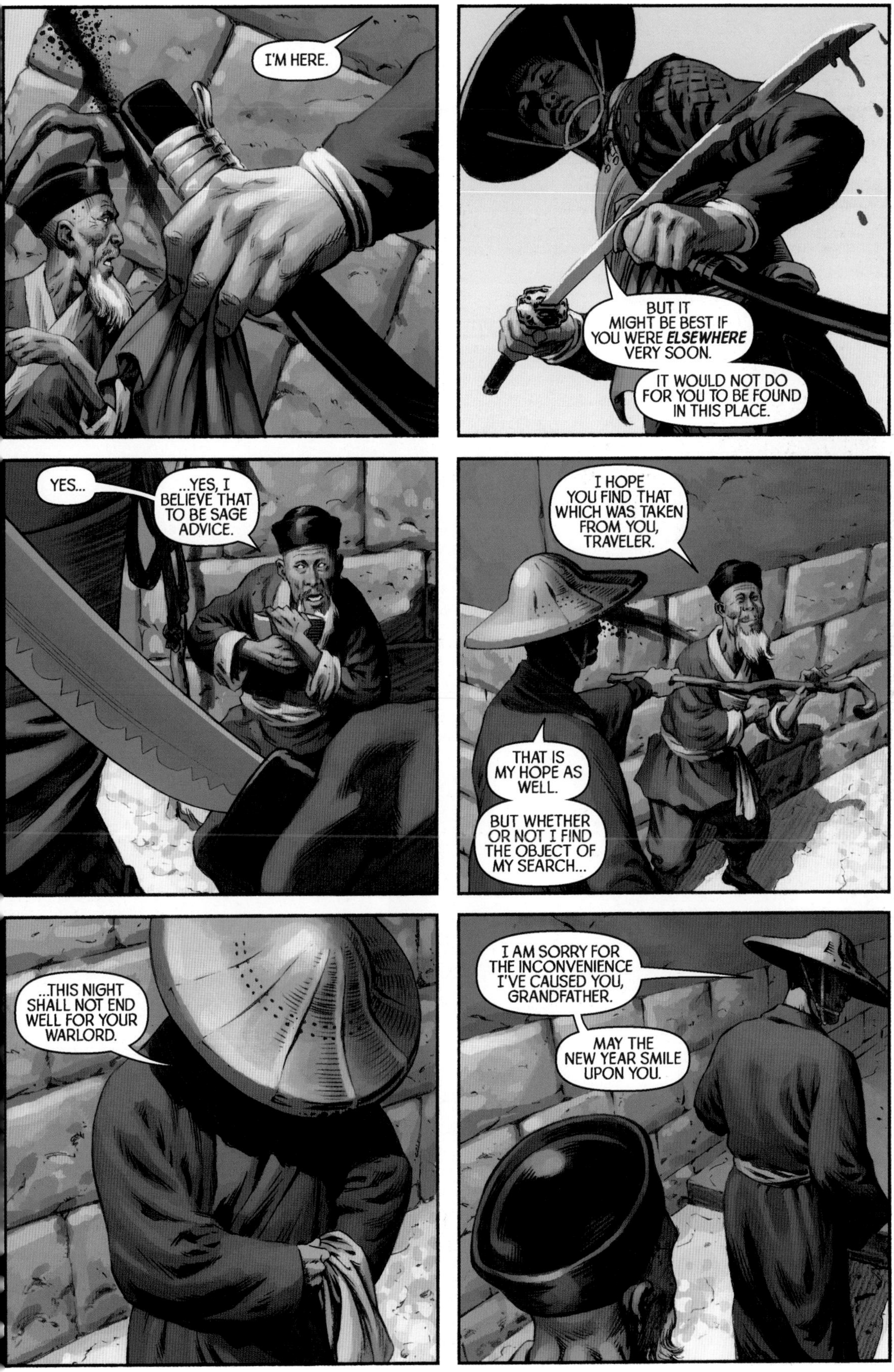
I'M HERE.
BUT IT MIGHT BE BEST IF YOU WERE *ELSEWHERE* VERY SOON.
IT WOULD NOT DO FOR YOU TO BE FOUND IN THIS PLACE.
YES...
...YES, I BELIEVE THAT TO BE SAGE ADVICE.
I HOPE YOU FIND THAT WHICH WAS TAKEN FROM YOU, TRAVELER.
THAT IS MY HOPE AS WELL.
BUT WHETHER OR NOT I FIND THE OBJECT OF MY SEARCH...
...THIS NIGHT SHALL NOT END WELL FOR YOUR WARLORD.
I AM SORRY FOR THE INCONVENIENCE I'VE CAUSED YOU, GRANDFATHER.
MAY THE NEW YEAR SMILE UPON YOU.

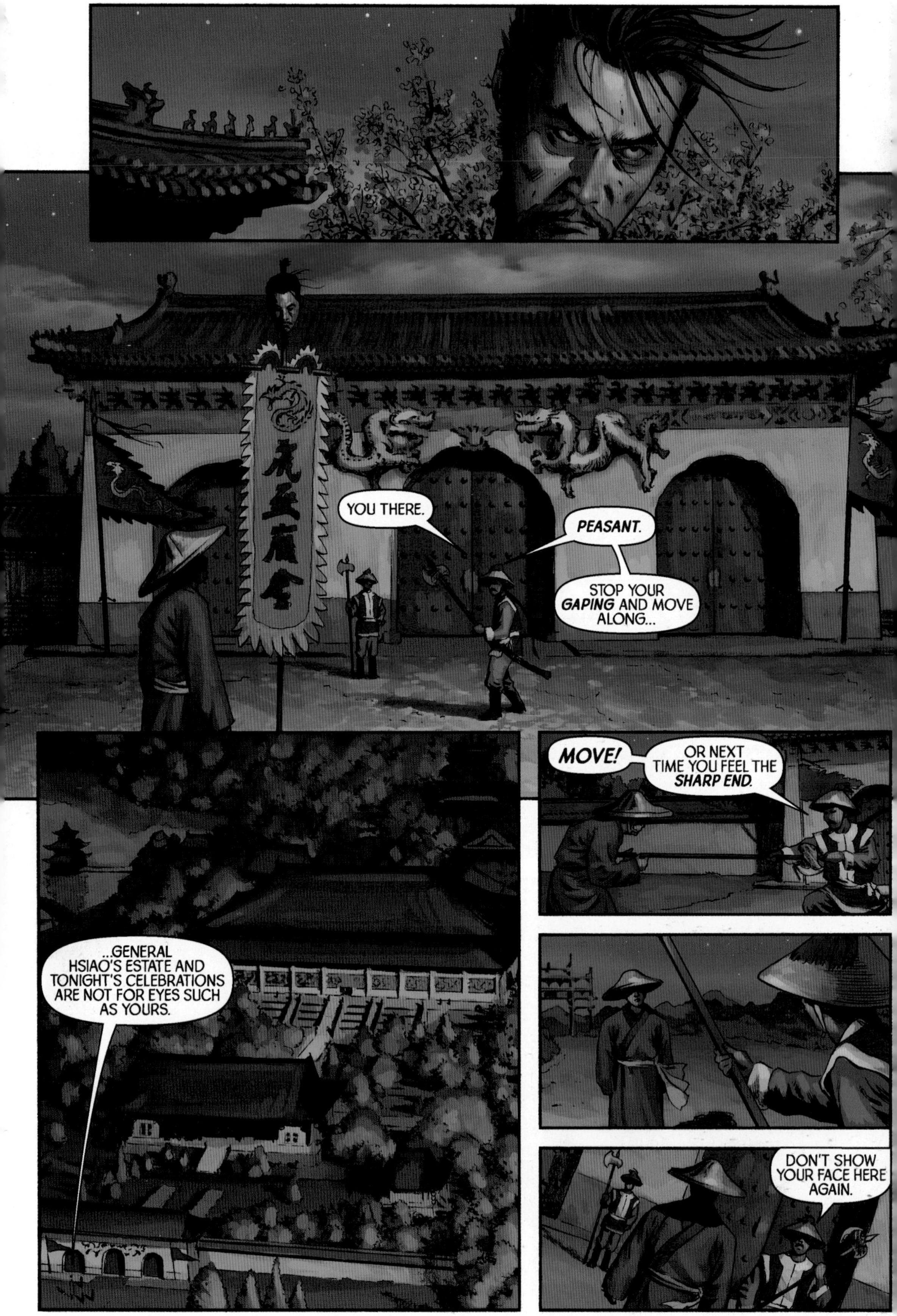
YOU THERE.
PEASANT.
STOP YOUR GAPING AND MOVE ALONG...
...GENERAL HSIAO'S ESTATE AND TONIGHT'S CELEBRATIONS ARE NOT FOR EYES SUCH AS YOURS.
MOVE!
OR NEXT TIME YOU FEEL THE SHARP END.
DON'T SHOW YOUR FACE HERE AGAIN.

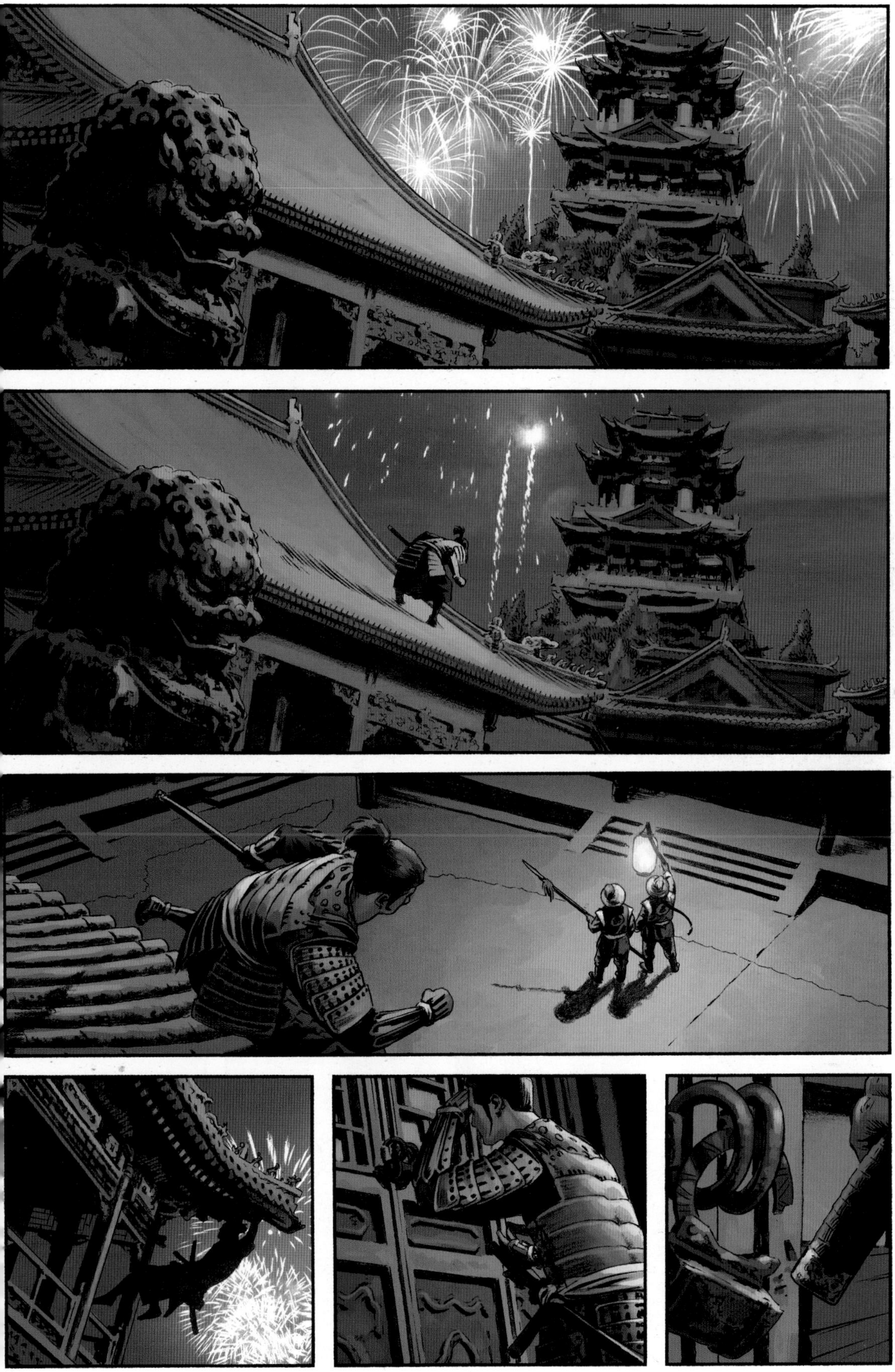

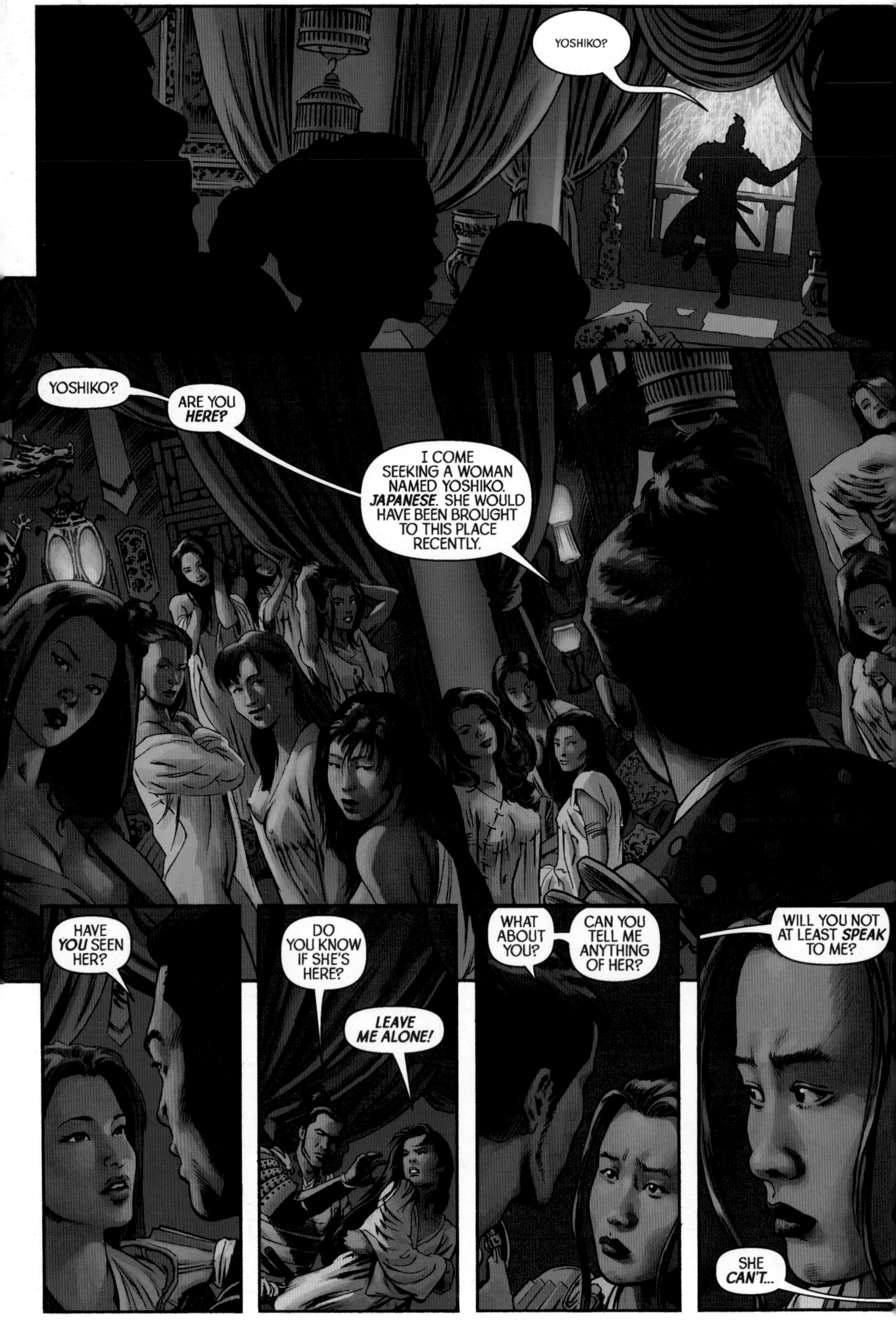

YOSHIKO?
YOSHIKO?
ARE YOU HERE?
I COME SEEKING A WOMAN NAMED YOSHIKO. JAPANESE. SHE WOULD HAVE BEEN BROUGHT TO THIS PLACE RECENTLY.
HAVE YOU SEEN HER?
DO YOU KNOW IF SHE'S HERE?
LEAVE ME ALONE!
WHAT ABOUT YOU?
CAN YOU TELL ME ANYTHING OF HER?
WILL YOU NOT AT LEAST SPEAK TO ME?
SHE CAN'T...

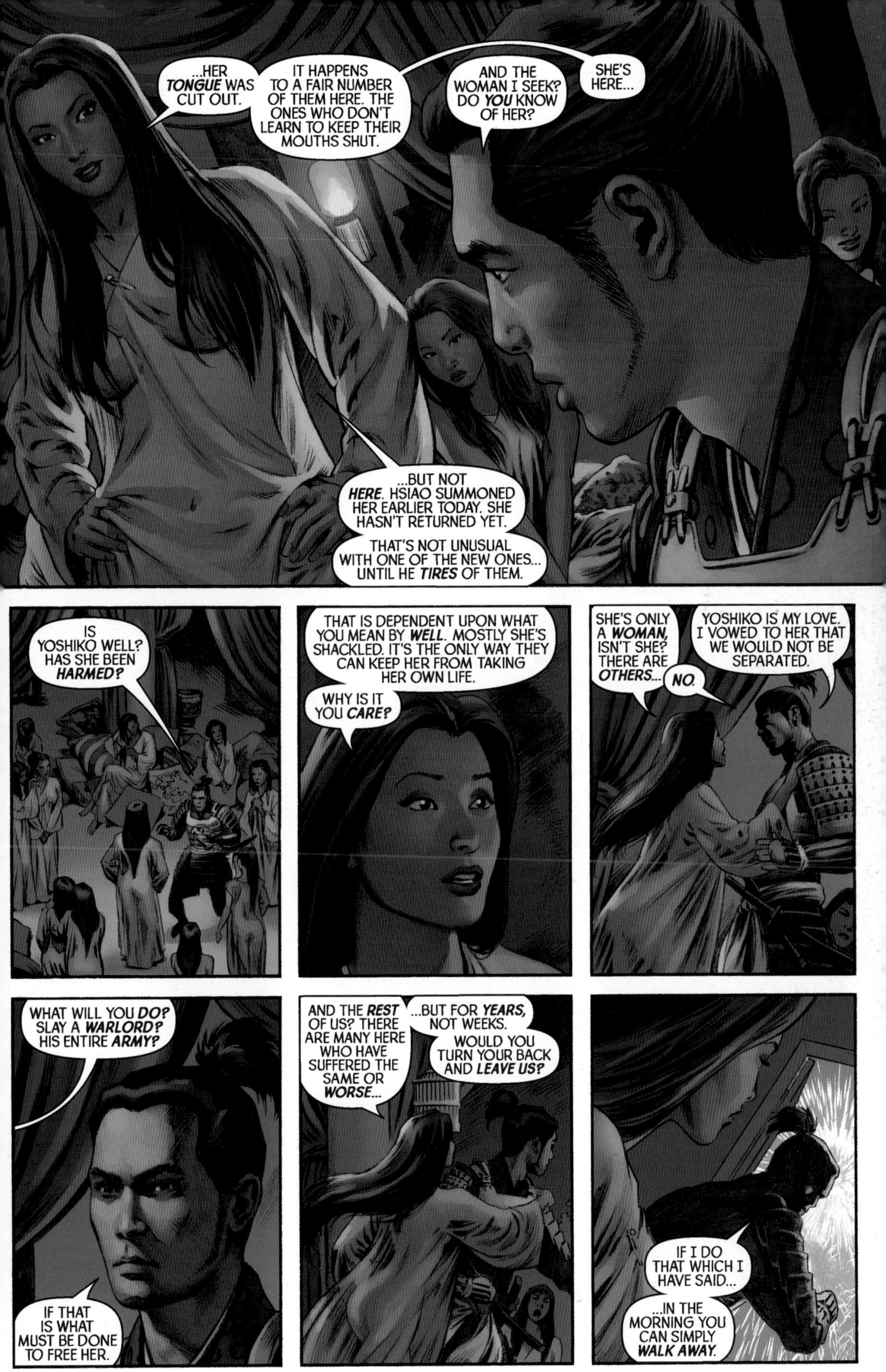
...HER TONGUE WAS CUT OUT.
IT HAPPENS TO A FAIR NUMBER OF THEM HERE. THE ONES WHO DON'T LEARN TO KEEP THEIR MOUTHS SHUT.
AND THE WOMAN I SEEK? DO YOU KNOW OF HER?
SHE'S HERE...
...BUT NOT HERE. HSIAO SUMMONED HER EARLIER TODAY. SHE HASN'T RETURNED YET.
THAT'S NOT UNUSUAL WITH ONE OF THE NEW ONES... UNTIL HE TIRES OF THEM.
IS YOSHIKO WELL? HAS SHE BEEN HARMED?
THAT IS DEPENDENT UPON WHAT YOU MEAN BY WELL. MOSTLY SHE'S SHACKLED. IT'S THE ONLY WAY THEY CAN KEEP HER FROM TAKING HER OWN LIFE.
WHY IS IT YOU CARE?
SHE'S ONLY A WOMAN, ISN'T SHE? THERE ARE OTHERS...
NO.
YOSHIKO IS MY LOVE. I VOWED TO HER THAT WE WOULD NOT BE SEPARATED.
WHAT WILL YOU DO? SLAY A WARLORD? HIS ENTIRE ARMY?
IF THAT IS WHAT MUST BE DONE TO FREE HER.
AND THE REST OF US? THERE ARE MANY HERE WHO HAVE SUFFERED THE SAME OR WORSE...
...BUT FOR YEARS, NOT WEEKS.
WOULD YOU TURN YOUR BACK AND LEAVE US?
IF I DO THAT WHICH I HAVE SAID...
...IN THE MORNING YOU CAN SIMPLY WALK AWAY.

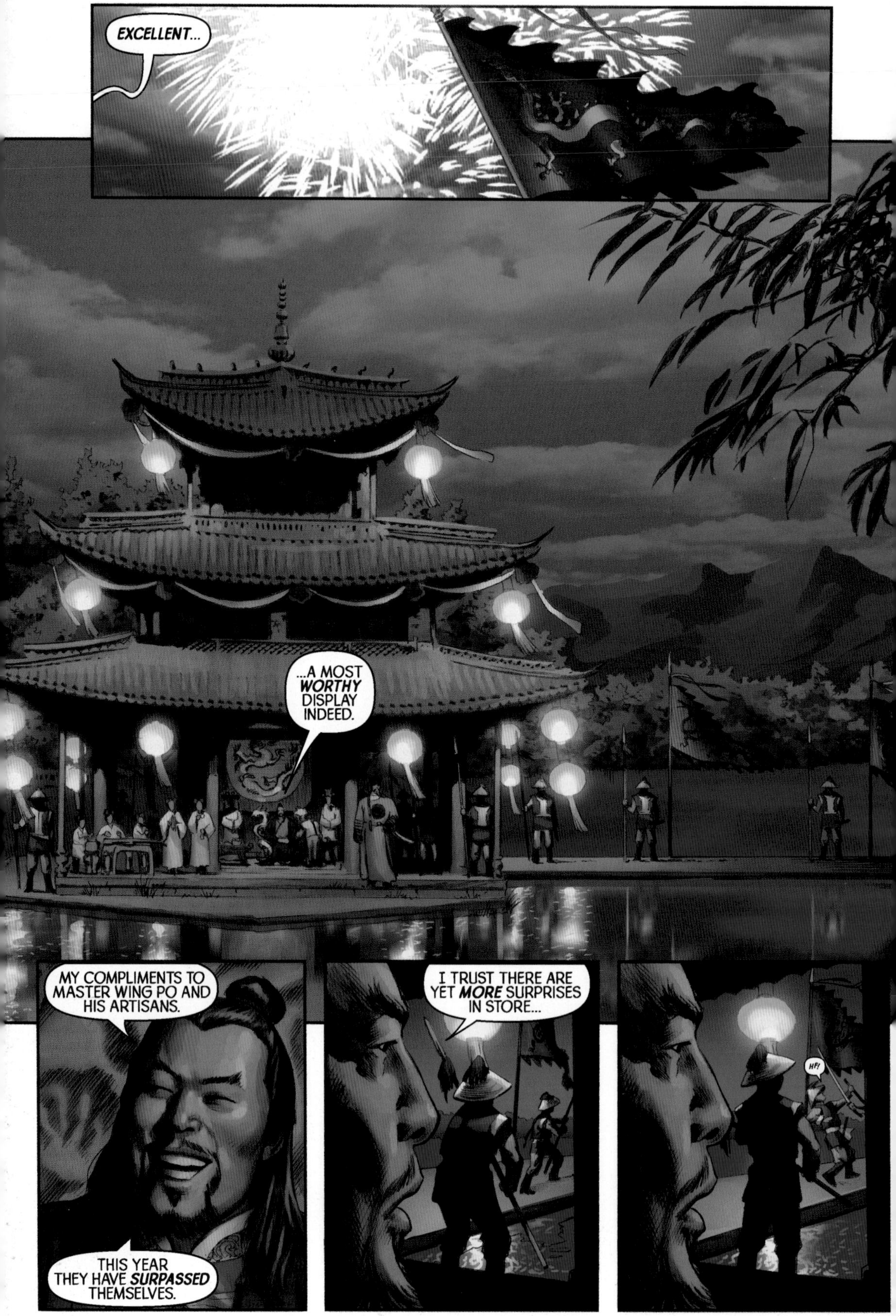
EXCELLENT...
...A MOST WORTHY DISPLAY INDEED.
MY COMPLIMENTS TO MASTER WING PO AND HIS ARTISANS.
THIS YEAR THEY HAVE SURPASSED THEMSELVES.
I TRUST THERE ARE YET MORE SURPRISES IN STORE...
HF!

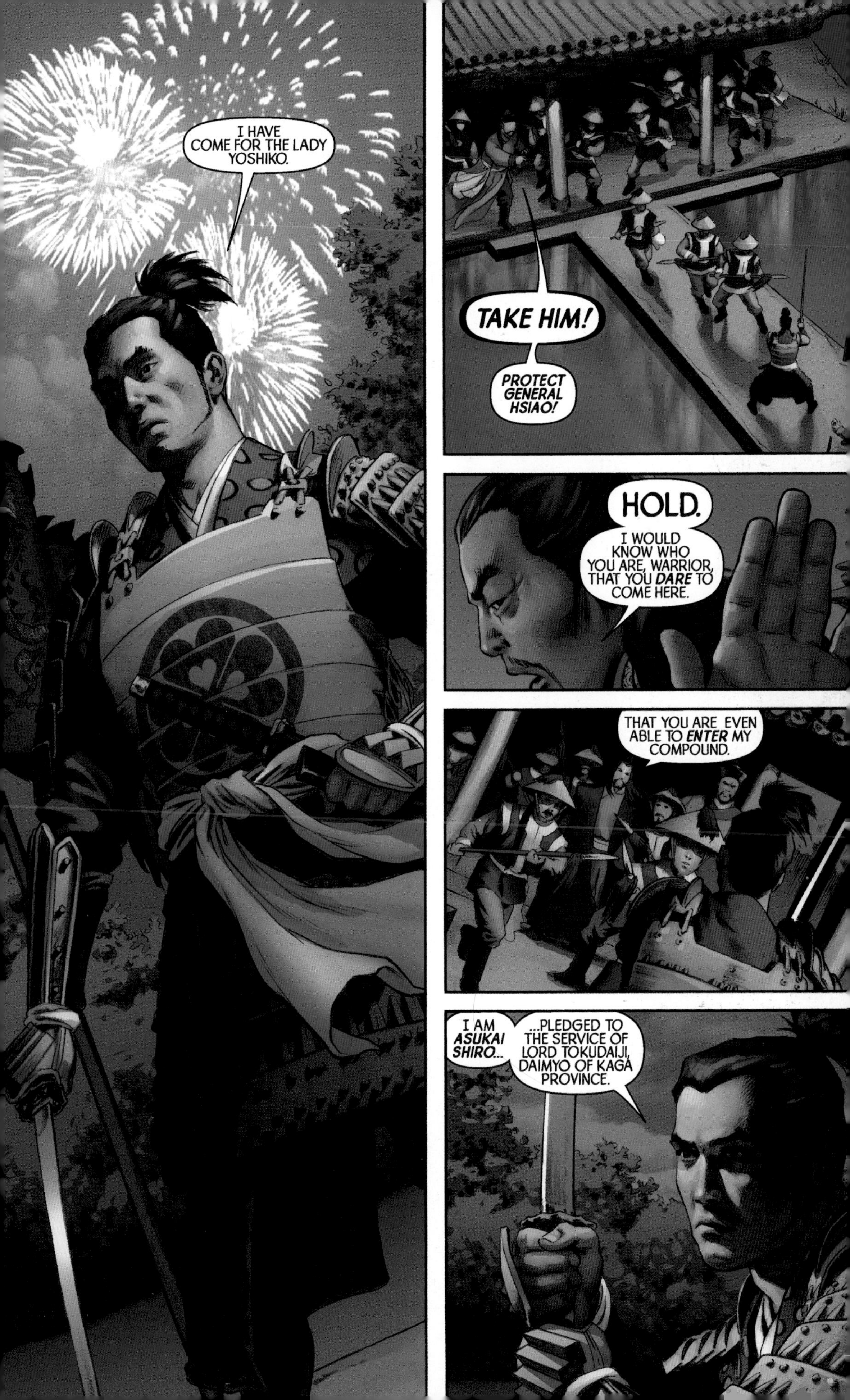
I HAVE COME FOR THE LADY YOSHIKO.
TAKE HIM!
PROTECT GENERAL HSIAO!
HOLD.
I WOULD KNOW WHO YOU ARE, WARRIOR, THAT YOU *DARE* TO COME HERE.
THAT YOU ARE EVEN ABLE TO *ENTER* MY COMPOUND.
I AM *ASUKAI SHIRO*...
...PLEDGED TO THE SERVICE OF LORD TOKUDAIJI, DAIMYO OF KAGA PROVINCE.

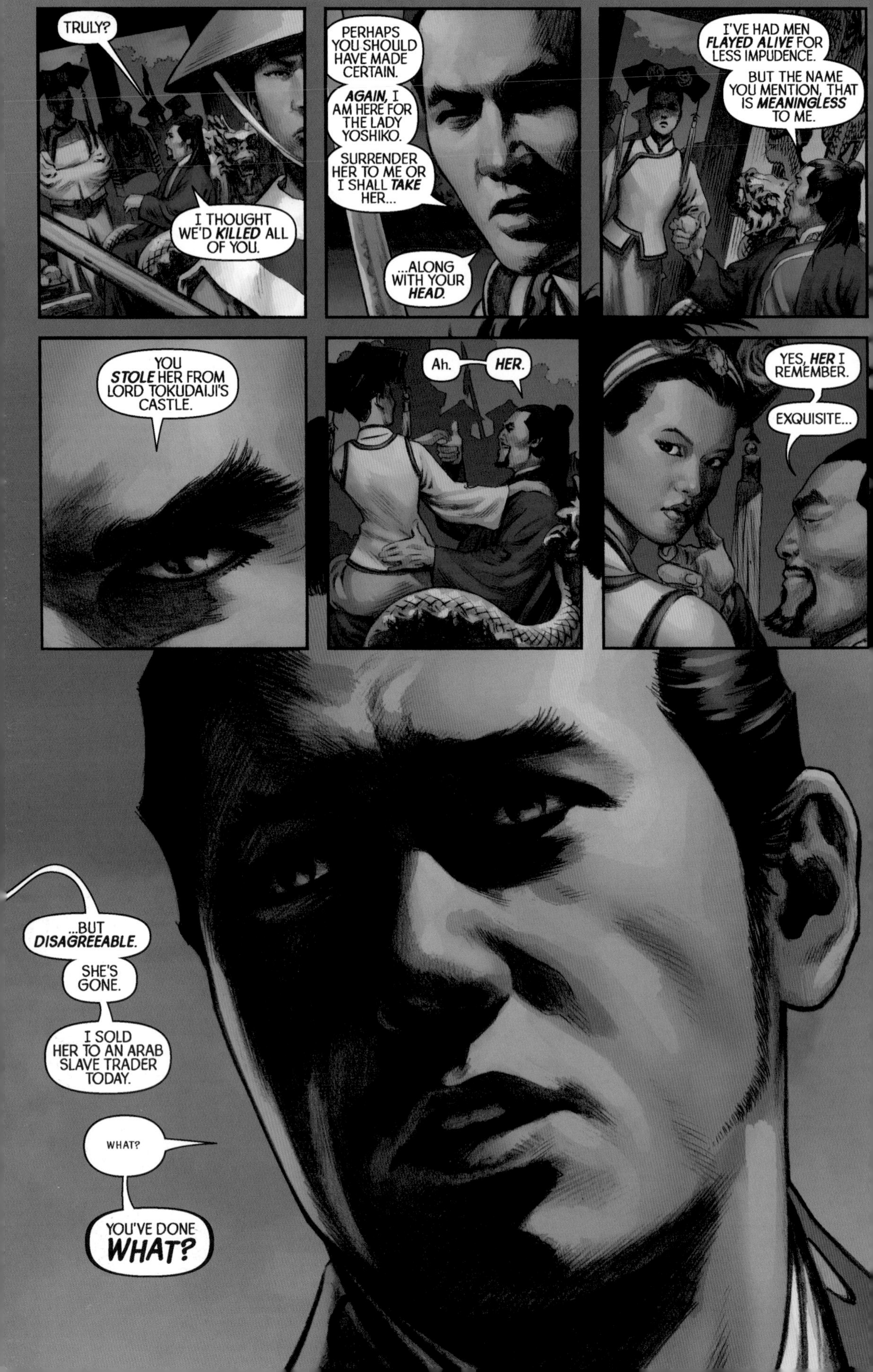
TRULY?
I THOUGHT WE'D KILLED ALL OF YOU.
PERHAPS YOU SHOULD HAVE MADE CERTAIN.
AGAIN, I AM HERE FOR THE LADY YOSHIKO.
SURRENDER HER TO ME OR I SHALL TAKE HER...
...ALONG WITH YOUR HEAD.
I'VE HAD MEN FLAYED ALIVE FOR LESS IMPUDENCE.
BUT THE NAME YOU MENTION, THAT IS MEANINGLESS TO ME.
YOU STOLE HER FROM LORD TOKUDAIJI'S CASTLE.
Ah.
HER.
YES, HER I REMEMBER.
EXQUISITE...
...BUT DISAGREEABLE.
SHE'S GONE.
I SOLD HER TO AN ARAB SLAVE TRADER TODAY.
WHAT?
YOU'VE DONE WHAT?

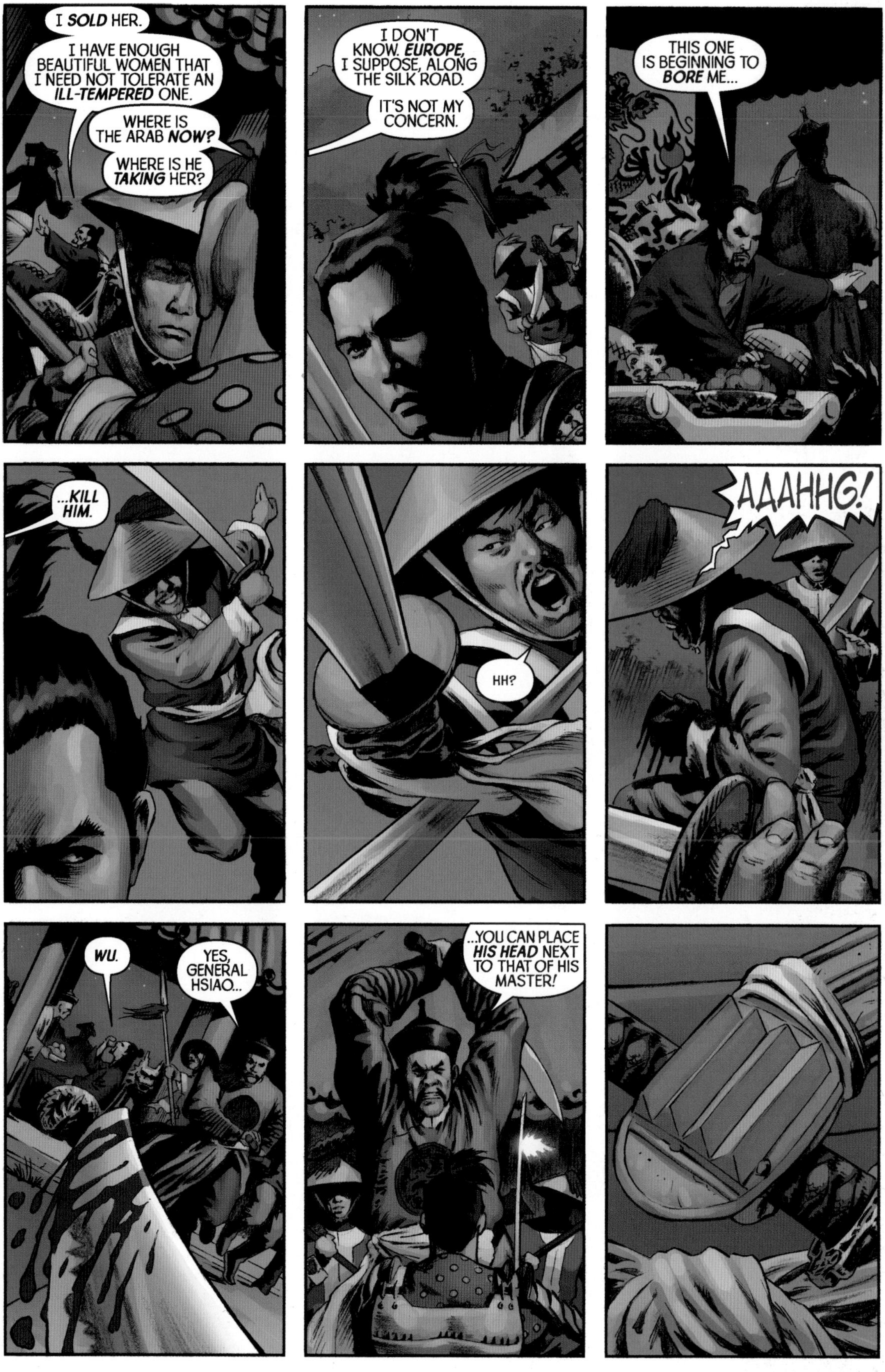
I **SOLD** HER.
I HAVE ENOUGH BEAUTIFUL WOMEN THAT I NEED NOT TOLERATE AN ***ILL-TEMPERED*** ONE.
WHERE IS THE ARAB ***NOW?***
WHERE IS HE ***TAKING*** HER?
I DON'T KNOW. ***EUROPE,*** I SUPPOSE, ALONG THE SILK ROAD.
IT'S NOT MY CONCERN.
THIS ONE IS BEGINNING TO ***BORE*** ME...
...***KILL HIM.***
HH?
AAAHHG!
WU.
YES, GENERAL HSIAO...
...YOU CAN PLACE ***HIS HEAD*** NEXT TO THAT OF HIS MASTER!

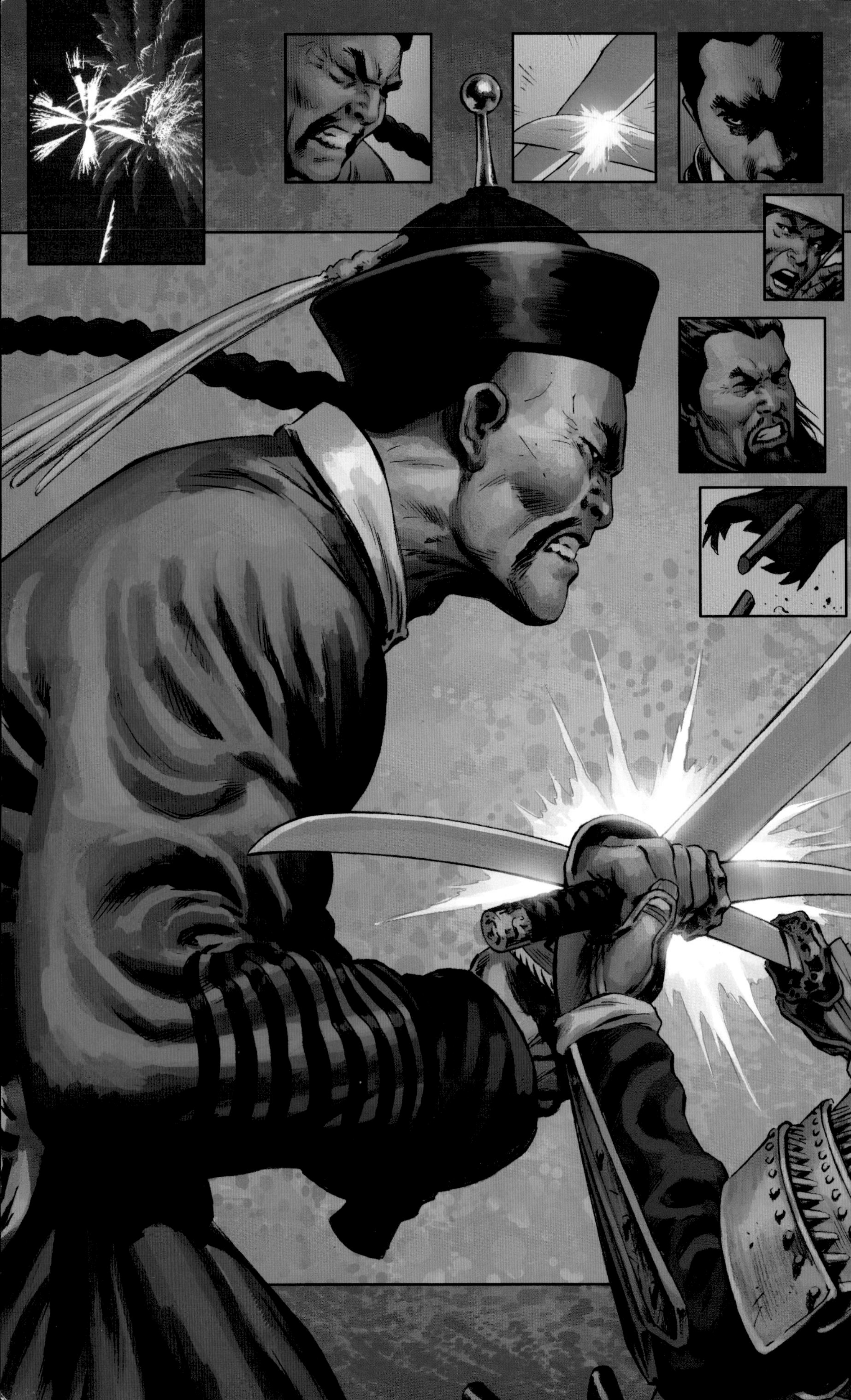

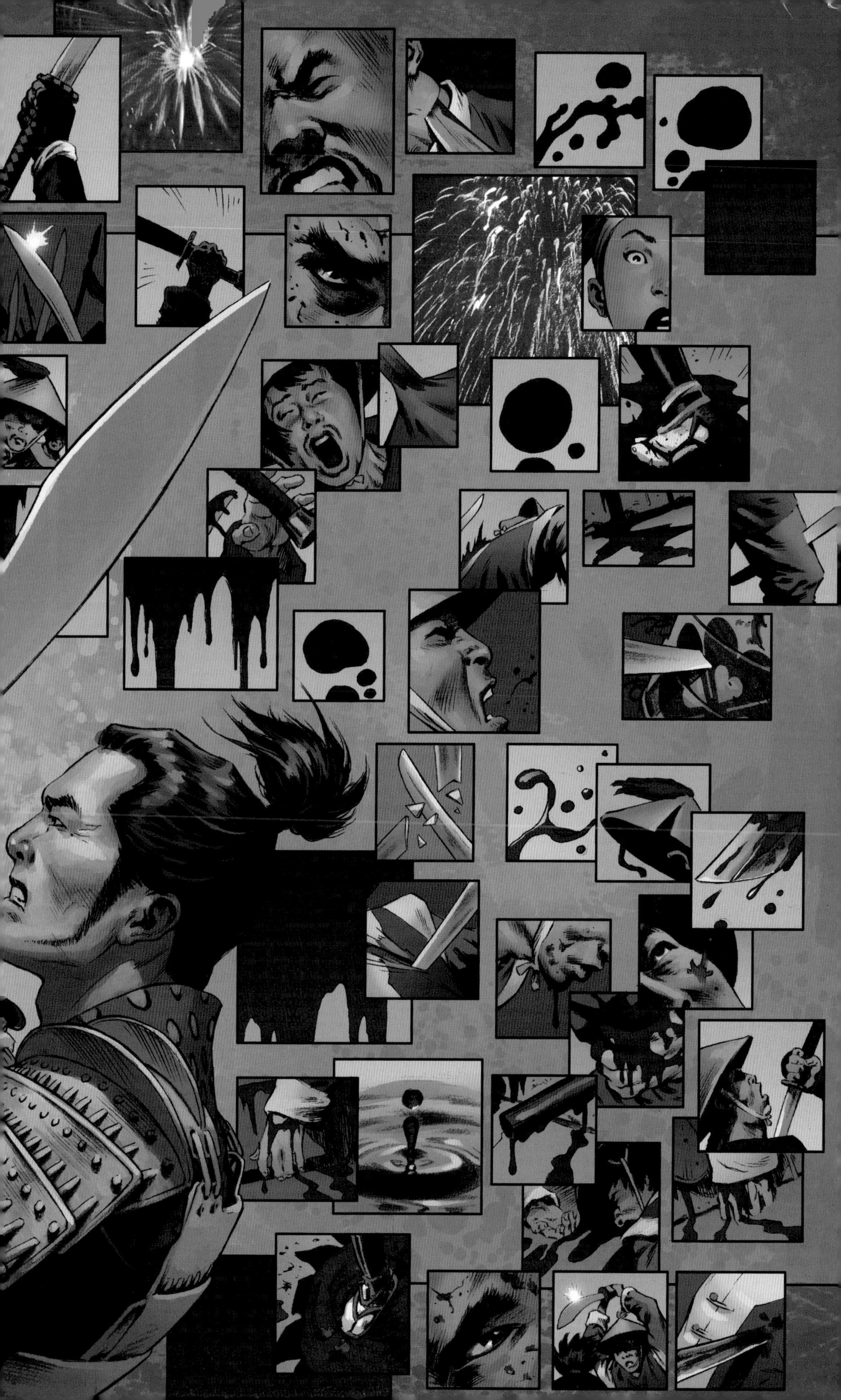

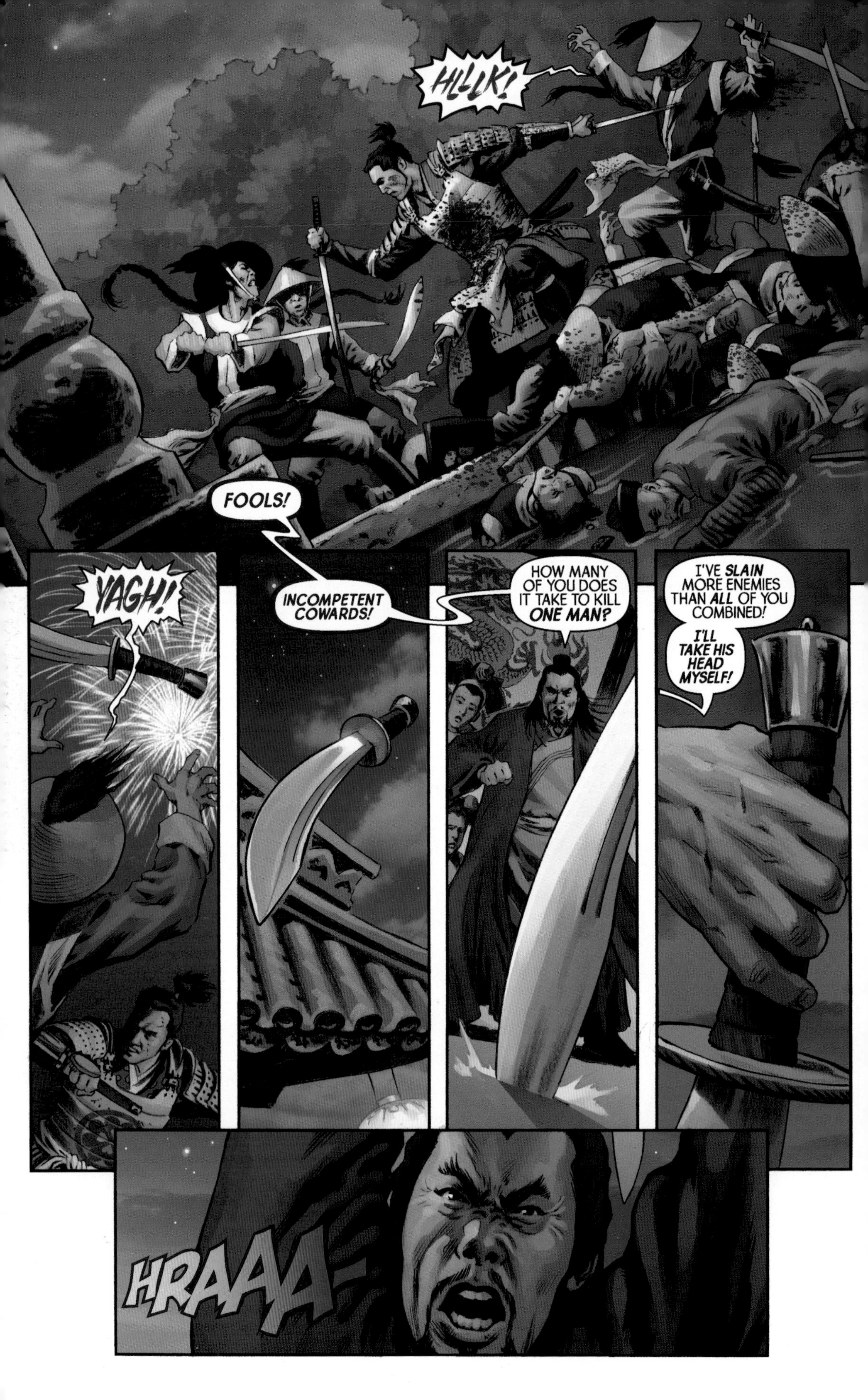
HLLLK!
FOOLS!
YAGH!
INCOMPETENT COWARDS!
HOW MANY OF YOU DOES IT TAKE TO KILL ONE MAN?
I'VE SLAIN MORE ENEMIES THAN ALL OF YOU COMBINED!
I'LL TAKE HIS HEAD MYSELF!
HRAAA

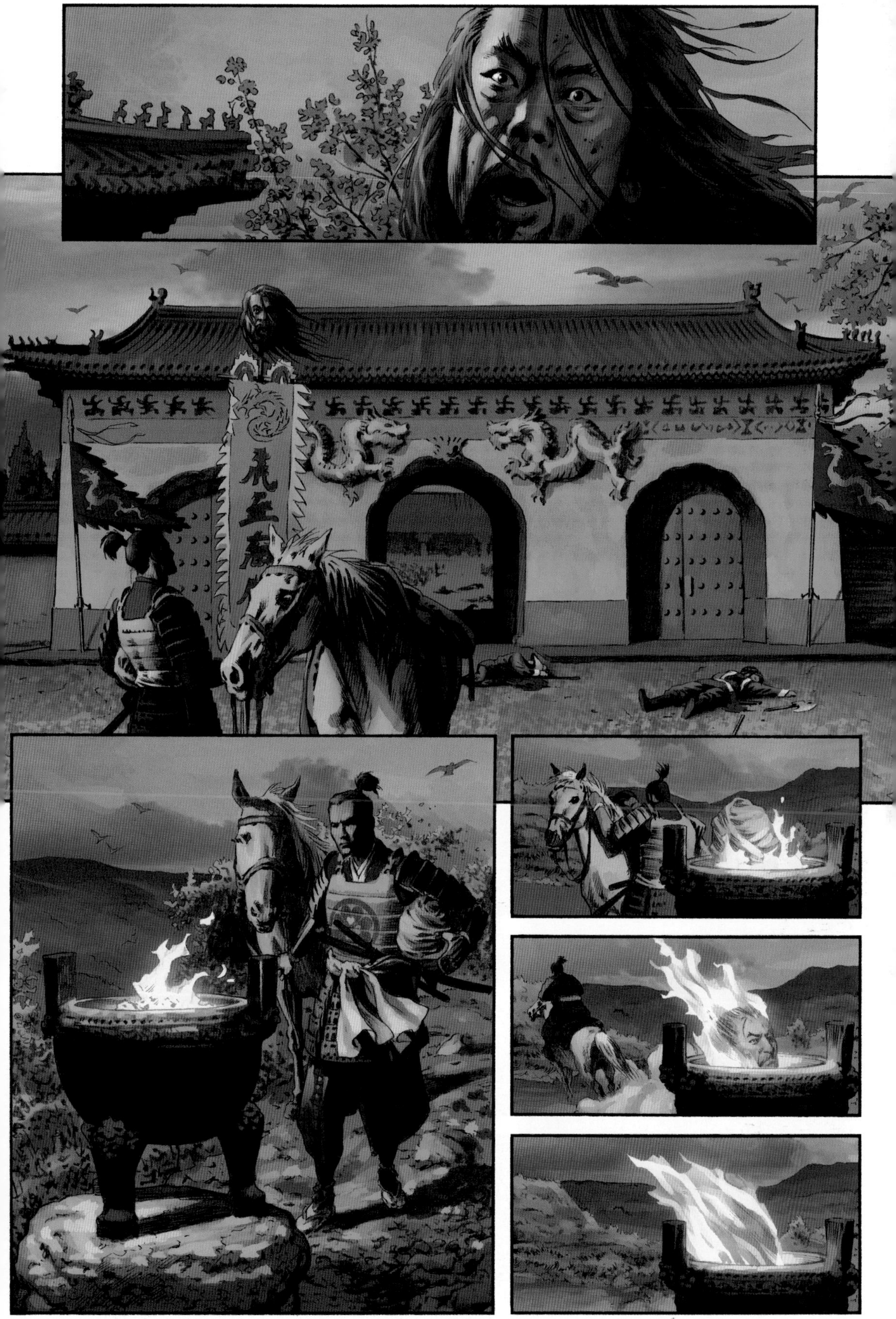

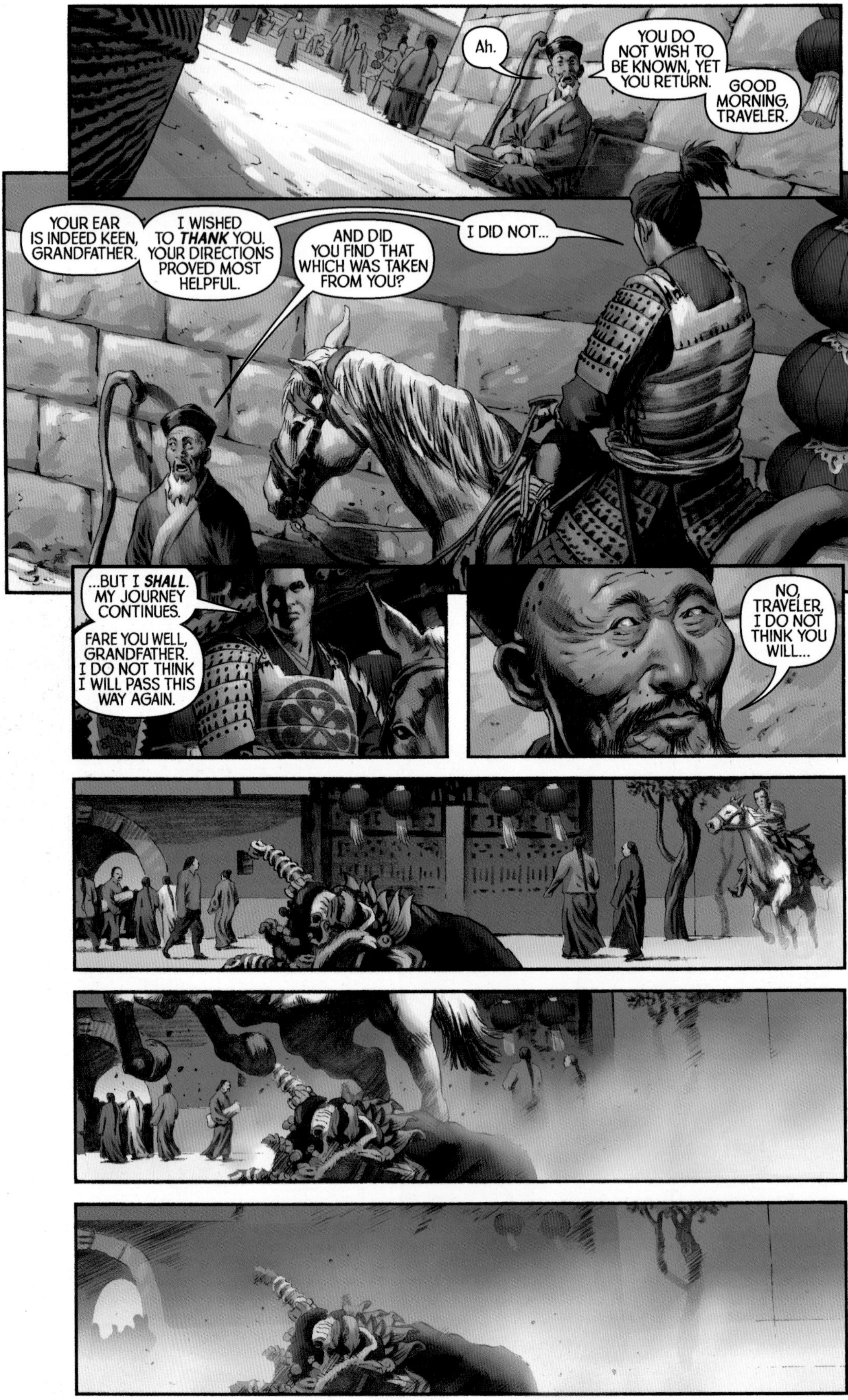
GOOD MORNING, TRAVELER.
YOU DO NOT WISH TO BE KNOWN, YET YOU RETURN.
Ah.
YOUR EAR IS INDEED KEEN, GRANDFATHER.
I WISHED TO THANK YOU. YOUR DIRECTIONS PROVED MOST HELPFUL.
AND DID YOU FIND THAT WHICH WAS TAKEN FROM YOU?
I DID NOT...
...BUT I SHALL. MY JOURNEY CONTINUES.
FARE YOU WELL, GRANDFATHER. I DO NOT THINK I WILL PASS THIS WAY AGAIN.
NO, TRAVELER, I DO NOT THINK YOU WILL...

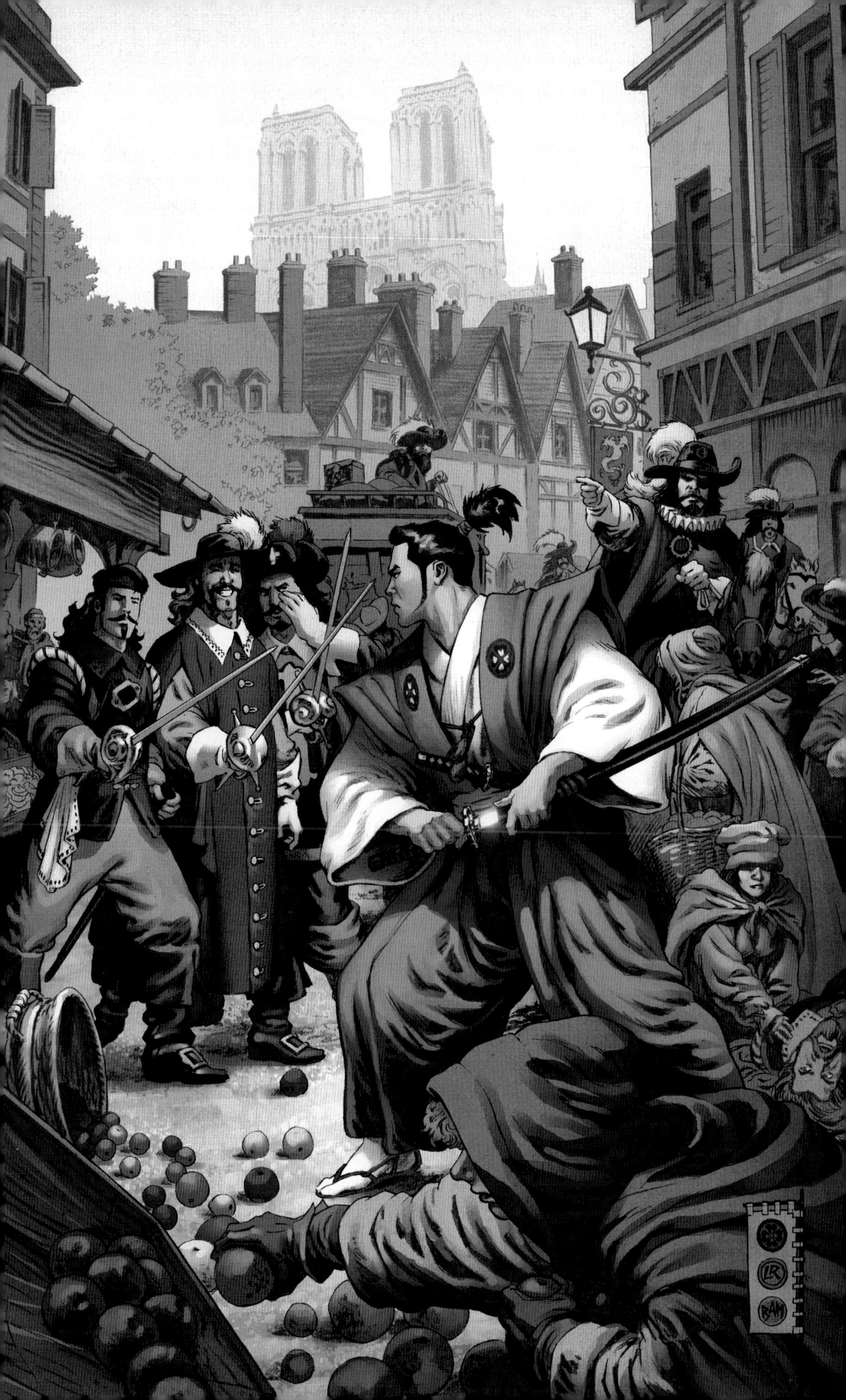

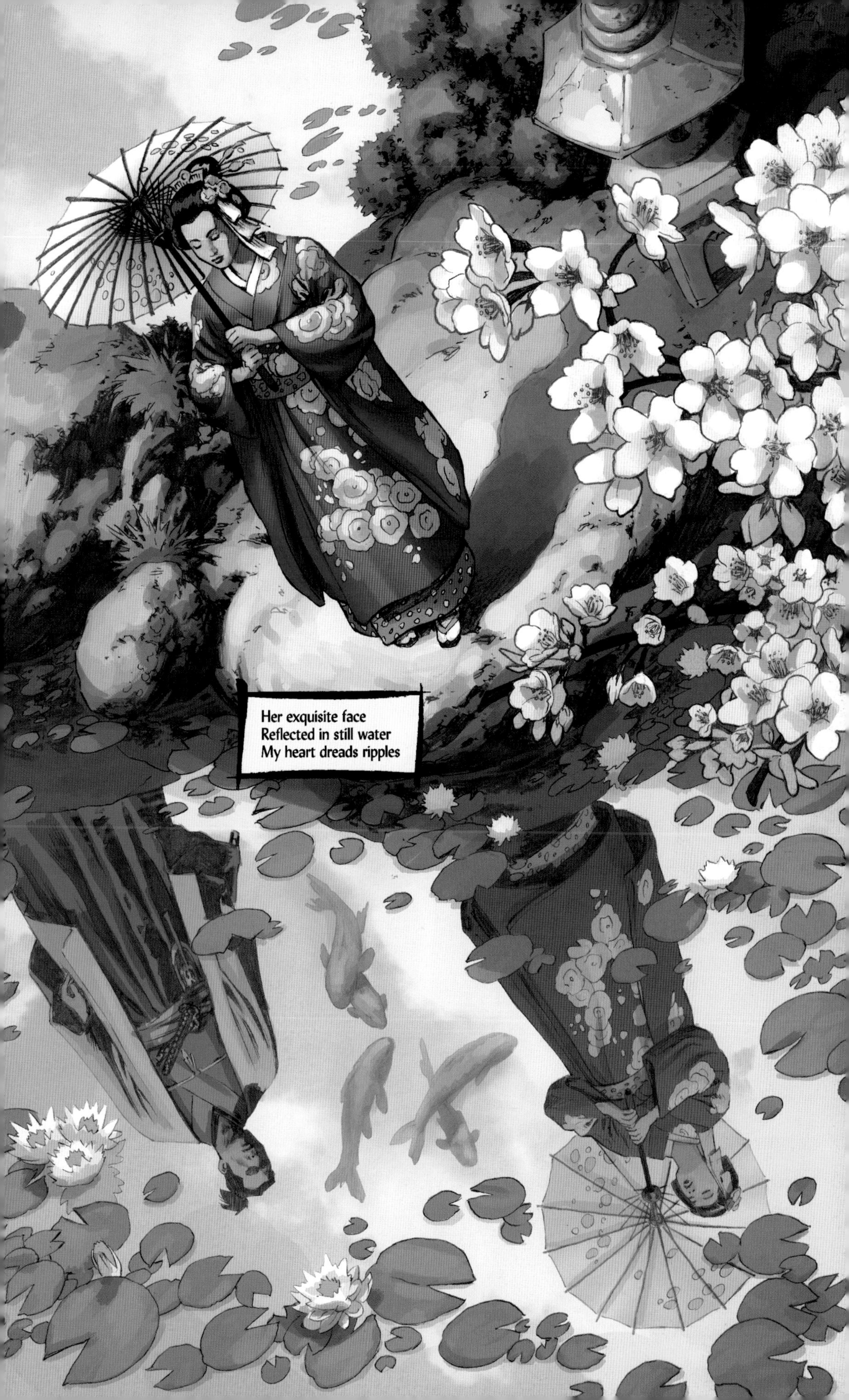
Her exquisite face
Reflected in still water
My heart dreads ripples

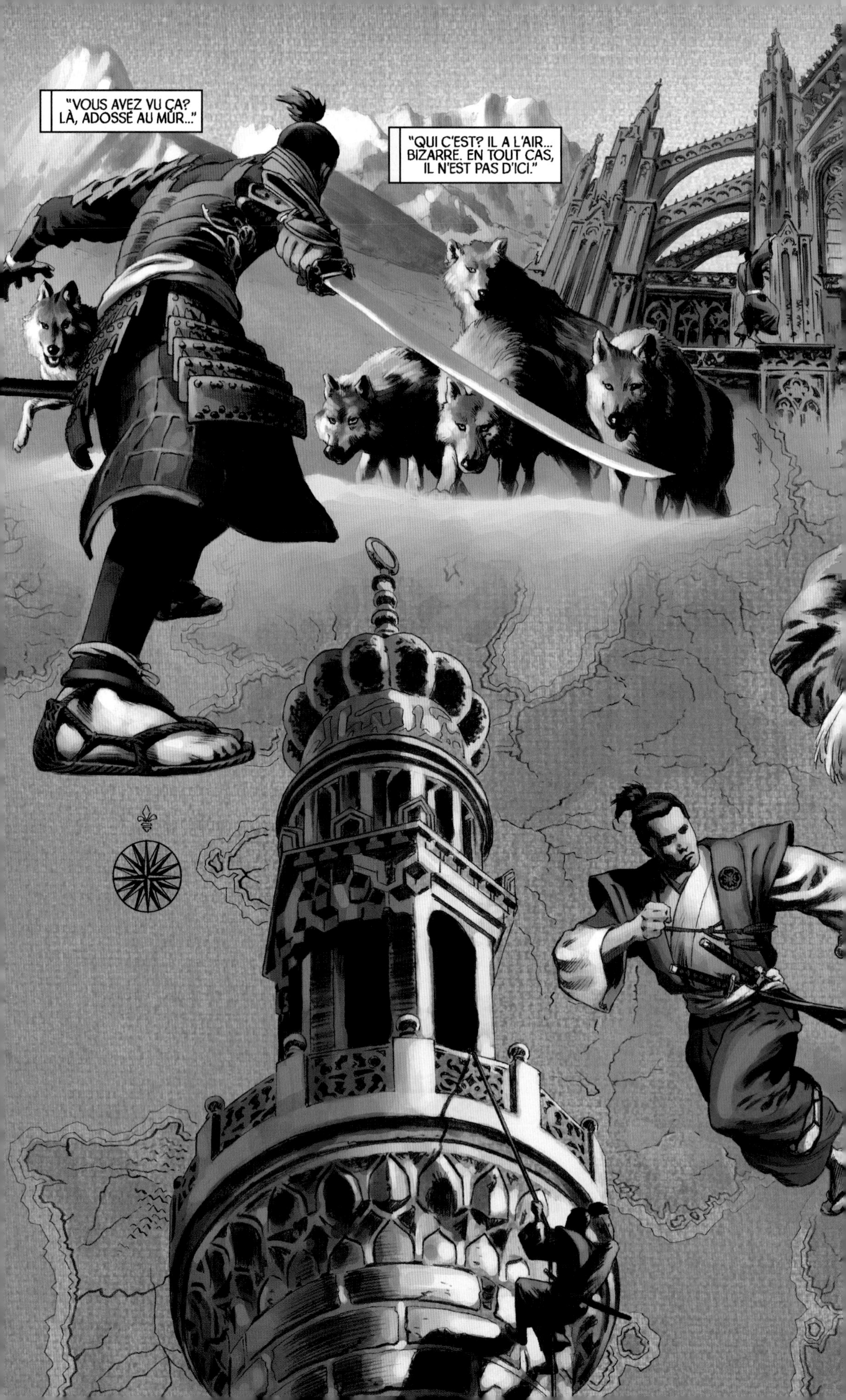
"VOUS AVEZ VU ÇA? LÀ, ADOSSÉ AU MUR..."
"QUI C'EST? IL A L'AIR... BIZARRE. EN TOUT CAS, IL N'EST PAS D'ICI."

"POUR SÛR. REGARDEZ-MOI CES DRÔLES D'HABITS. IL VIENT DES INDES."
"CHINOIS. MOI, J'DIS QU'IL EST CHINOIS."
"MAIS, QU'EST-CE QU'IL FAIT LÀ?"
A New & Exact Map of
EUROPE AND ASIA
Compiled from Surveys
& authentic Journals of
Thierry Mornpt, in service to his
"IL DORT À L'OMBRE DE NOTRE-DAME. VOILÀ C'QU'IL FAIT.
"IL EST DÉGOÛTANT. IL N'A VRAIMENT AUCUN RESPECT."
"RÉVEILLE-LE. ÇA LUI APPRENDRA."

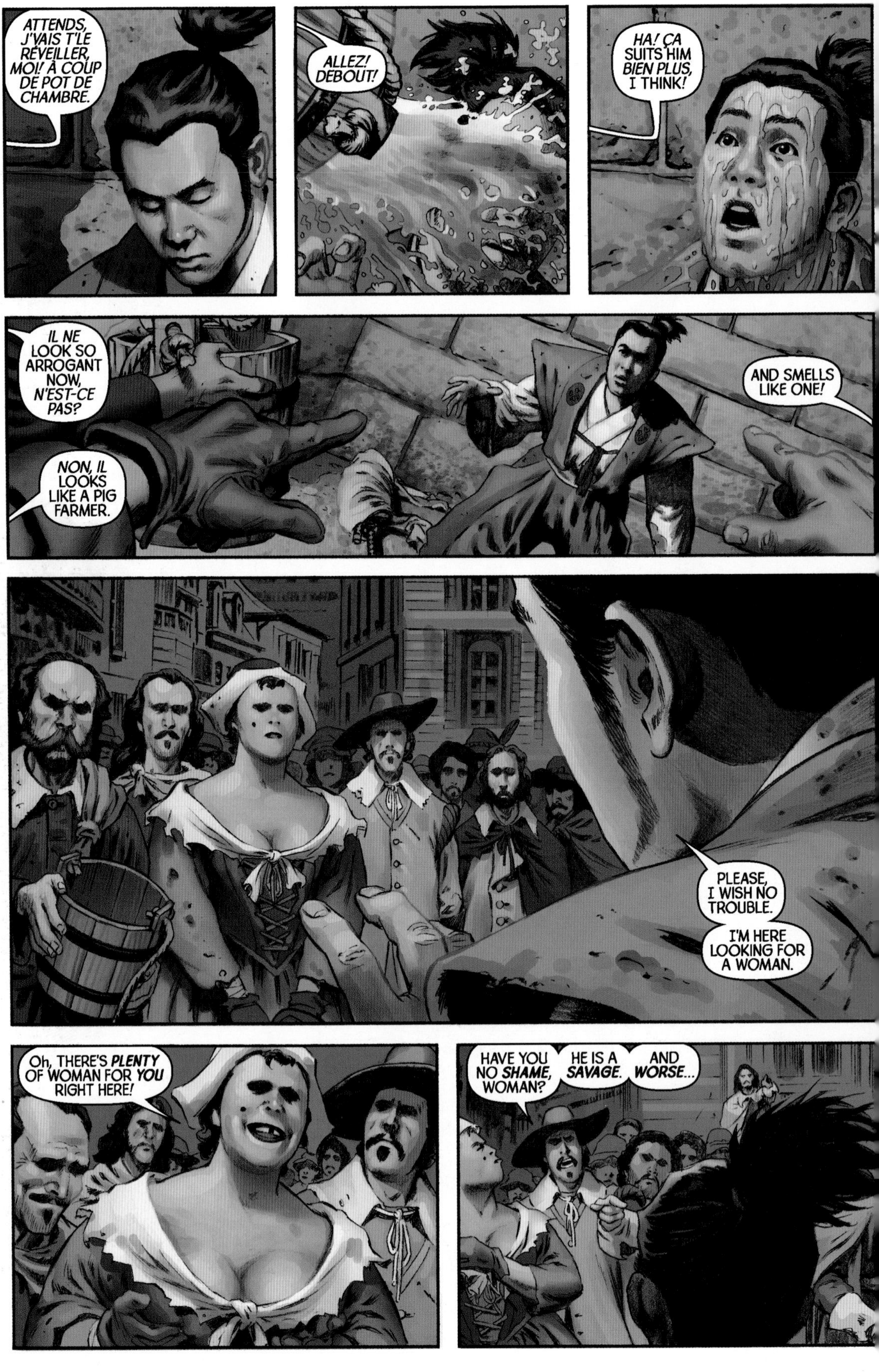
ATTENDS, J'VAIS T'LE RÉVEILLER, MOI! À COUP DE POT DE CHAMBRE.
ALLEZ! DEBOUT!
HA! ÇA SUITS HIM BIEN PLUS, I THINK!
IL NE LOOK SO ARROGANT NOW, N'EST-CE PAS?
NON, IL LOOKS LIKE A PIG FARMER.
AND SMELLS LIKE ONE!
PLEASE, I WISH NO TROUBLE.
I'M HERE LOOKING FOR A WOMAN.
Oh, THERE'S PLENTY OF WOMAN FOR YOU RIGHT HERE!
HAVE YOU NO SHAME, WOMAN?
HE IS A SAVAGE.
AND WORSE...

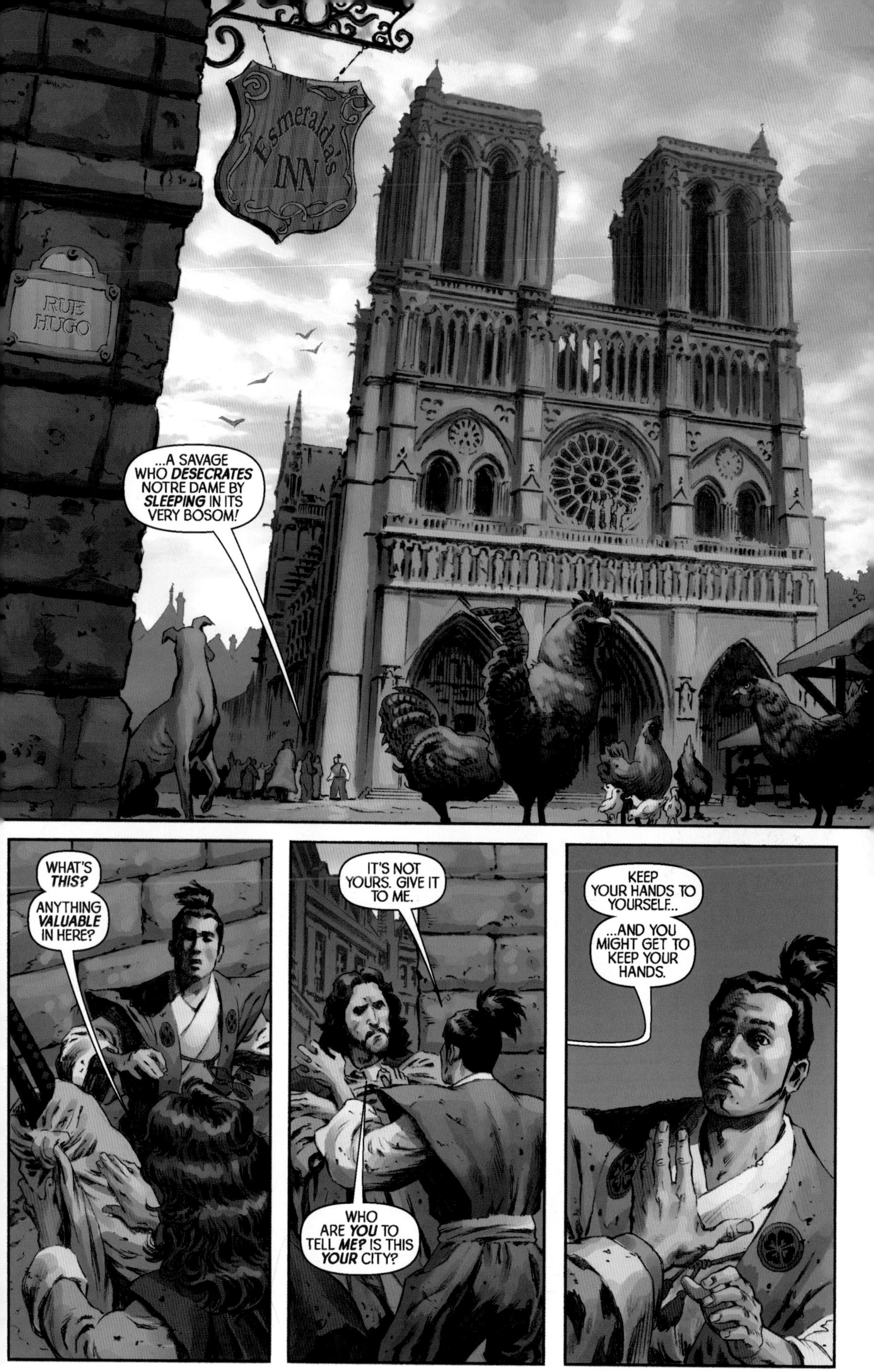
Esmeralda's INN
RUE HUGO
...A SAVAGE WHO *DESECRATES* NOTRE DAME BY *SLEEPING* IN ITS VERY BOSOM!
WHAT'S *THIS?*
ANYTHING *VALUABLE* IN HERE?
IT'S NOT YOURS. GIVE IT TO ME.
WHO ARE *YOU* TO TELL *ME?* IS THIS *YOUR* CITY?
KEEP YOUR HANDS TO YOURSELF...
...AND YOU MIGHT GET TO KEEP YOUR HANDS.

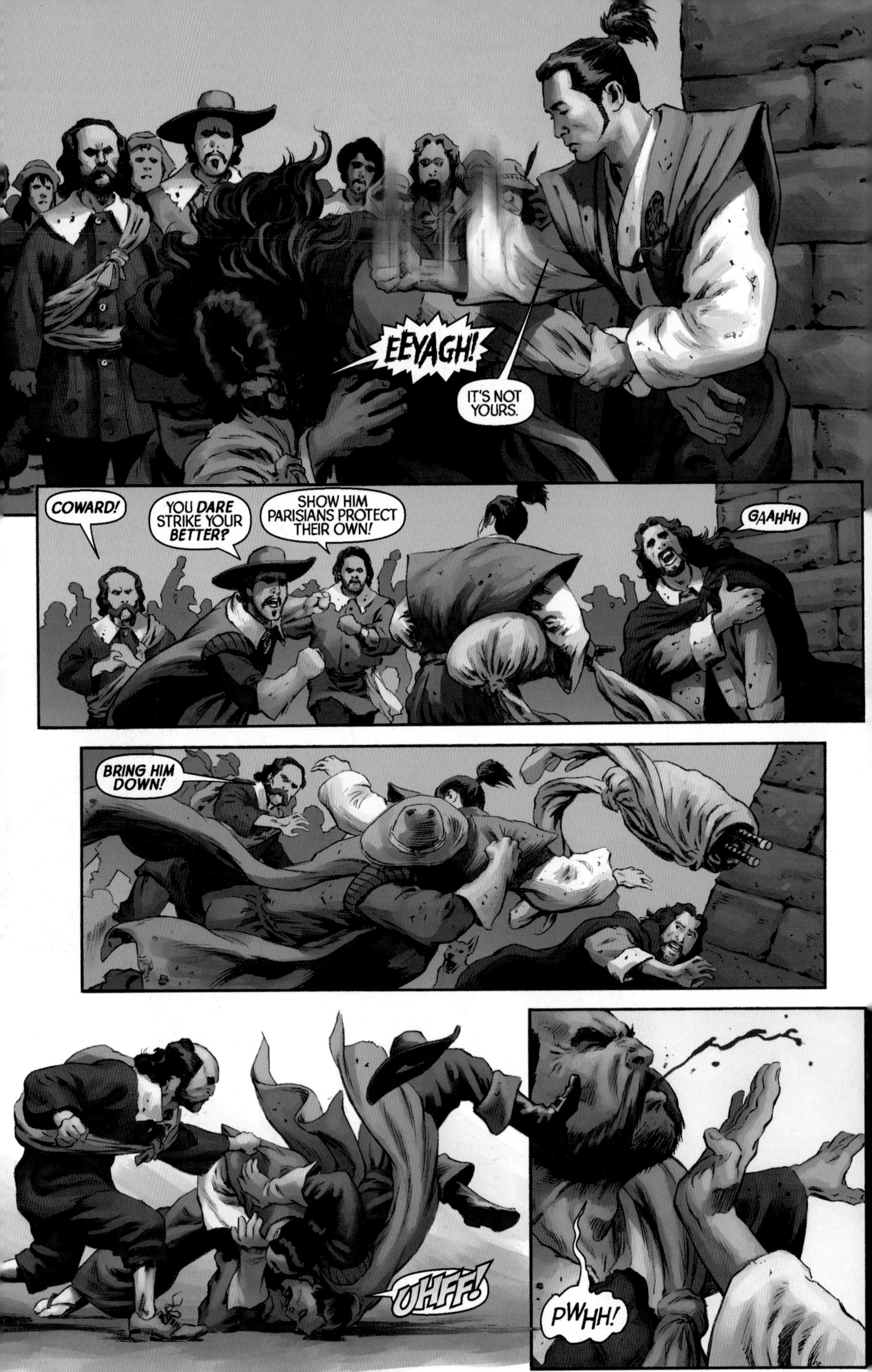
EEYAGH!
IT'S NOT YOURS.
COWARD!
YOU DARE STRIKE YOUR BETTER?
SHOW HIM PARISIANS PROTECT THEIR OWN!
GAAHHH
BRING HIM DOWN!
OHFF!
PWHH!

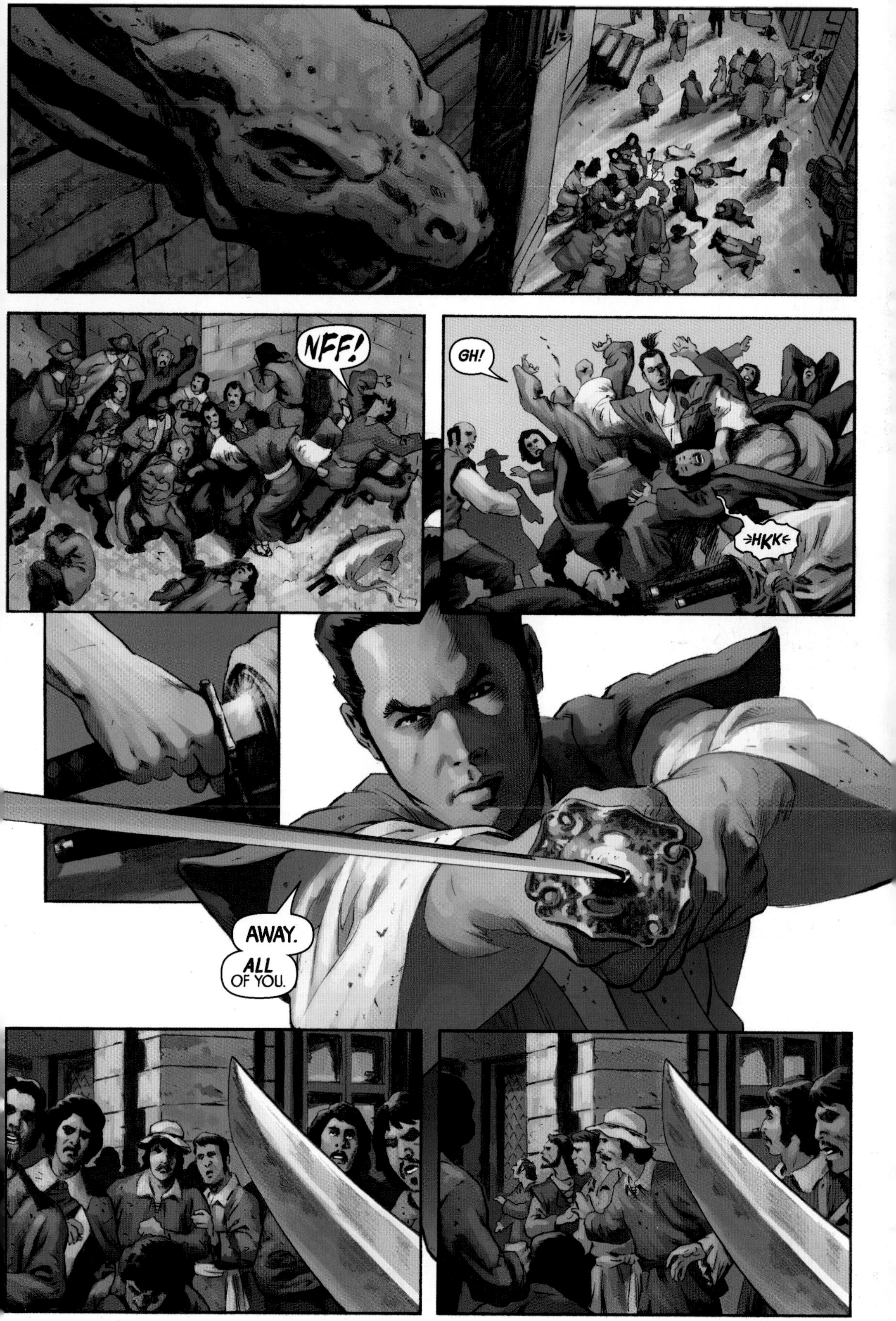
NFF!
GH!
HKK
AWAY.
ALL OF YOU.

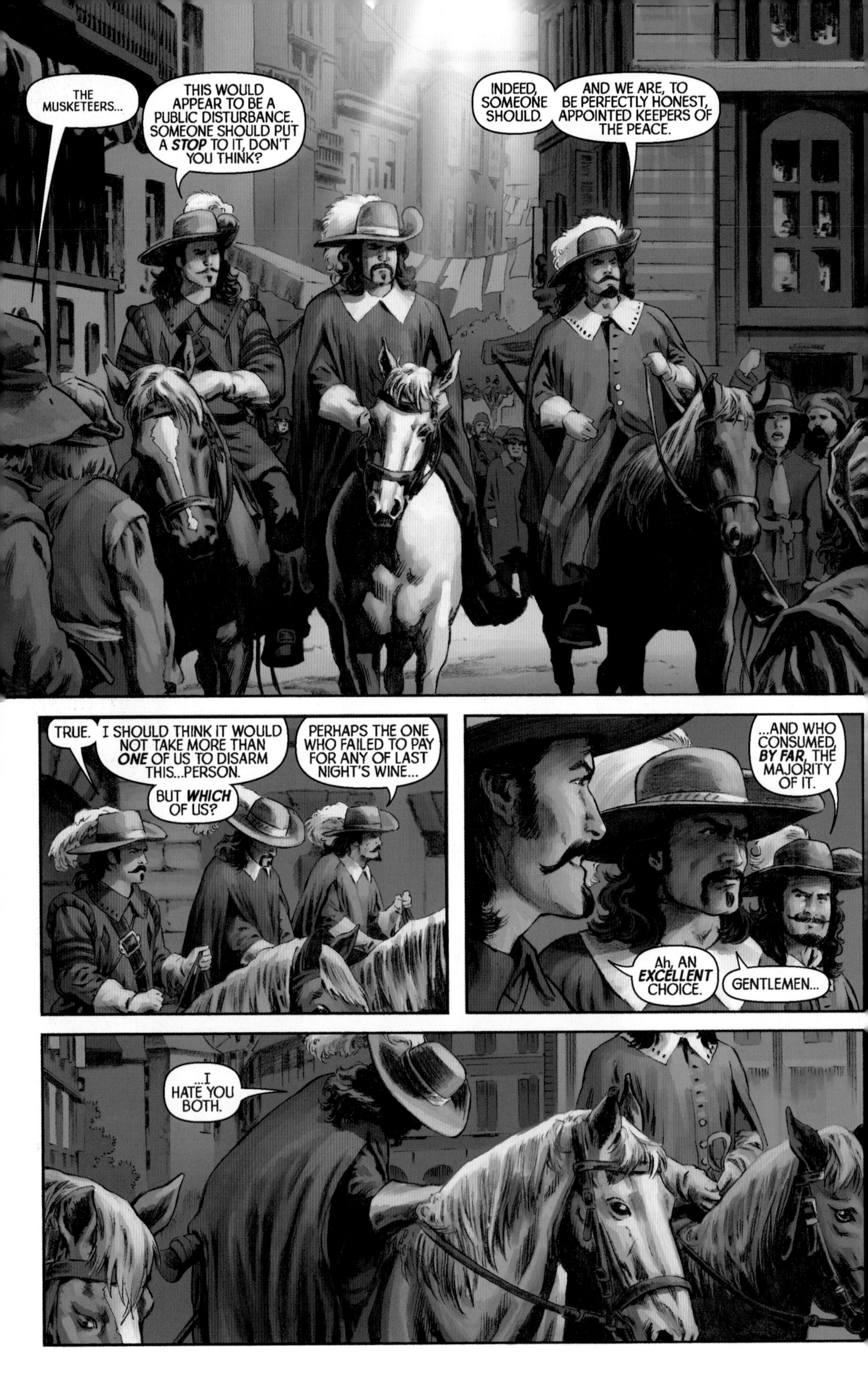
THE MUSKETEERS...
THIS WOULD APPEAR TO BE A PUBLIC DISTURBANCE. SOMEONE SHOULD PUT A **STOP** TO IT, DON'T YOU THINK?
INDEED, SOMEONE SHOULD.
AND WE ARE, TO BE PERFECTLY HONEST, APPOINTED KEEPERS OF THE PEACE.
TRUE.
I SHOULD THINK IT WOULD NOT TAKE MORE THAN **ONE** OF US TO DISARM THIS...PERSON.
BUT **WHICH** OF US?
PERHAPS THE ONE WHO FAILED TO PAY FOR ANY OF LAST NIGHT'S WINE...
...AND WHO CONSUMED, **BY FAR**, THE MAJORITY OF IT.
Ah, AN **EXCELLENT** CHOICE.
GENTLEMEN...
...I HATE YOU BOTH.

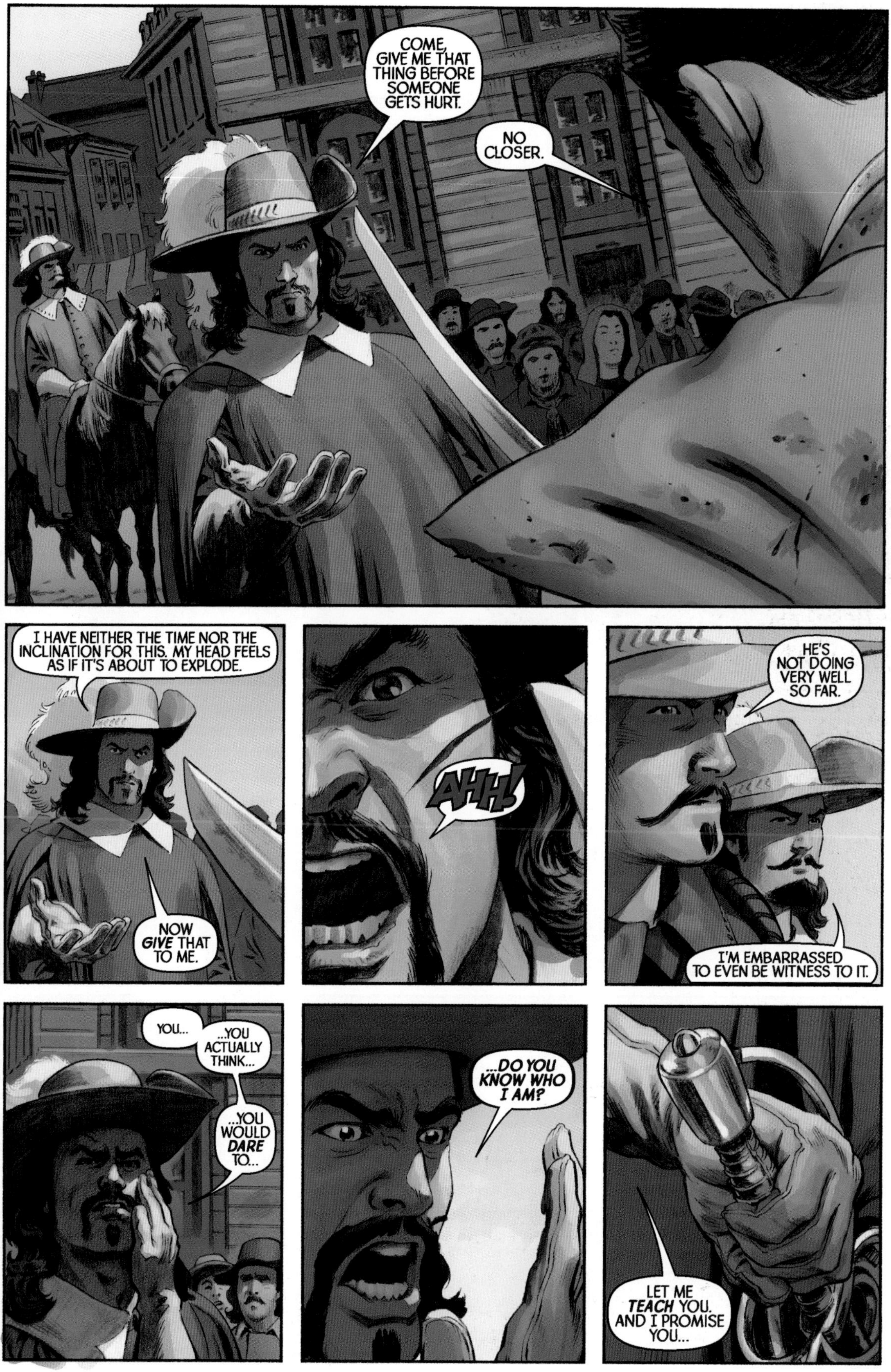
COME, GIVE ME THAT THING BEFORE SOMEONE GETS HURT.
NO CLOSER.
I HAVE NEITHER THE TIME NOR THE INCLINATION FOR THIS. MY HEAD FEELS AS IF IT'S ABOUT TO EXPLODE.
NOW *GIVE* THAT TO ME.
AHH!
HE'S NOT DOING VERY WELL SO FAR.
I'M EMBARRASSED TO EVEN BE WITNESS TO IT.
YOU...
...YOU ACTUALLY THINK...
...YOU WOULD *DARE* TO...
...DO YOU KNOW WHO I AM?
LET ME *TEACH* YOU. AND I PROMISE YOU...

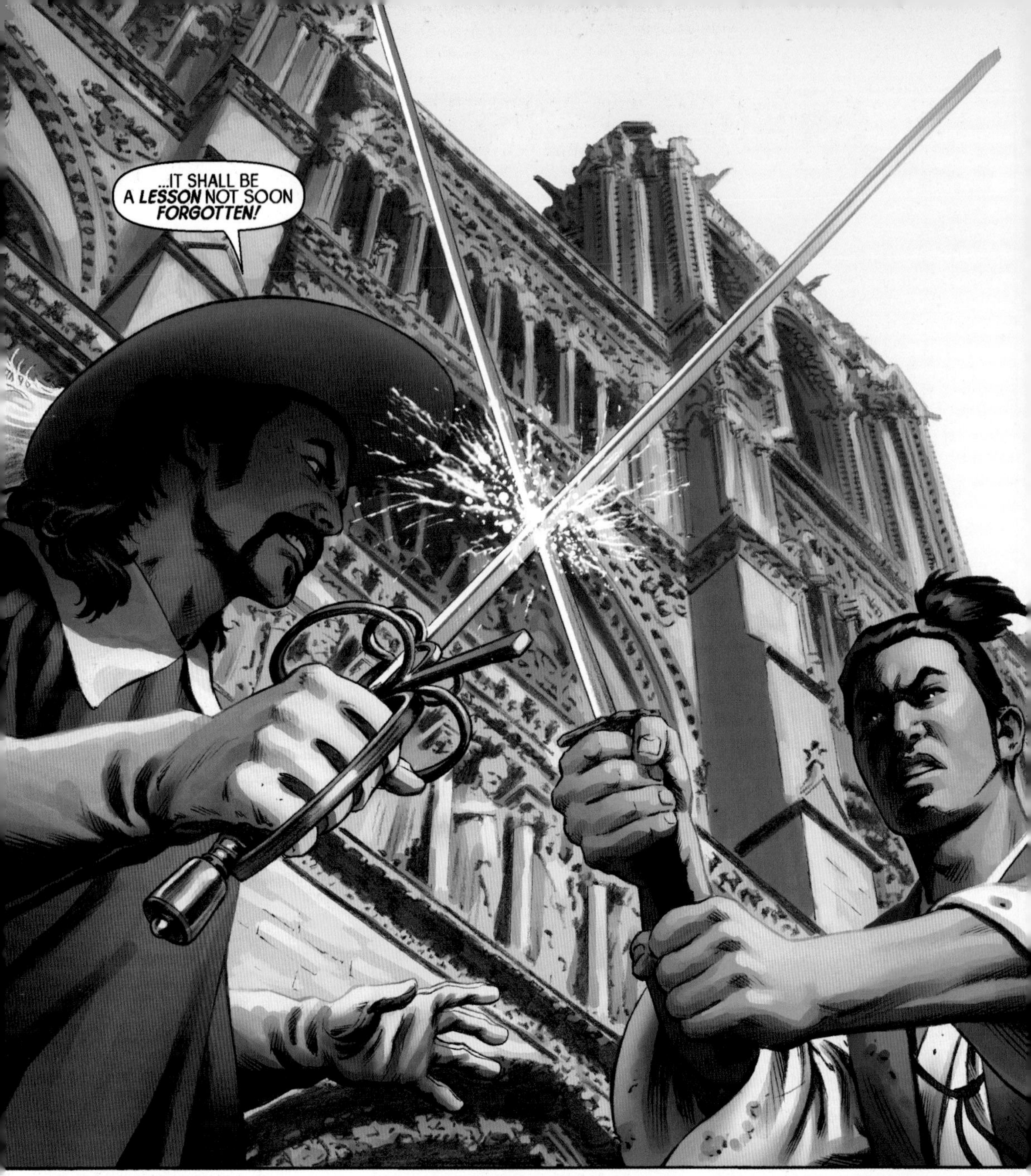
...IT SHALL BE A *LESSON* NOT SOON *FORGOTTEN!*

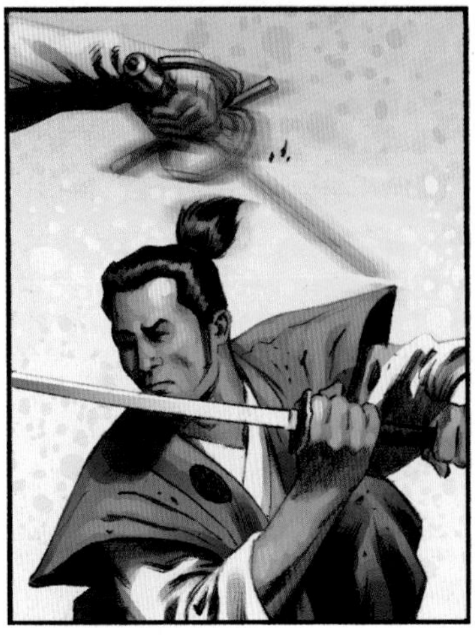

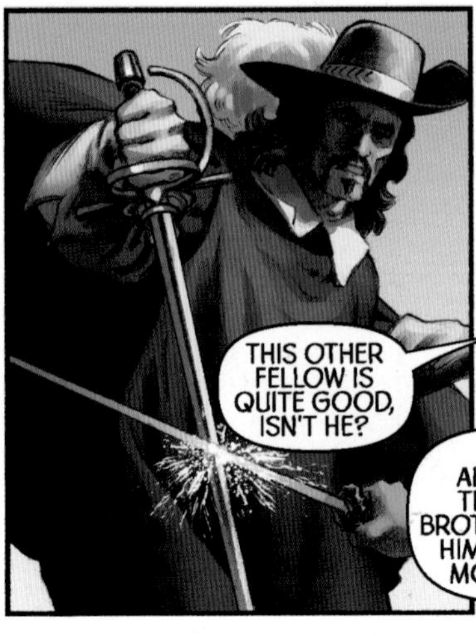
THIS OTHER FELLOW IS QUITE GOOD, ISN'T HE?
EVEN ALLOWING THAT OUR BROTHER IS NOT HIMSELF THIS MORNING...

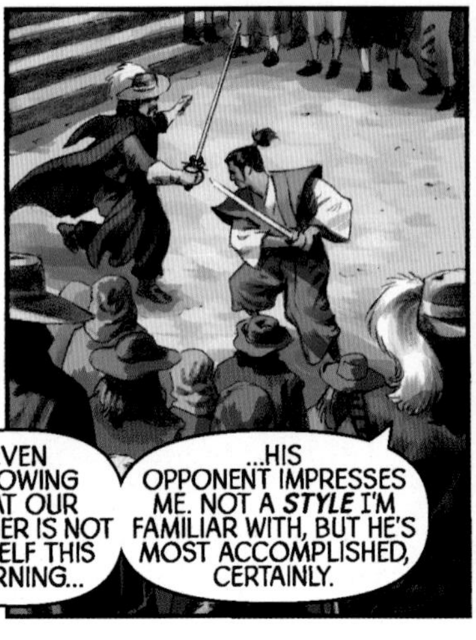
...HIS OPPONENT IMPRESSES ME. NOT A *STYLE* I'M FAMILIAR WITH, BUT HE'S MOST ACCOMPLISHED, CERTAINLY.

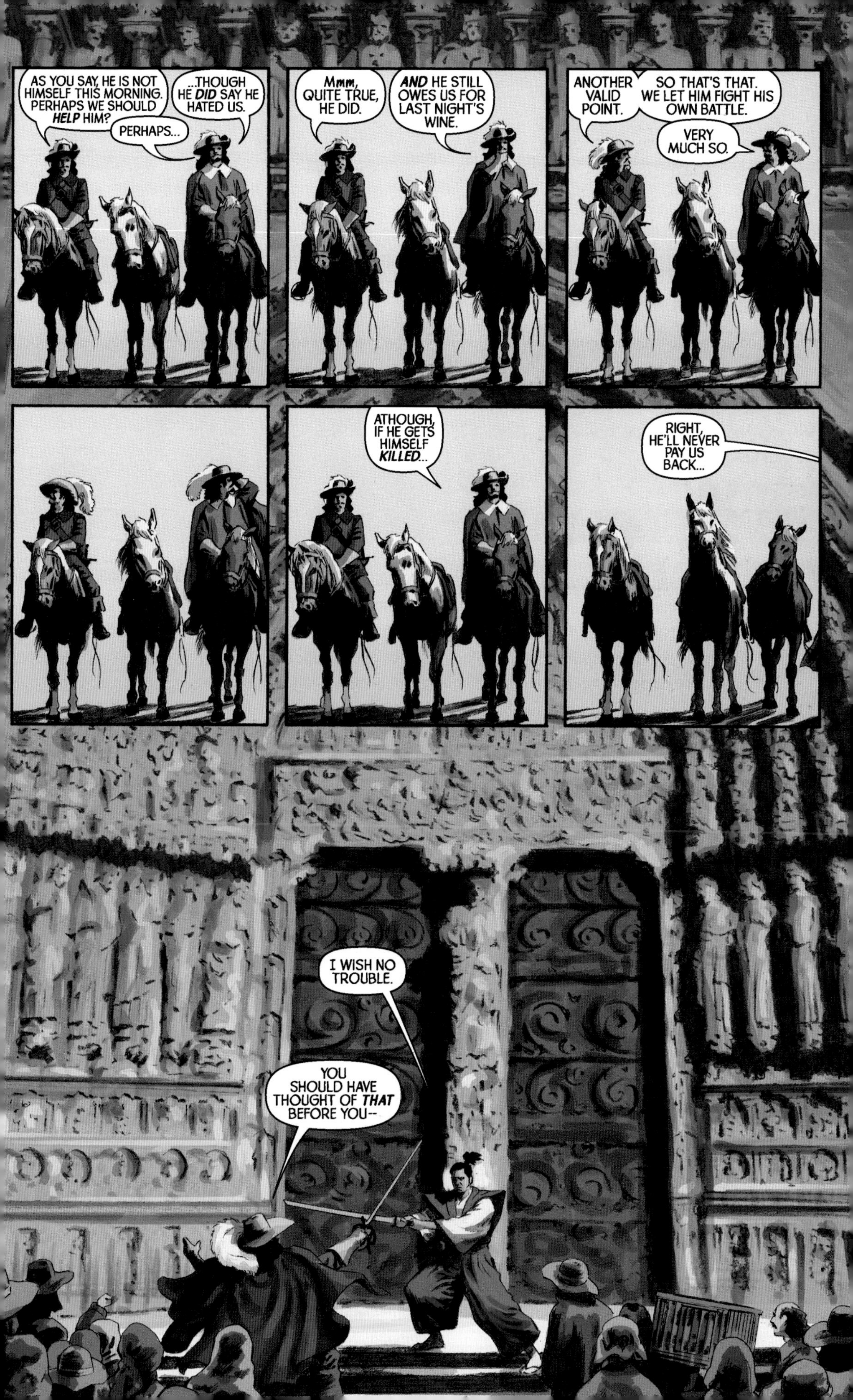
AS YOU SAY, HE IS NOT HIMSELF THIS MORNING. PERHAPS WE SHOULD *HELP* HIM?
...THOUGH HE *DID* SAY HE HATED US.
PERHAPS...
Mmm, QUITE TRUE, HE DID.
AND HE STILL OWES US FOR LAST NIGHT'S WINE.
ANOTHER VALID POINT.
SO THAT'S THAT. WE LET HIM FIGHT HIS OWN BATTLE.
VERY MUCH SO.
ATHOUGH, IF HE GETS HIMSELF *KILLED*...
RIGHT, HE'LL NEVER PAY US BACK...
I WISH NO TROUBLE.
YOU SHOULD HAVE THOUGHT OF *THAT* BEFORE YOU--

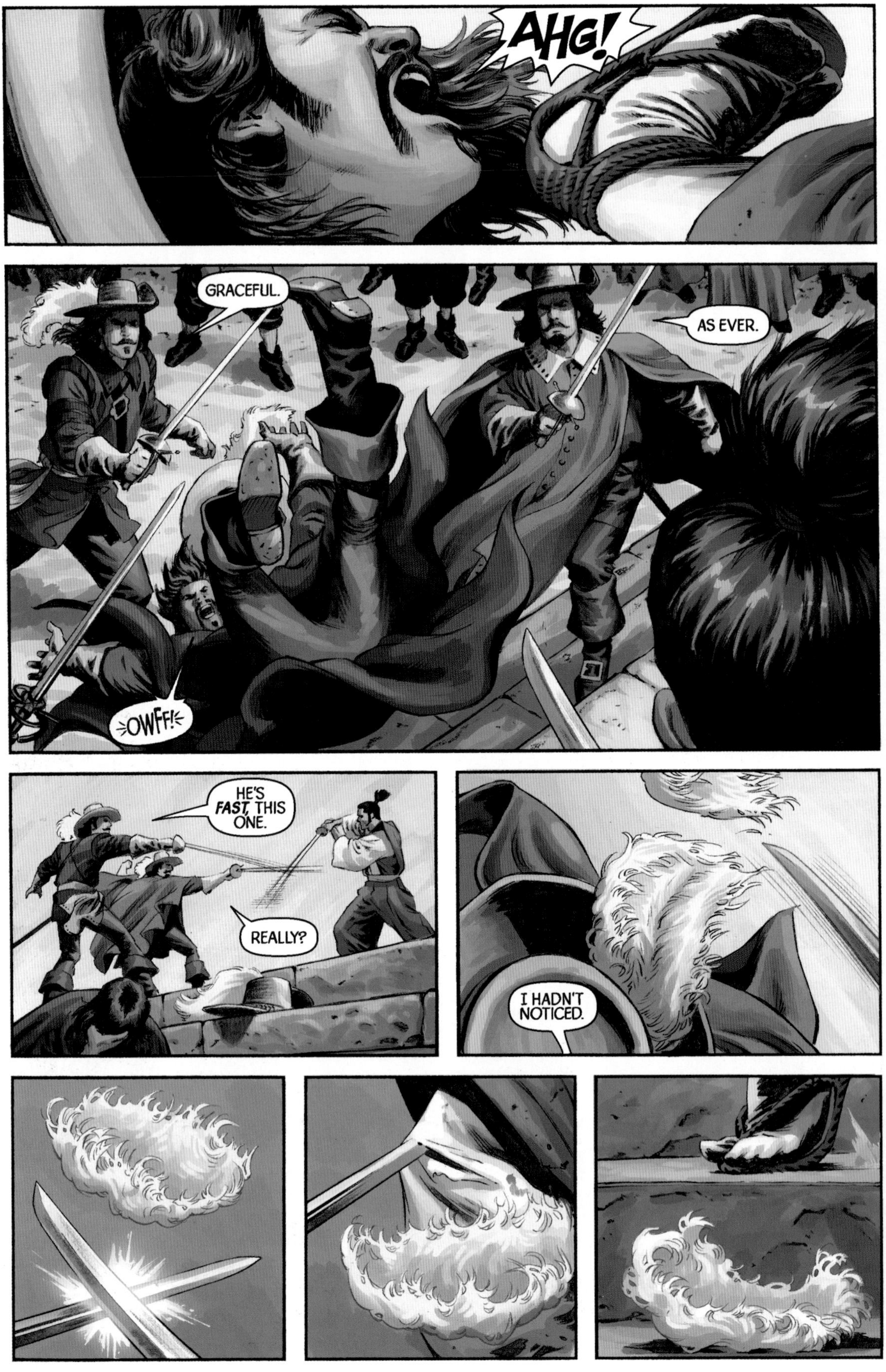
AHG!
GRACEFUL.
AS EVER.
OWFF!
HE'S *FAST,* THIS ONE.
REALLY?
I HADN'T NOTICED.

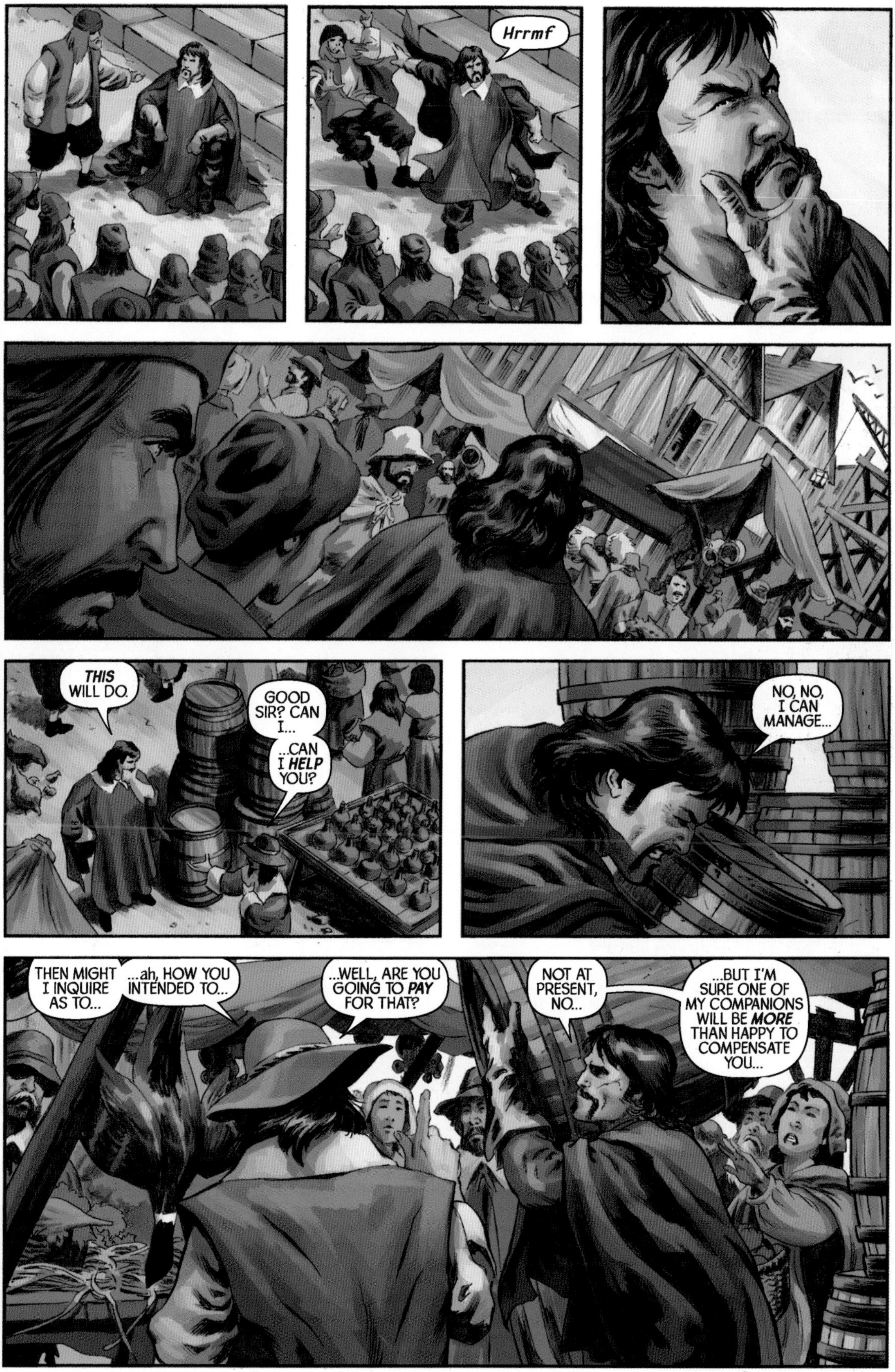
Hrrmf
THIS WILL DO.
GOOD SIR? CAN I...
...CAN I HELP YOU?
NO, NO, I CAN MANAGE...
THEN MIGHT I INQUIRE AS TO...
...ah, HOW YOU INTENDED TO...
...WELL, ARE YOU GOING TO PAY FOR THAT?
NOT AT PRESENT, NO...
...BUT I'M SURE ONE OF MY COMPANIONS WILL BE MORE THAN HAPPY TO COMPENSATE YOU...

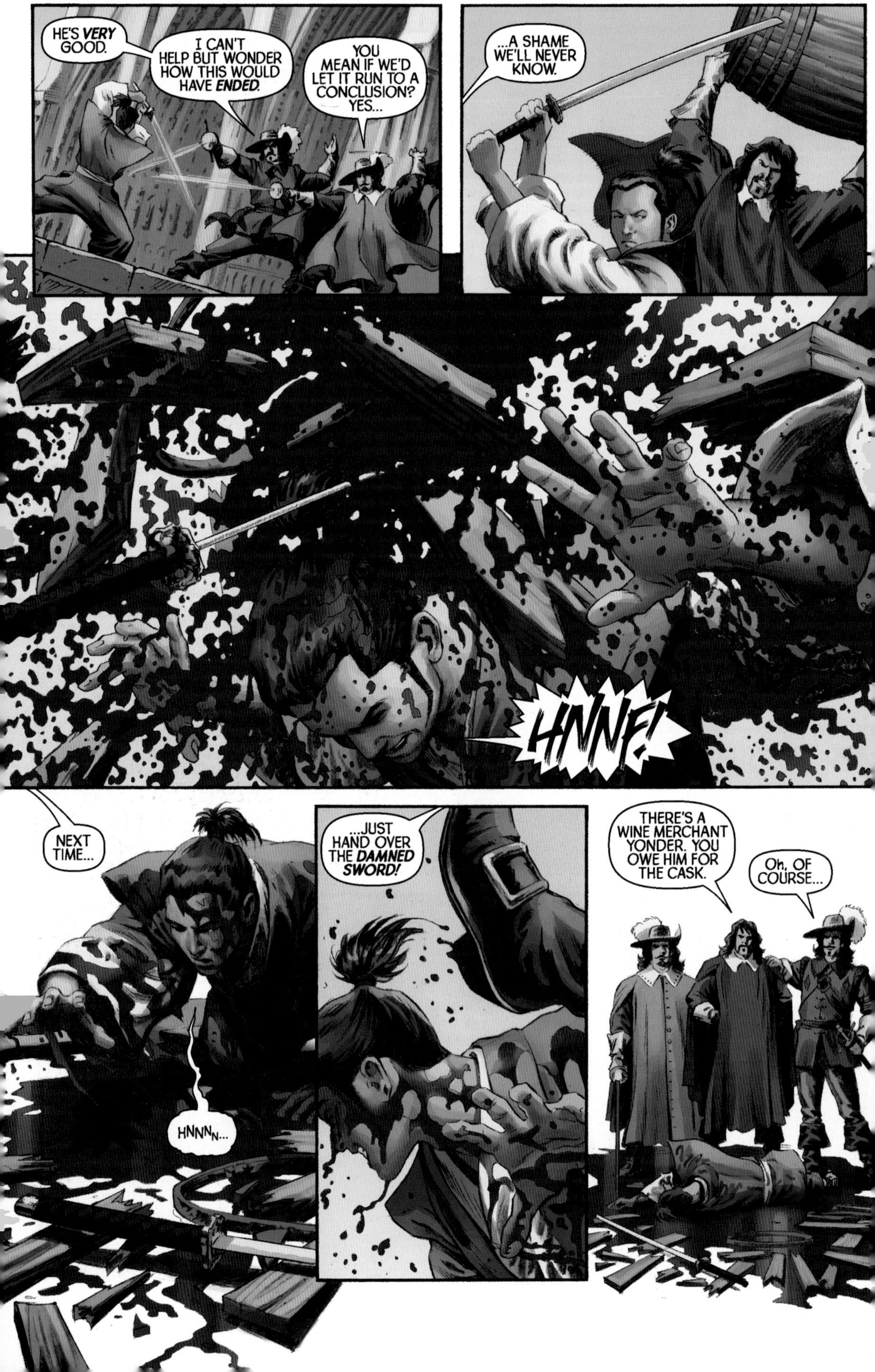
HE'S **VERY** GOOD.
I CAN'T HELP BUT WONDER HOW THIS WOULD HAVE **ENDED**.
YOU MEAN IF WE'D LET IT RUN TO A CONCLUSION? YES...
...A SHAME WE'LL NEVER KNOW.
HNNF!
NEXT TIME...
HNNNN...
...JUST HAND OVER THE **DAMNED SWORD!**
THERE'S A WINE MERCHANT YONDER. YOU OWE HIM FOR THE CASK.
Oh, OF COURSE...

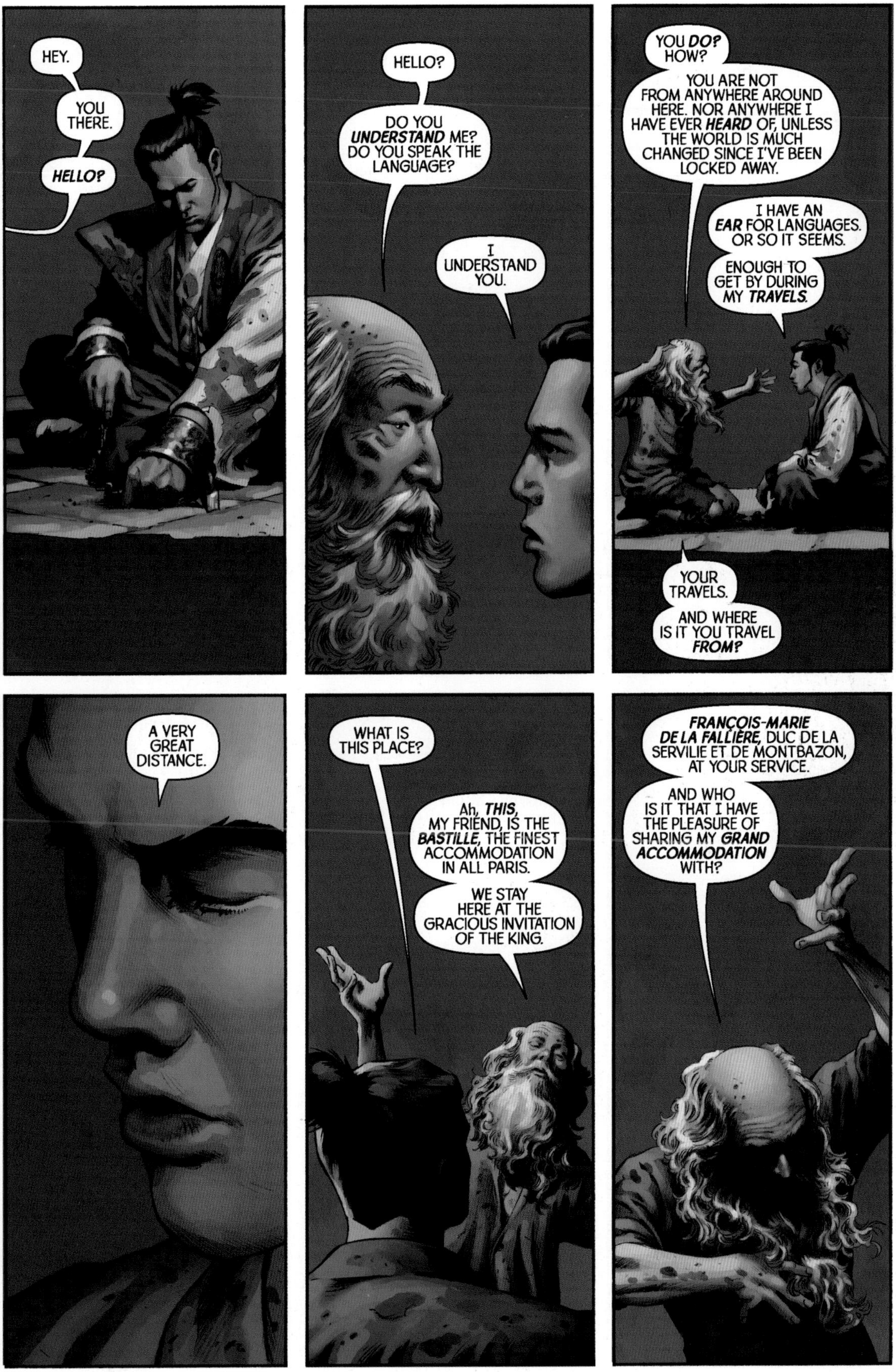
HEY.
YOU THERE.
HELLO?
HELLO?
DO YOU UNDERSTAND ME? DO YOU SPEAK THE LANGUAGE?
I UNDERSTAND YOU.
YOU DO? HOW?
YOU ARE NOT FROM ANYWHERE AROUND HERE. NOR ANYWHERE I HAVE EVER HEARD OF, UNLESS THE WORLD IS MUCH CHANGED SINCE I'VE BEEN LOCKED AWAY.
I HAVE AN EAR FOR LANGUAGES. OR SO IT SEEMS.
ENOUGH TO GET BY DURING MY TRAVELS.
YOUR TRAVELS.
AND WHERE IS IT YOU TRAVEL FROM?
A VERY GREAT DISTANCE.
WHAT IS THIS PLACE?
Ah, THIS, MY FRIEND, IS THE BASTILLE, THE FINEST ACCOMMODATION IN ALL PARIS.
WE STAY HERE AT THE GRACIOUS INVITATION OF THE KING.
FRANÇOIS-MARIE DE LA FALLIÈRE, DUC DE LA SERVILIE ET DE MONTBAZON, AT YOUR SERVICE.
AND WHO IS IT THAT I HAVE THE PLEASURE OF SHARING MY GRAND ACCOMMODATION WITH?

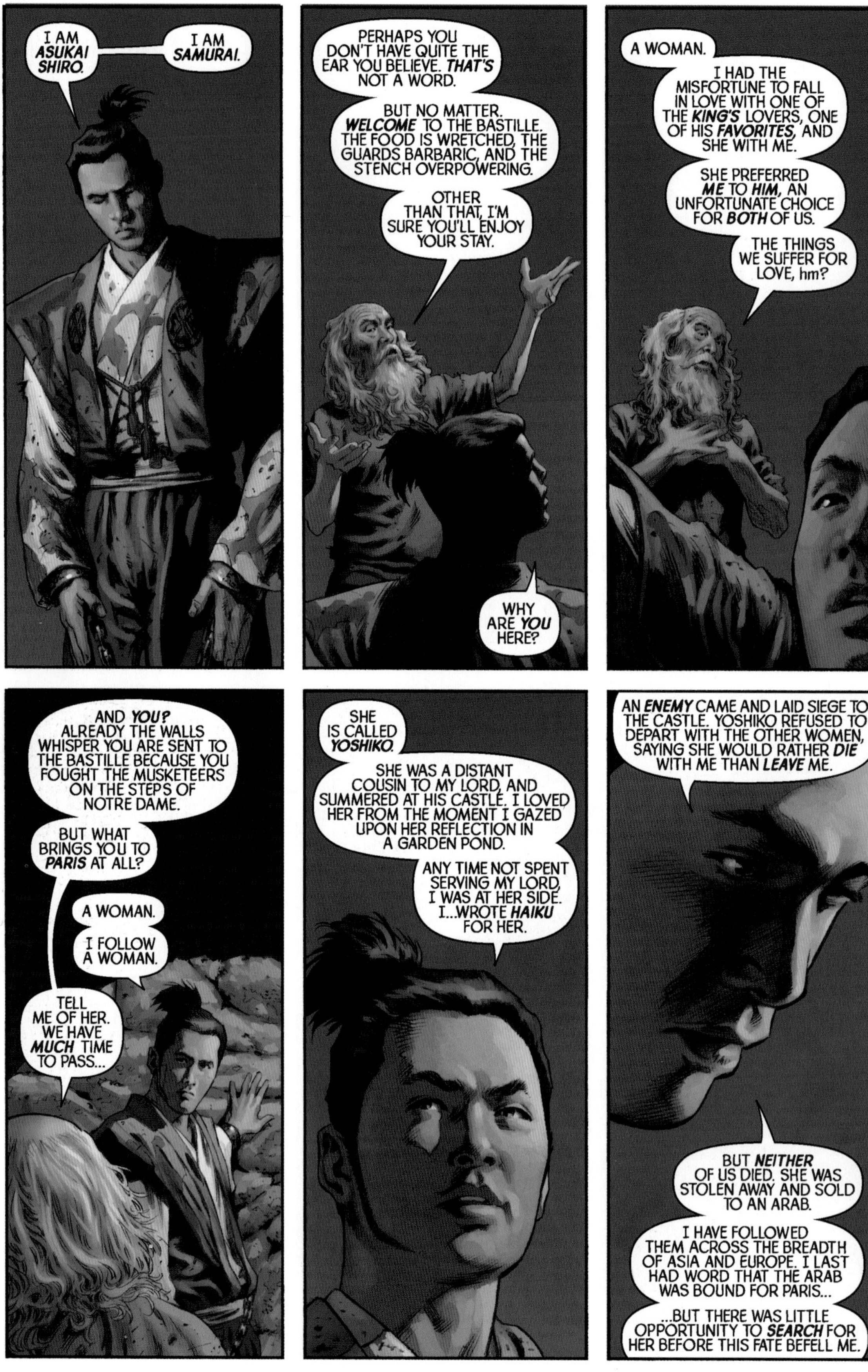
I AM ASUKAI SHIRO.
I AM SAMURAI.
PERHAPS YOU DON'T HAVE QUITE THE EAR YOU BELIEVE. THAT'S NOT A WORD.
BUT NO MATTER. WELCOME TO THE BASTILLE. THE FOOD IS WRETCHED, THE GUARDS BARBARIC, AND THE STENCH OVERPOWERING.
OTHER THAN THAT, I'M SURE YOU'LL ENJOY YOUR STAY.
WHY ARE YOU HERE?
A WOMAN.
I HAD THE MISFORTUNE TO FALL IN LOVE WITH ONE OF THE KING'S LOVERS, ONE OF HIS FAVORITES, AND SHE WITH ME.
SHE PREFERRED ME TO HIM, AN UNFORTUNATE CHOICE FOR BOTH OF US.
THE THINGS WE SUFFER FOR LOVE, hm?
AND YOU? ALREADY THE WALLS WHISPER YOU ARE SENT TO THE BASTILLE BECAUSE YOU FOUGHT THE MUSKETEERS ON THE STEPS OF NOTRE DAME.
BUT WHAT BRINGS YOU TO PARIS AT ALL?
A WOMAN.
I FOLLOW A WOMAN.
TELL ME OF HER. WE HAVE MUCH TIME TO PASS...
SHE IS CALLED YOSHIKO.
SHE WAS A DISTANT COUSIN TO MY LORD, AND SUMMERED AT HIS CASTLE. I LOVED HER FROM THE MOMENT I GAZED UPON HER REFLECTION IN A GARDEN POND.
ANY TIME NOT SPENT SERVING MY LORD, I WAS AT HER SIDE. I...WROTE HAIKU FOR HER.
AN ENEMY CAME AND LAID SIEGE TO THE CASTLE. YOSHIKO REFUSED TO DEPART WITH THE OTHER WOMEN, SAYING SHE WOULD RATHER DIE WITH ME THAN LEAVE ME.
BUT NEITHER OF US DIED. SHE WAS STOLEN AWAY AND SOLD TO AN ARAB.
I HAVE FOLLOWED THEM ACROSS THE BREADTH OF ASIA AND EUROPE. I LAST HAD WORD THAT THE ARAB WAS BOUND FOR PARIS...
...BUT THERE WAS LITTLE OPPORTUNITY TO SEARCH FOR HER BEFORE THIS FATE BEFELL ME.

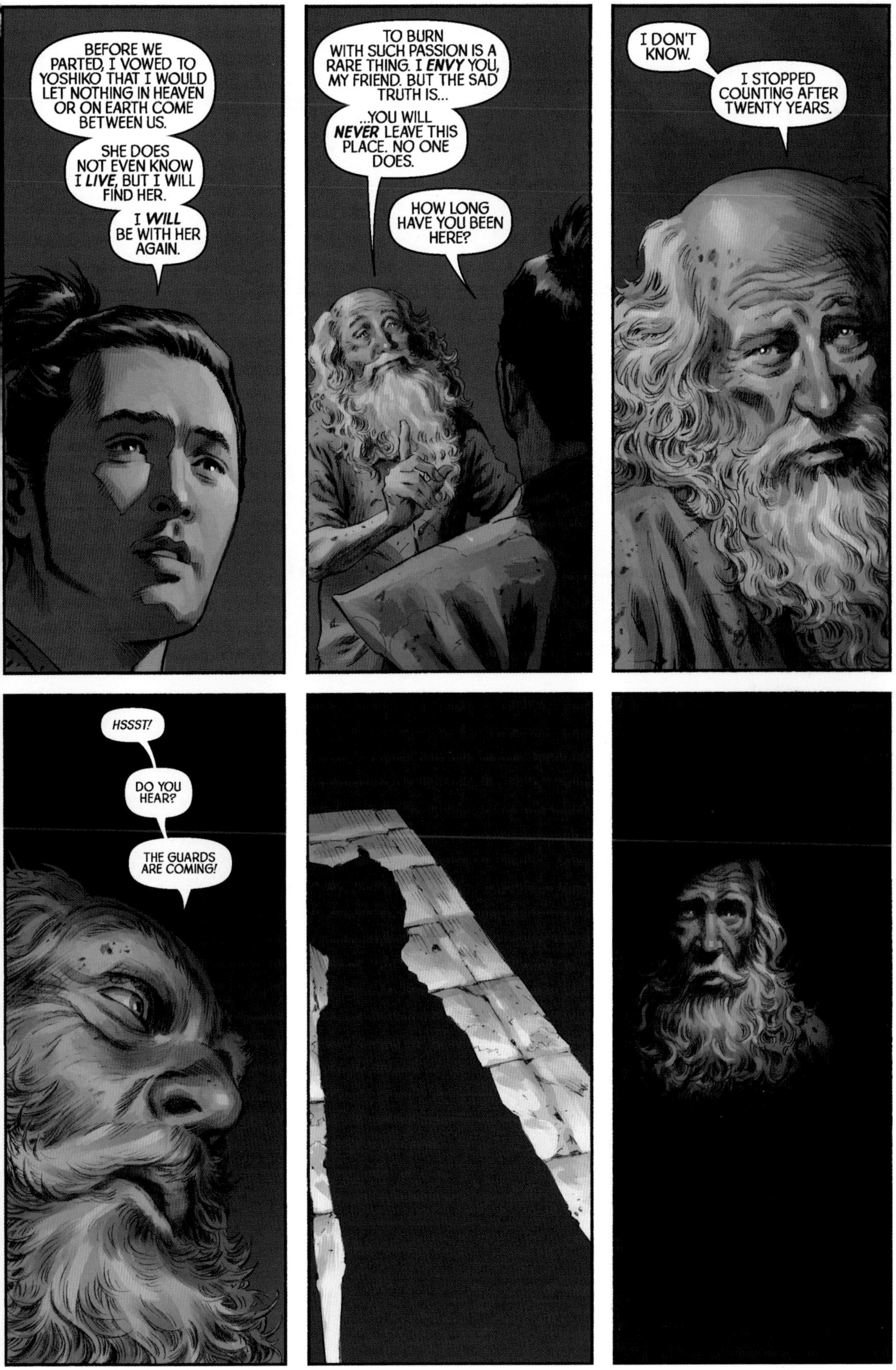
BEFORE WE PARTED, I VOWED TO YOSHIKO THAT I WOULD LET NOTHING IN HEAVEN OR ON EARTH COME BETWEEN US.
SHE DOES NOT EVEN KNOW I *LIVE*, BUT I WILL FIND HER.
I ***WILL*** BE WITH HER AGAIN.
TO BURN WITH SUCH PASSION IS A RARE THING. I ***ENVY*** YOU, MY FRIEND. BUT THE SAD TRUTH IS...
...YOU WILL ***NEVER*** LEAVE THIS PLACE. NO ONE DOES.
HOW LONG HAVE YOU BEEN HERE?
I DON'T KNOW.
I STOPPED COUNTING AFTER TWENTY YEARS.
HSSST!
DO YOU HEAR?
THE GUARDS ARE COMING!

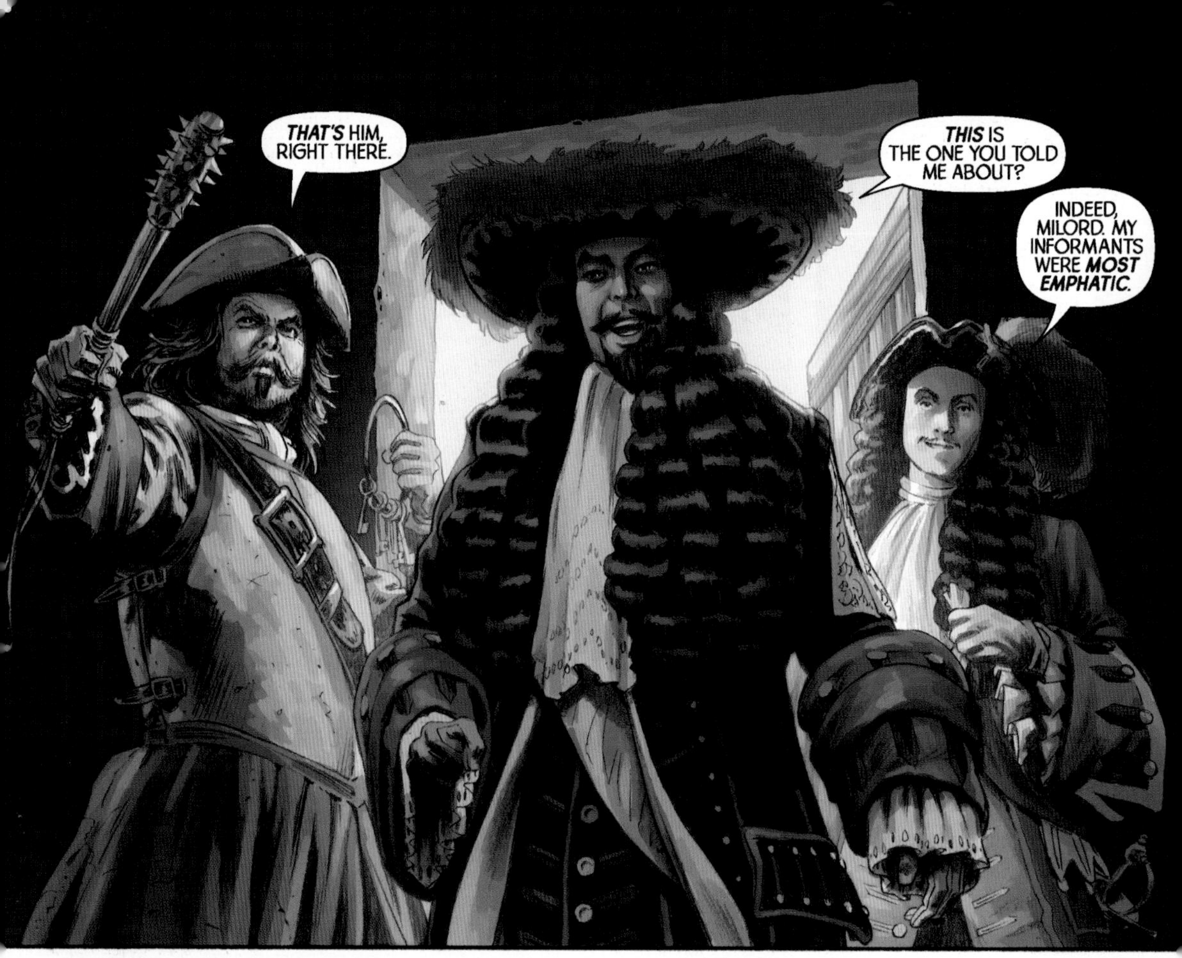
THAT'S HIM, RIGHT THERE.
THIS IS THE ONE YOU TOLD ME ABOUT?
INDEED, MILORD. MY INFORMANTS WERE MOST EMPHATIC.

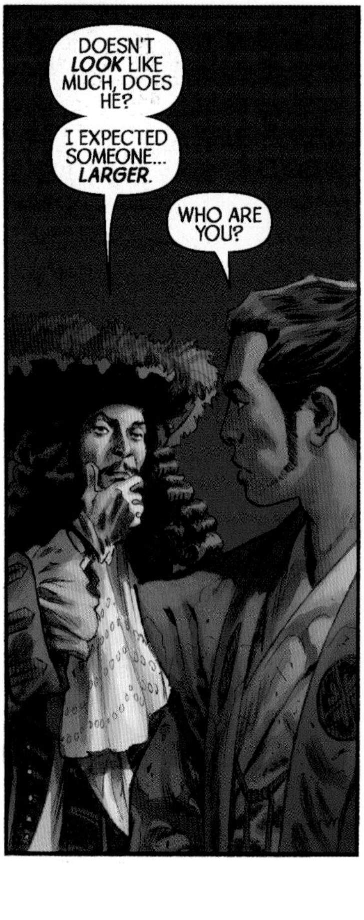
DOESN'T LOOK LIKE MUCH, DOES HE?
I EXPECTED SOMEONE... LARGER.
WHO ARE YOU?

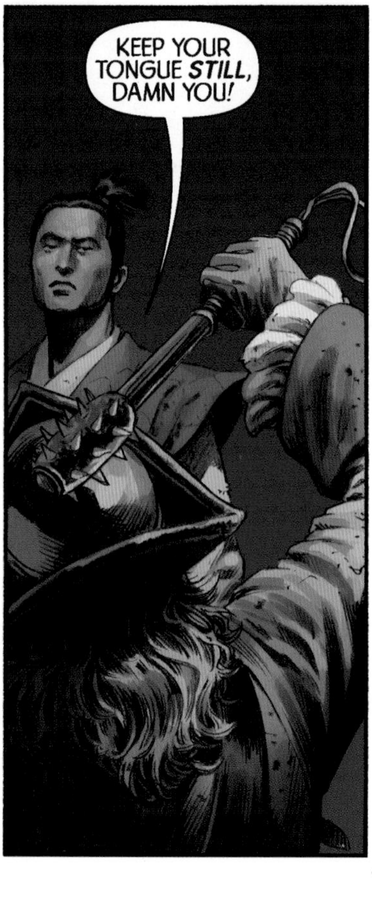
KEEP YOUR TONGUE STILL, DAMN YOU!

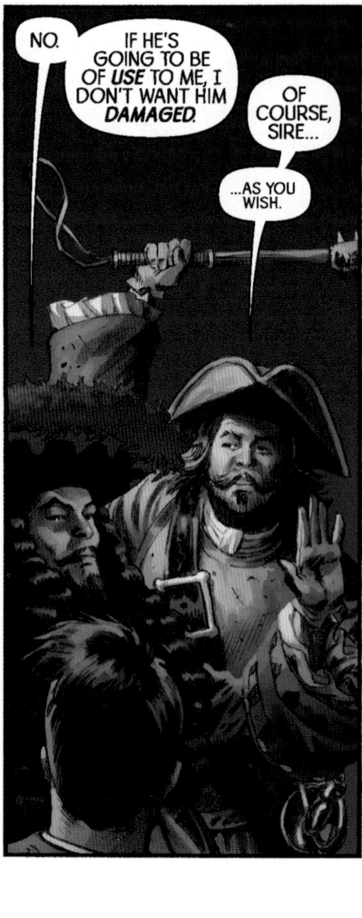
NO.
IF HE'S GOING TO BE OF USE TO ME, I DON'T WANT HIM DAMAGED.
OF COURSE, SIRE...
...AS YOU WISH.

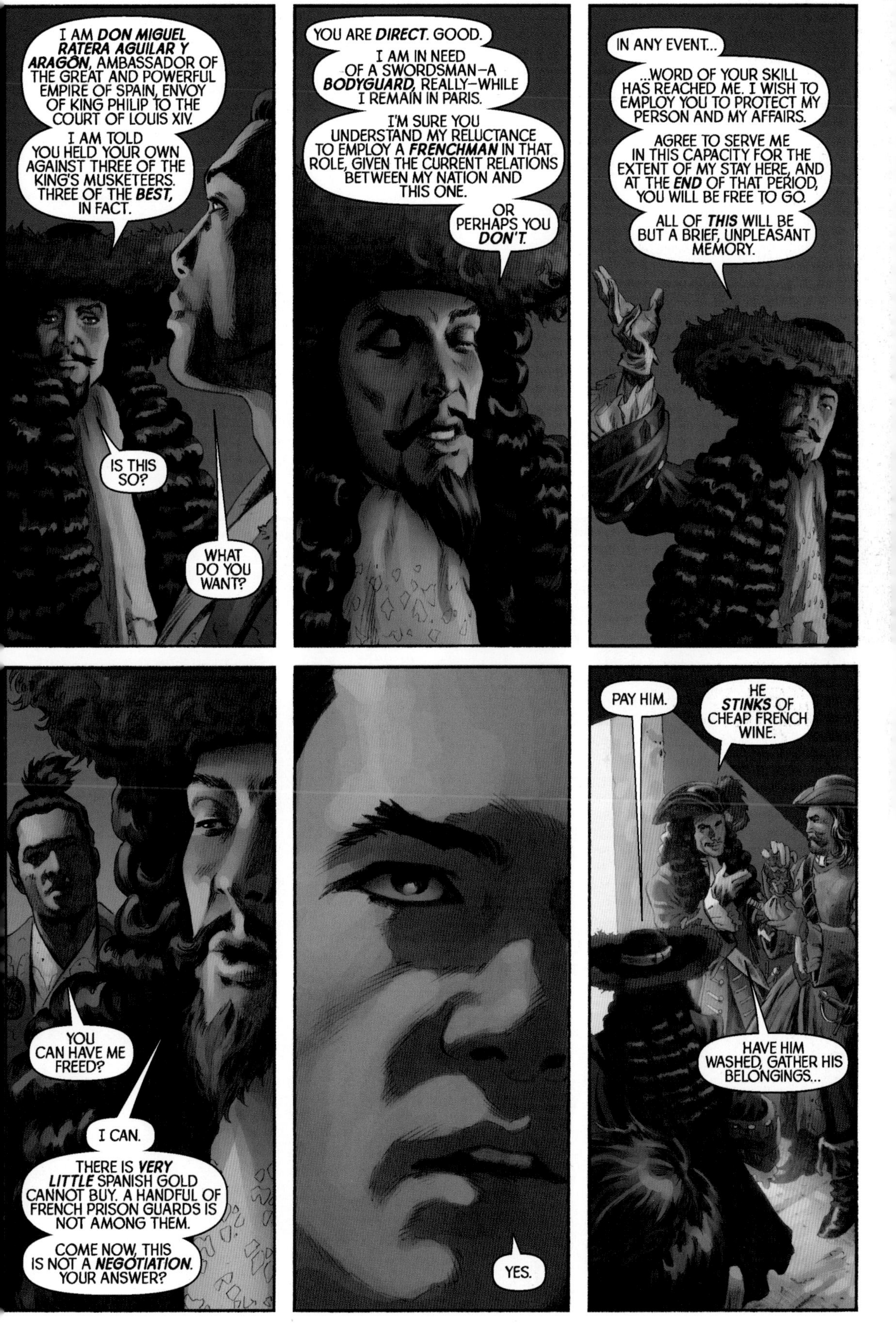
I AM DON MIGUEL RATERA AGUILAR Y ARAGÓN, AMBASSADOR OF THE GREAT AND POWERFUL EMPIRE OF SPAIN, ENVOY OF KING PHILIP TO THE COURT OF LOUIS XIV.
I AM TOLD YOU HELD YOUR OWN AGAINST THREE OF THE KING'S MUSKETEERS. THREE OF THE BEST, IN FACT.
IS THIS SO?
WHAT DO YOU WANT?
YOU ARE DIRECT. GOOD.
I AM IN NEED OF A SWORDSMAN—A BODYGUARD, REALLY—WHILE I REMAIN IN PARIS.
I'M SURE YOU UNDERSTAND MY RELUCTANCE TO EMPLOY A FRENCHMAN IN THAT ROLE, GIVEN THE CURRENT RELATIONS BETWEEN MY NATION AND THIS ONE.
OR PERHAPS YOU DON'T.
IN ANY EVENT...
...WORD OF YOUR SKILL HAS REACHED ME. I WISH TO EMPLOY YOU TO PROTECT MY PERSON AND MY AFFAIRS.
AGREE TO SERVE ME IN THIS CAPACITY FOR THE EXTENT OF MY STAY HERE, AND AT THE END OF THAT PERIOD, YOU WILL BE FREE TO GO.
ALL OF THIS WILL BE BUT A BRIEF, UNPLEASANT MEMORY.
YOU CAN HAVE ME FREED?
I CAN.
THERE IS VERY LITTLE SPANISH GOLD CANNOT BUY. A HANDFUL OF FRENCH PRISON GUARDS IS NOT AMONG THEM.
COME NOW, THIS IS NOT A NEGOTIATION. YOUR ANSWER?
YES.
PAY HIM.
HE STINKS OF CHEAP FRENCH WINE.
HAVE HIM WASHED, GATHER HIS BELONGINGS...

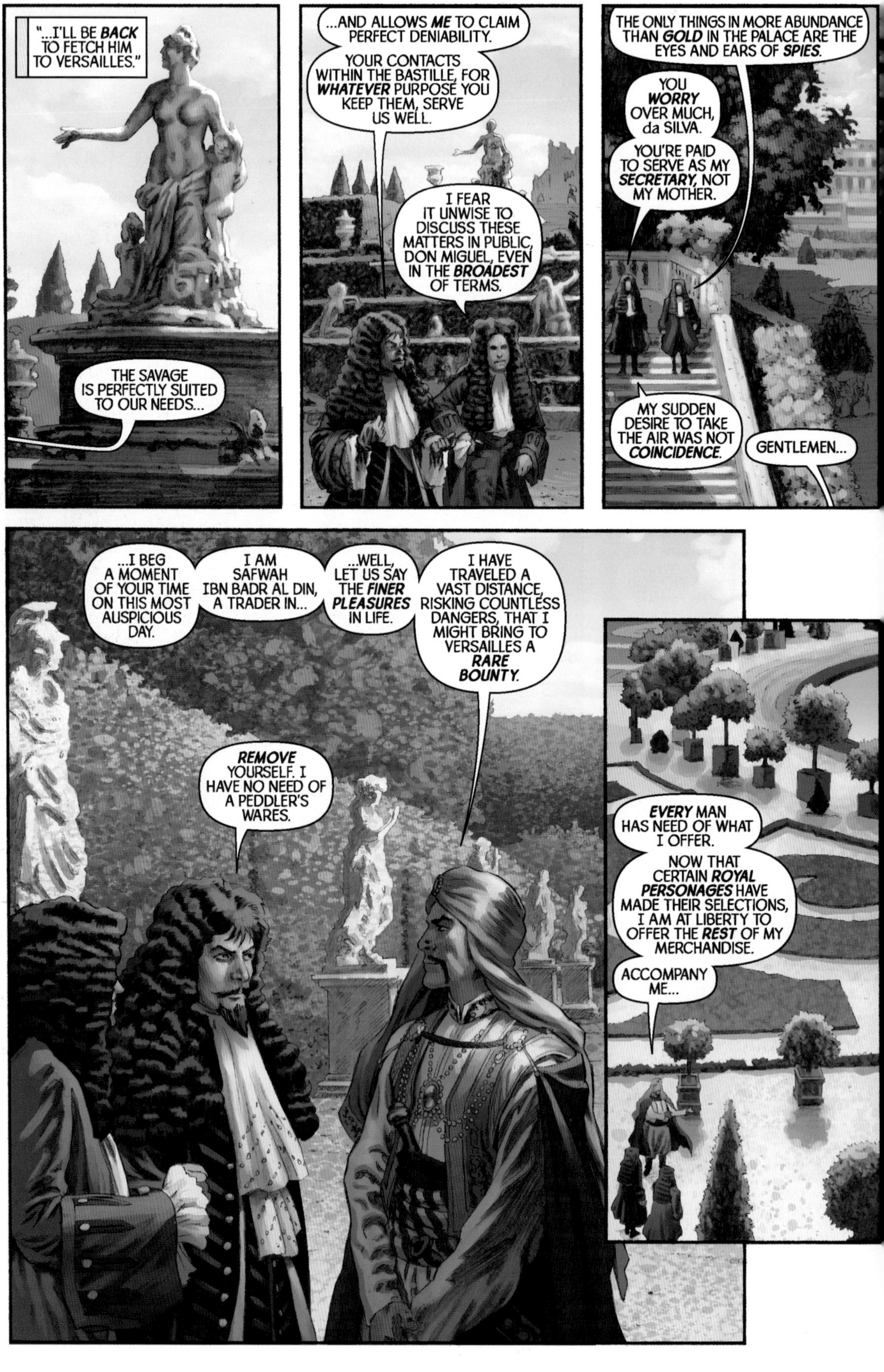
"...I'LL BE BACK TO FETCH HIM TO VERSAILLES."
THE SAVAGE IS PERFECTLY SUITED TO OUR NEEDS...
...AND ALLOWS ME TO CLAIM PERFECT DENIABILITY.
YOUR CONTACTS WITHIN THE BASTILLE, FOR WHATEVER PURPOSE YOU KEEP THEM, SERVE US WELL.
I FEAR IT UNWISE TO DISCUSS THESE MATTERS IN PUBLIC, DON MIGUEL, EVEN IN THE BROADEST OF TERMS.
THE ONLY THINGS IN MORE ABUNDANCE THAN GOLD IN THE PALACE ARE THE EYES AND EARS OF SPIES.
YOU WORRY OVER MUCH, da SILVA.
YOU'RE PAID TO SERVE AS MY SECRETARY, NOT MY MOTHER.
MY SUDDEN DESIRE TO TAKE THE AIR WAS NOT COINCIDENCE.
GENTLEMEN...
...I BEG A MOMENT OF YOUR TIME ON THIS MOST AUSPICIOUS DAY.
I AM SAFWAH IBN BADR AL DIN, A TRADER IN...
...WELL, LET US SAY THE FINER PLEASURES IN LIFE.
I HAVE TRAVELED A VAST DISTANCE, RISKING COUNTLESS DANGERS, THAT I MIGHT BRING TO VERSAILLES A RARE BOUNTY.
REMOVE YOURSELF. I HAVE NO NEED OF A PEDDLER'S WARES.
EVERY MAN HAS NEED OF WHAT I OFFER.
NOW THAT CERTAIN ROYAL PERSONAGES HAVE MADE THEIR SELECTIONS, I AM AT LIBERTY TO OFFER THE REST OF MY MERCHANDISE.
ACCOMPANY ME...

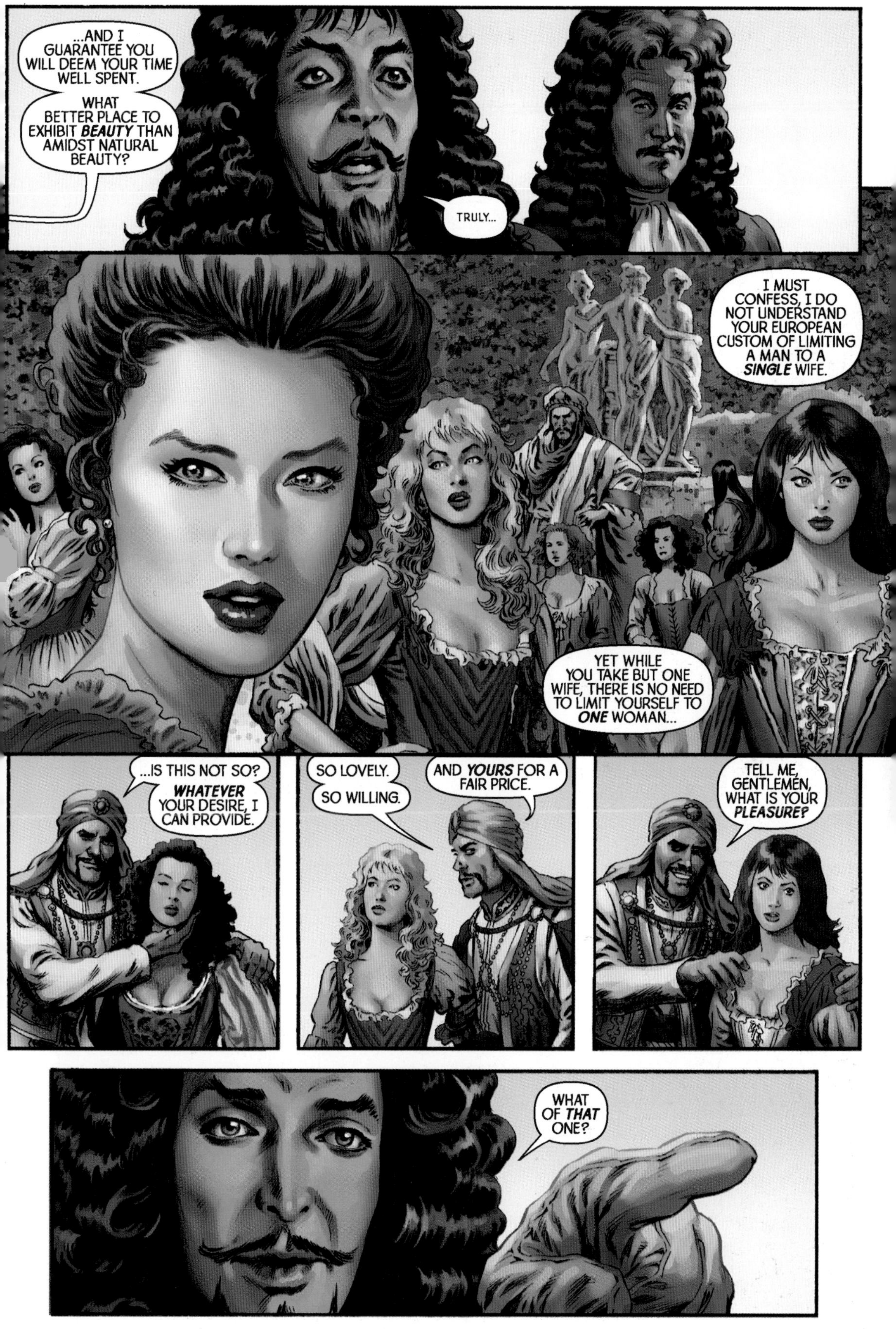

...AND I GUARANTEE YOU WILL DEEM YOUR TIME WELL SPENT.
WHAT BETTER PLACE TO EXHIBIT BEAUTY THAN AMIDST NATURAL BEAUTY?
TRULY...
I MUST CONFESS, I DO NOT UNDERSTAND YOUR EUROPEAN CUSTOM OF LIMITING A MAN TO A SINGLE WIFE.
YET WHILE YOU TAKE BUT ONE WIFE, THERE IS NO NEED TO LIMIT YOURSELF TO ONE WOMAN...
...IS THIS NOT SO? WHATEVER YOUR DESIRE, I CAN PROVIDE.
SO LOVELY.
SO WILLING.
AND YOURS FOR A FAIR PRICE.
TELL ME, GENTLEMEN, WHAT IS YOUR PLEASURE?
WHAT OF THAT ONE?

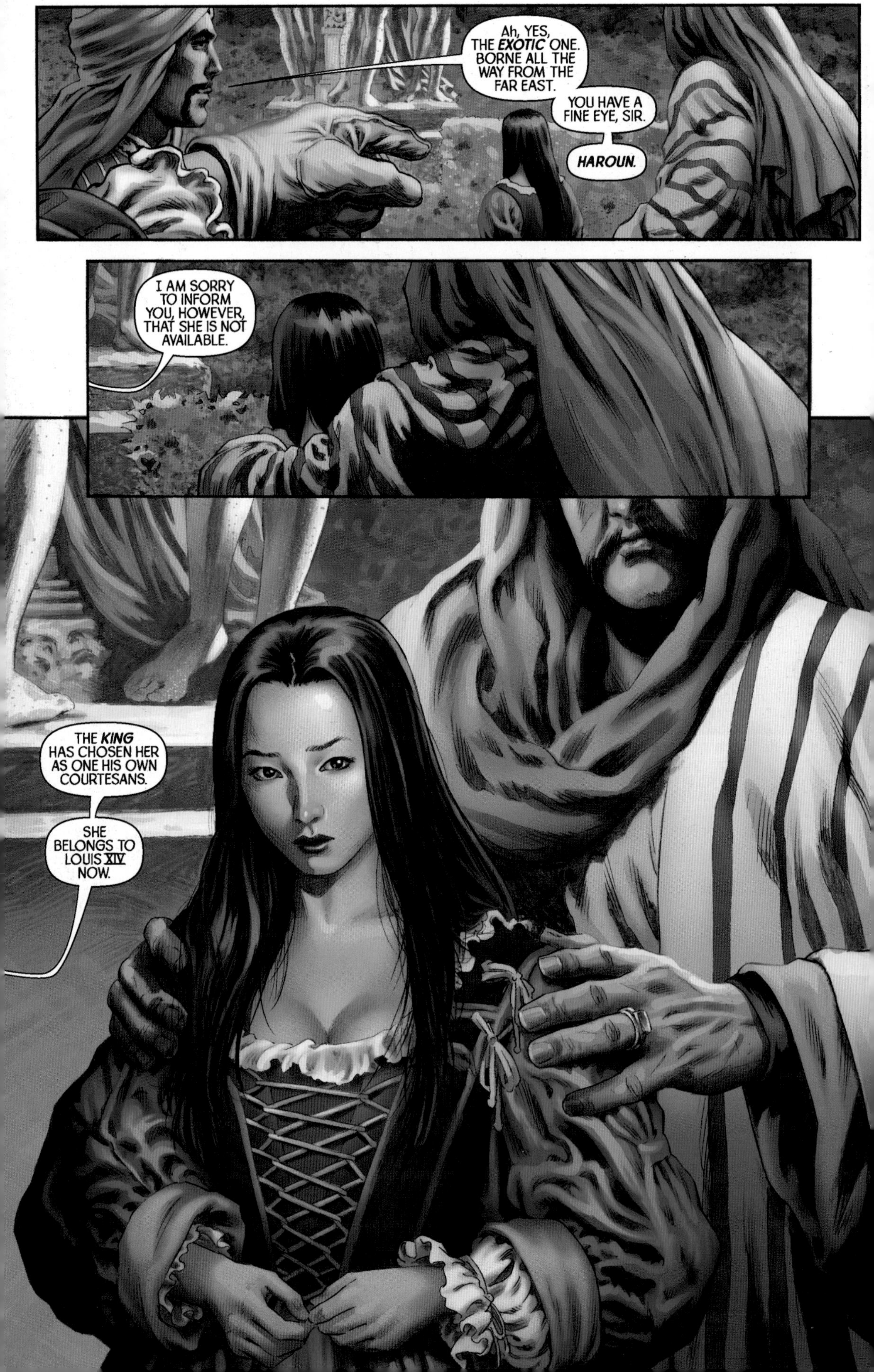

Ah, YES, THE EXOTIC ONE. BORNE ALL THE WAY FROM THE FAR EAST.
YOU HAVE A FINE EYE, SIR.
HAROUN.
I AM SORRY TO INFORM YOU, HOWEVER, THAT SHE IS NOT AVAILABLE.
THE KING HAS CHOSEN HER AS ONE HIS OWN COURTESANS.
SHE BELONGS TO LOUIS XIV NOW.

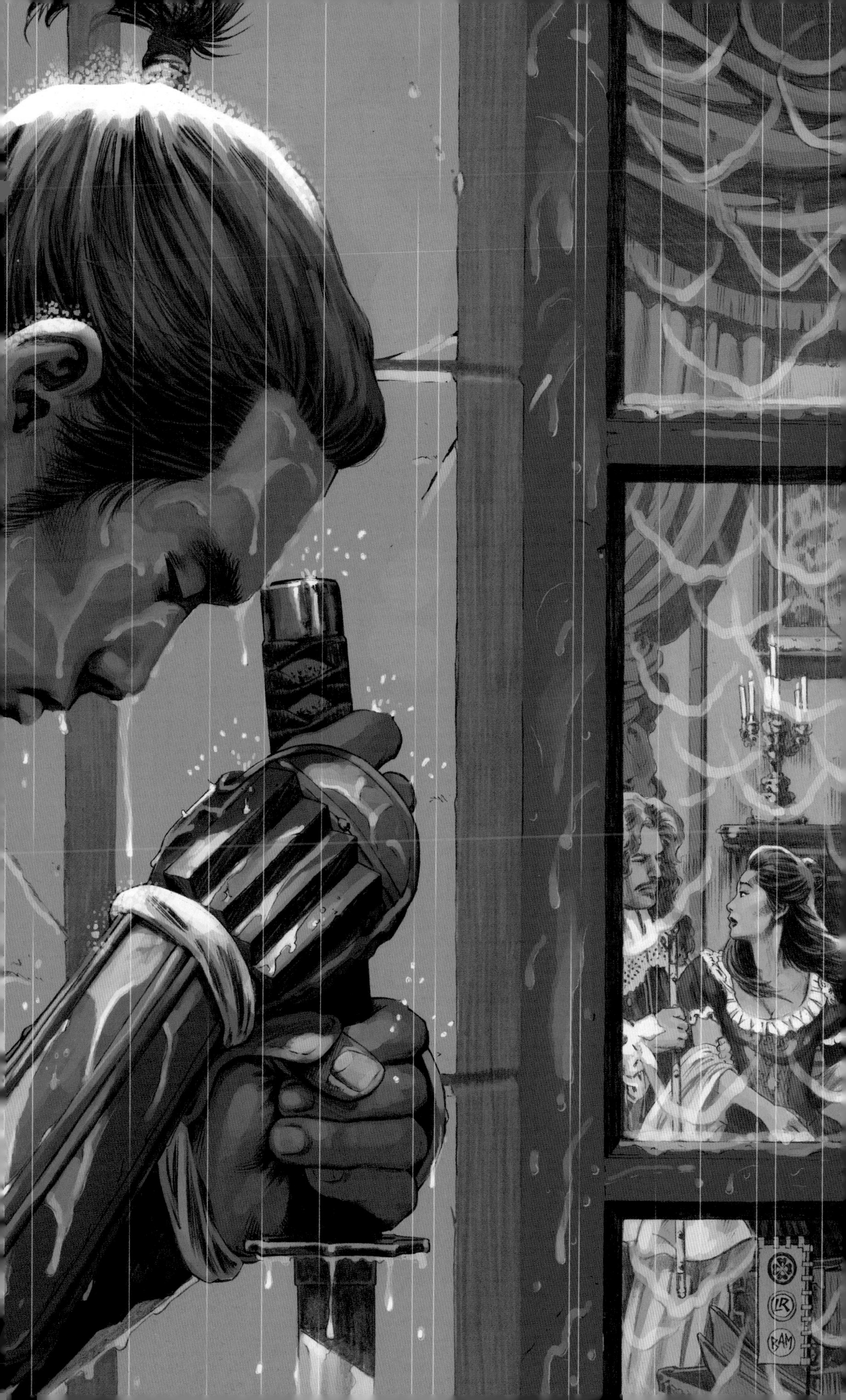

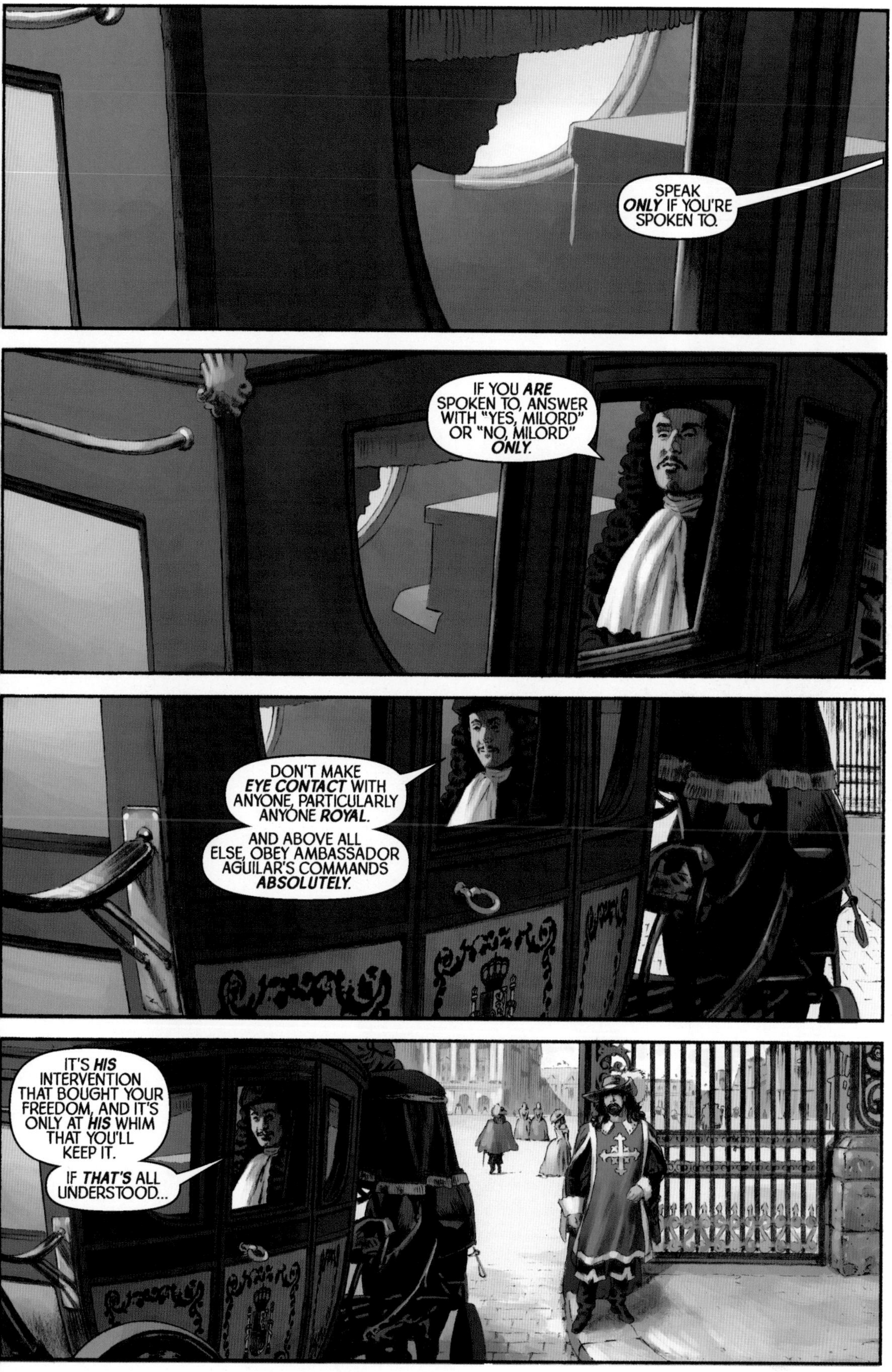
SPEAK ONLY IF YOU'RE SPOKEN TO.
IF YOU ARE SPOKEN TO, ANSWER WITH "YES, MILORD" OR "NO, MILORD" ONLY.
DON'T MAKE EYE CONTACT WITH ANYONE, PARTICULARLY ANYONE ROYAL.
AND ABOVE ALL ELSE, OBEY AMBASSADOR AGUILAR'S COMMANDS ABSOLUTELY.
IT'S HIS INTERVENTION THAT BOUGHT YOUR FREEDOM, AND IT'S ONLY AT HIS WHIM THAT YOU'LL KEEP IT.
IF THAT'S ALL UNDERSTOOD...

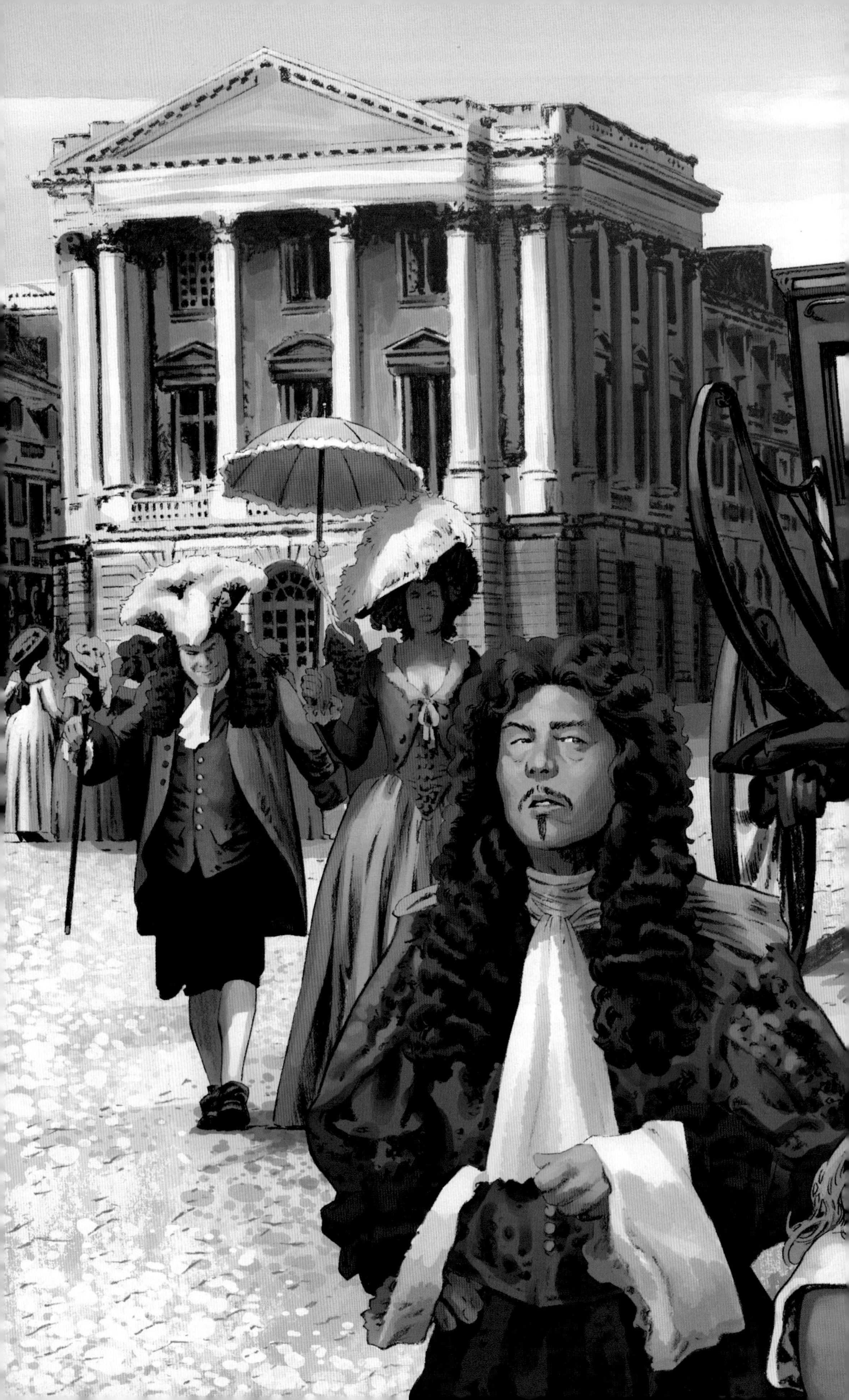

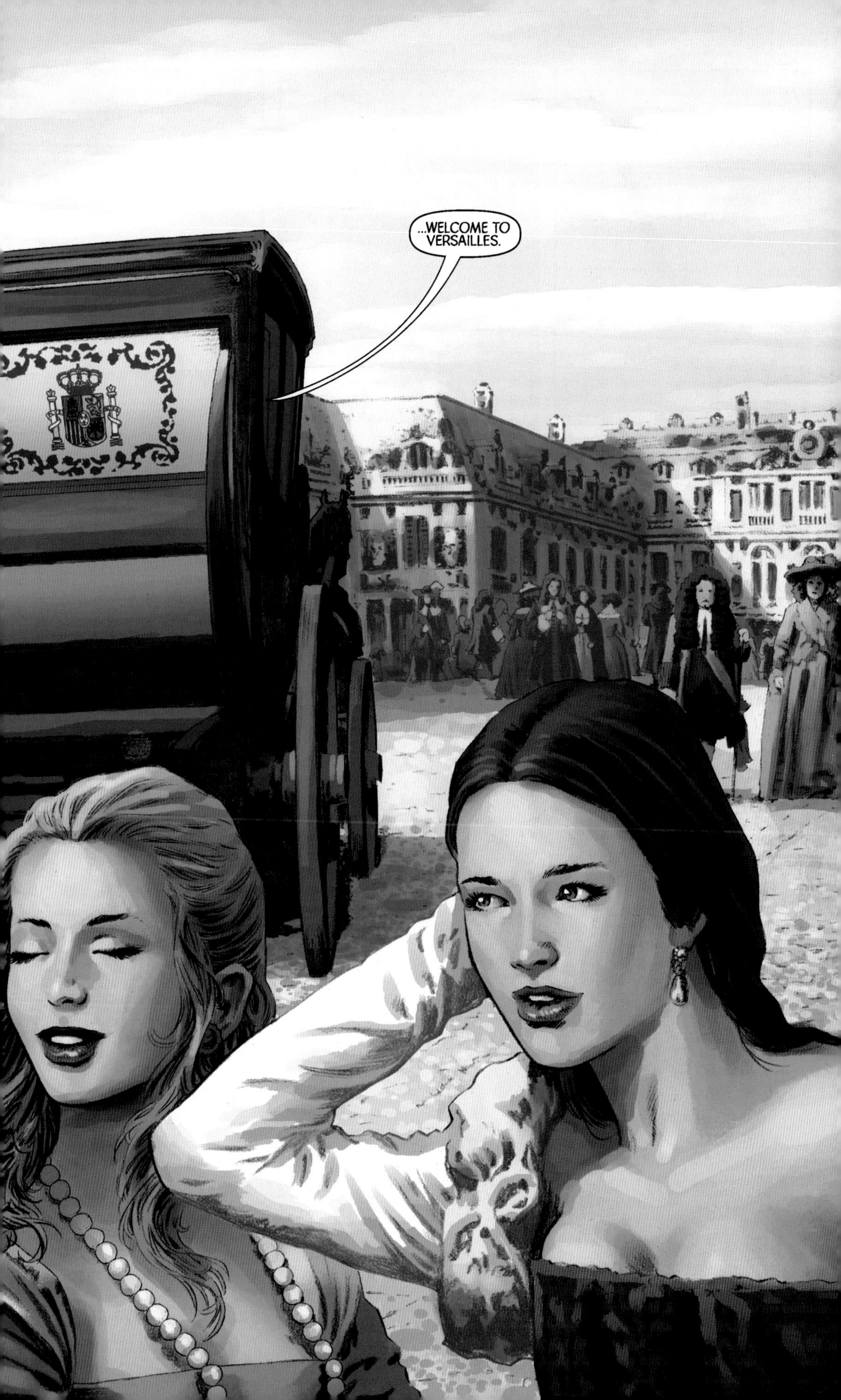
...WELCOME TO VERSAILLES.

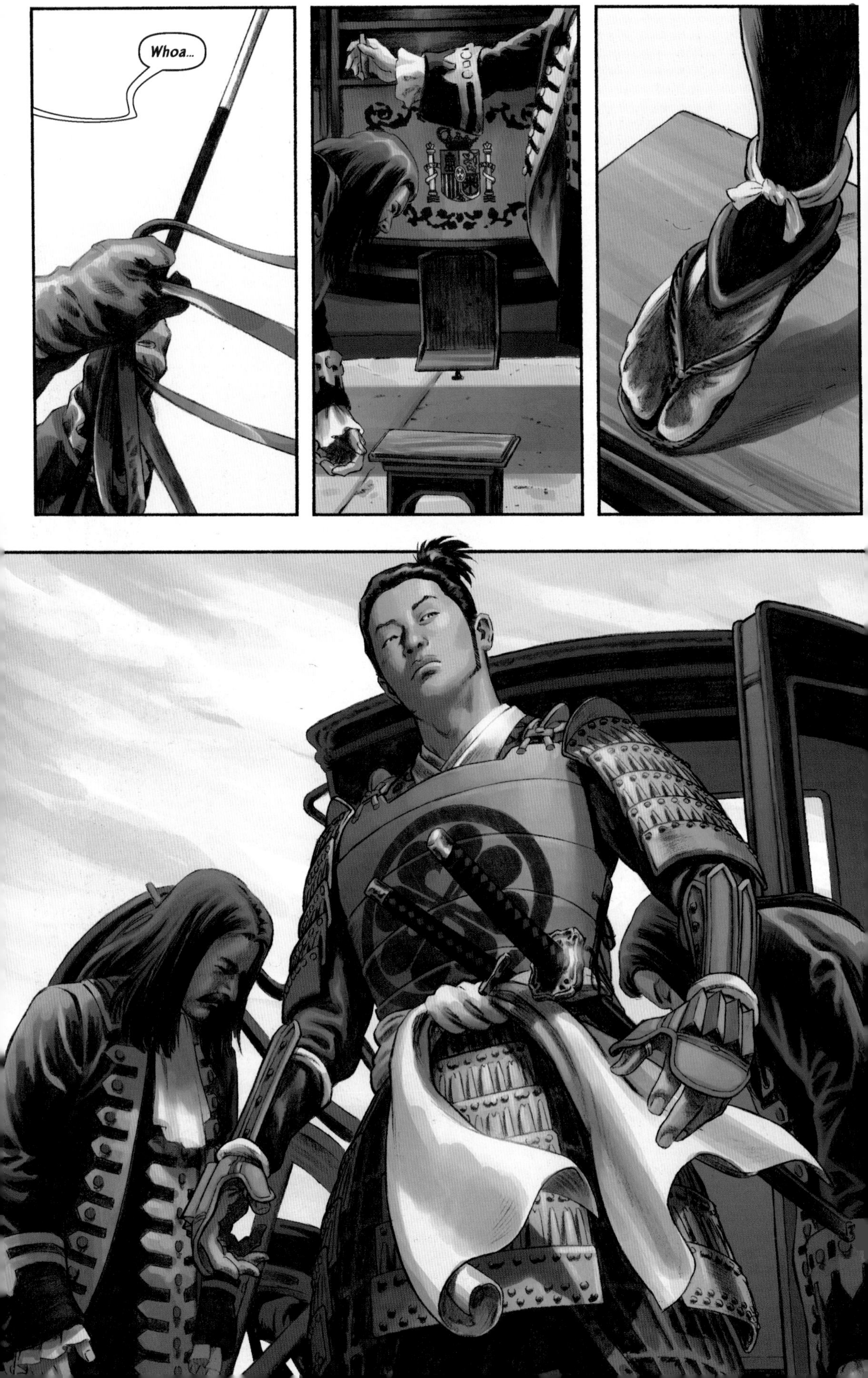
Whoa...

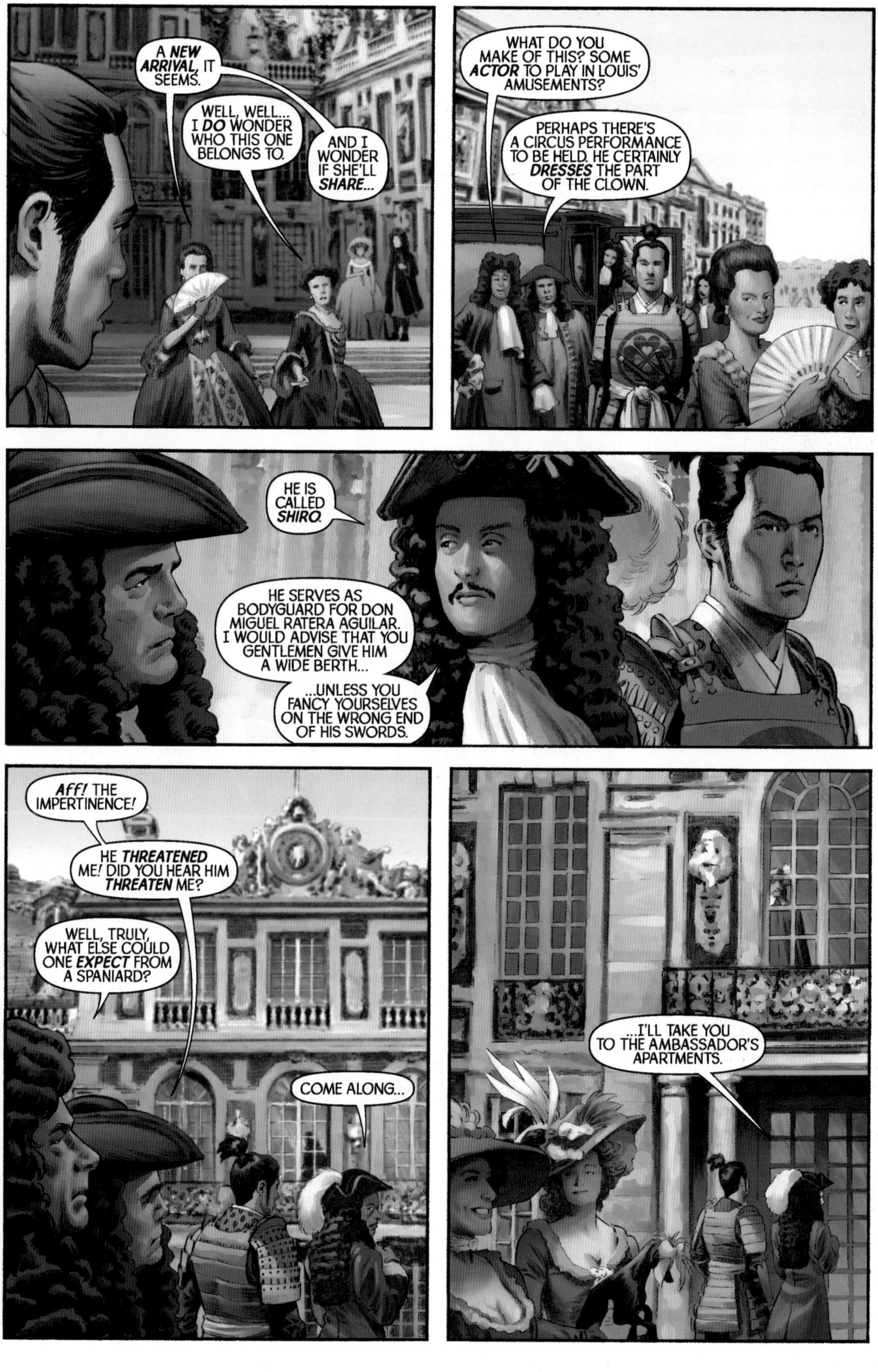
A NEW ARRIVAL, IT SEEMS.
WELL, WELL... I DO WONDER WHO THIS ONE BELONGS TO.
AND I WONDER IF SHE'LL SHARE...
WHAT DO YOU MAKE OF THIS? SOME ACTOR TO PLAY IN LOUIS' AMUSEMENTS?
PERHAPS THERE'S A CIRCUS PERFORMANCE TO BE HELD. HE CERTAINLY DRESSES THE PART OF THE CLOWN.
HE IS CALLED SHIRO.
HE SERVES AS BODYGUARD FOR DON MIGUEL RATERA AGUILAR. I WOULD ADVISE THAT YOU GENTLEMEN GIVE HIM A WIDE BERTH...
...UNLESS YOU FANCY YOURSELVES ON THE WRONG END OF HIS SWORDS.
AFF! THE IMPERTINENCE!
HE THREATENED ME! DID YOU HEAR HIM THREATEN ME?
WELL, TRULY, WHAT ELSE COULD ONE EXPECT FROM A SPANIARD?
COME ALONG...
...I'LL TAKE YOU TO THE AMBASSADOR'S APARTMENTS.

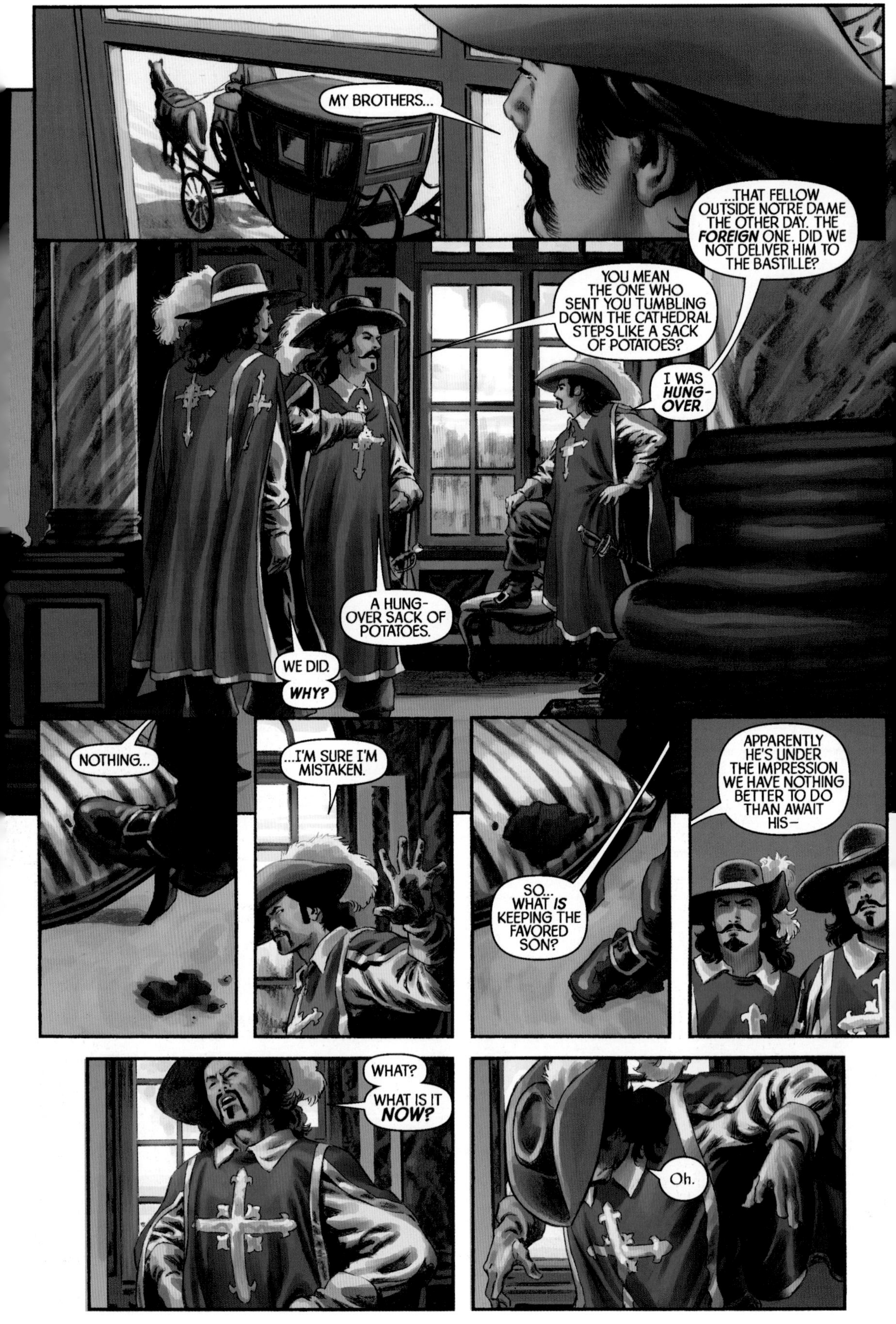

MY BROTHERS...
...THAT FELLOW OUTSIDE NOTRE DAME THE OTHER DAY. THE **FOREIGN** ONE. DID WE NOT DELIVER HIM TO THE BASTILLE?
YOU MEAN THE ONE WHO SENT YOU TUMBLING DOWN THE CATHEDRAL STEPS LIKE A SACK OF POTATOES?
I WAS **HUNG-OVER**.
A HUNG-OVER SACK OF POTATOES.
WE DID.
WHY?
NOTHING...
...I'M SURE I'M MISTAKEN.
SO... WHAT **IS** KEEPING THE FAVORED SON?
APPARENTLY HE'S UNDER THE IMPRESSION WE HAVE NOTHING BETTER TO DO THAN AWAIT HIS—
WHAT?
WHAT IS IT **NOW?**
Oh.

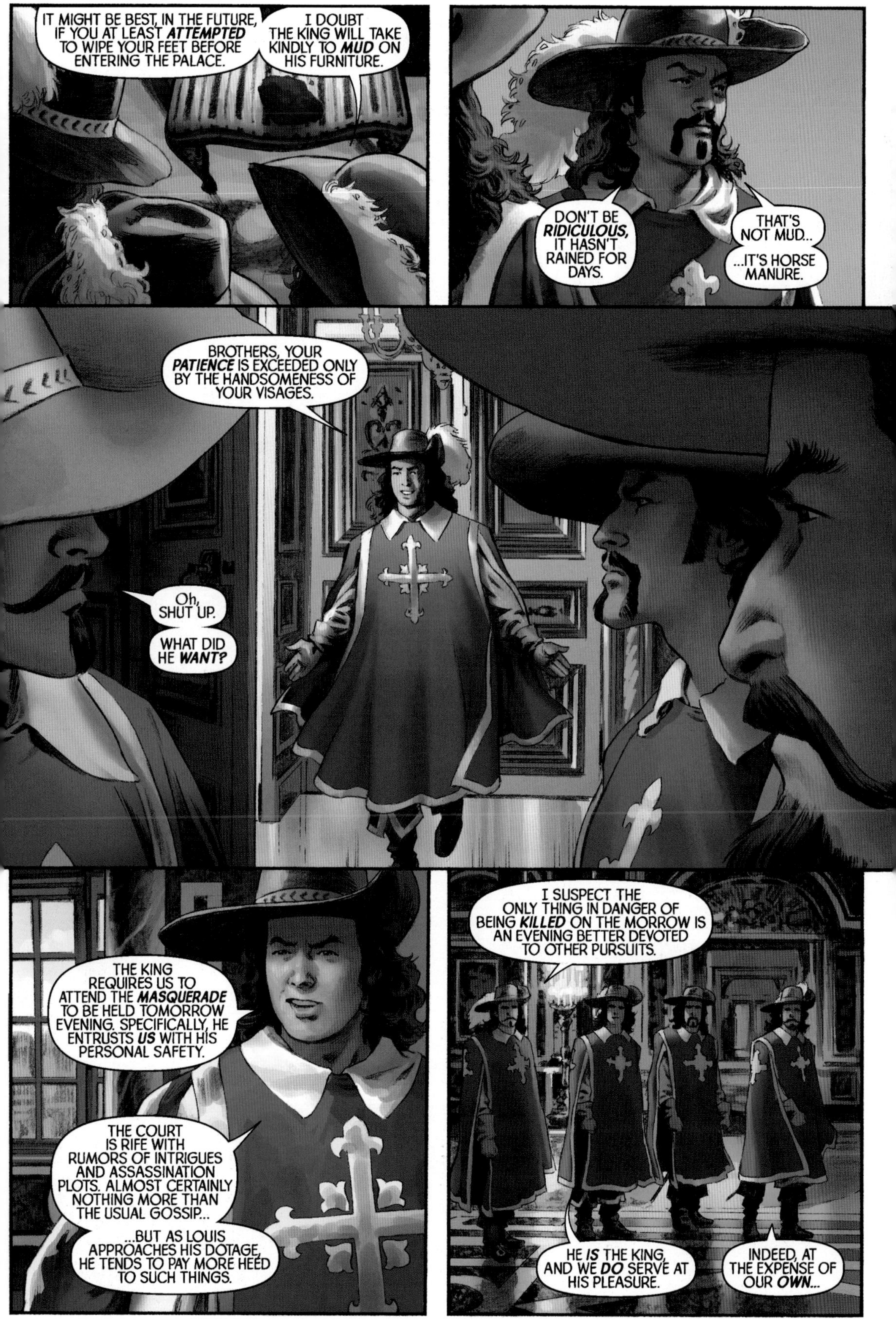
IT MIGHT BE BEST, IN THE FUTURE, IF YOU AT LEAST ATTEMPTED TO WIPE YOUR FEET BEFORE ENTERING THE PALACE.
I DOUBT THE KING WILL TAKE KINDLY TO MUD ON HIS FURNITURE.
DON'T BE RIDICULOUS, IT HASN'T RAINED FOR DAYS.
THAT'S NOT MUD...
...IT'S HORSE MANURE.
BROTHERS, YOUR PATIENCE IS EXCEEDED ONLY BY THE HANDSOMENESS OF YOUR VISAGES.
Oh, SHUT UP.
WHAT DID HE WANT?
THE KING REQUIRES US TO ATTEND THE MASQUERADE TO BE HELD TOMORROW EVENING. SPECIFICALLY, HE ENTRUSTS US WITH HIS PERSONAL SAFETY.
THE COURT IS RIFE WITH RUMORS OF INTRIGUES AND ASSASSINATION PLOTS. ALMOST CERTAINLY NOTHING MORE THAN THE USUAL GOSSIP...
...BUT AS LOUIS APPROACHES HIS DOTAGE, HE TENDS TO PAY MORE HEED TO SUCH THINGS.
I SUSPECT THE ONLY THING IN DANGER OF BEING KILLED ON THE MORROW IS AN EVENING BETTER DEVOTED TO OTHER PURSUITS.
HE IS THE KING, AND WE DO SERVE AT HIS PLEASURE.
INDEED, AT THE EXPENSE OF OUR OWN...

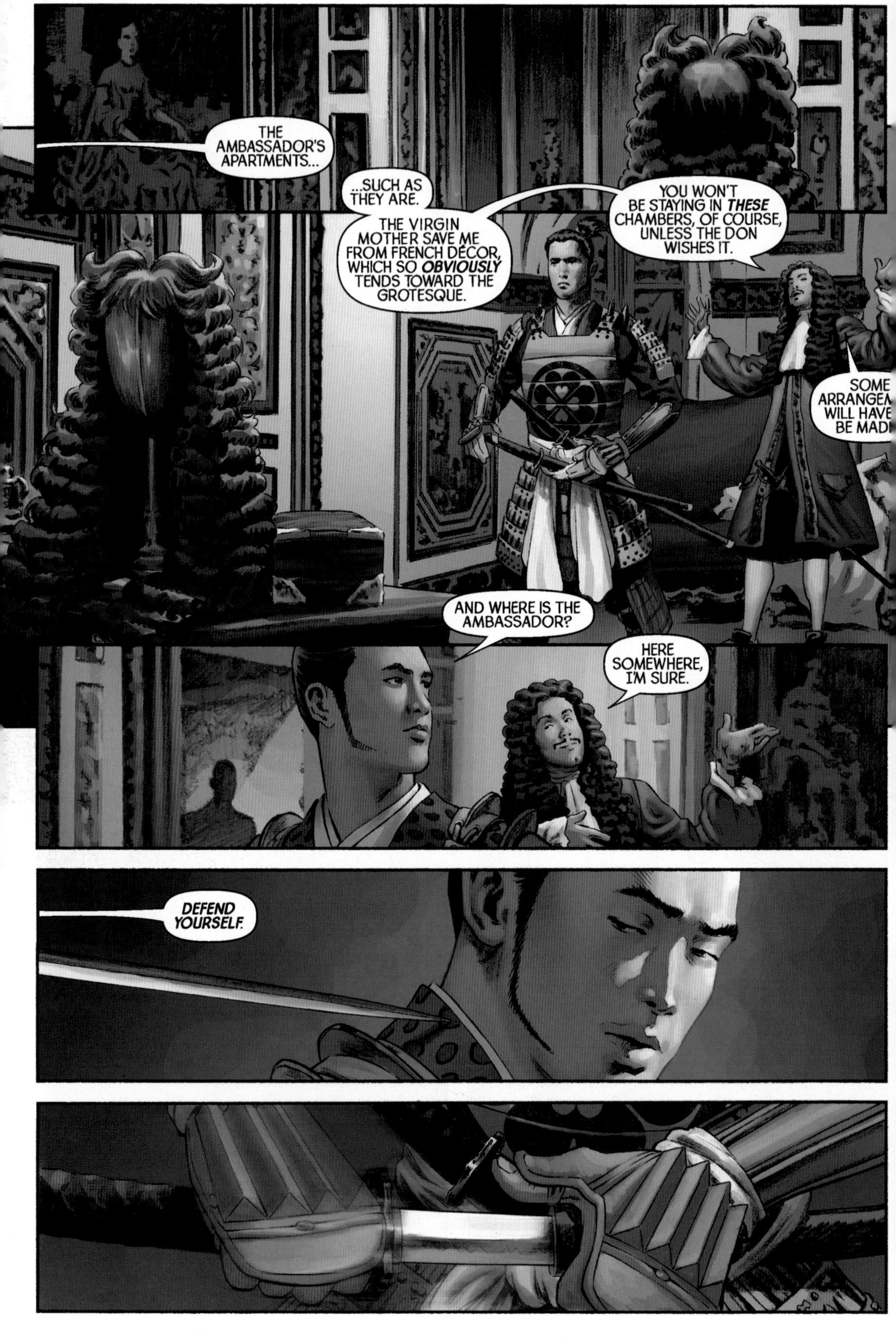
THE AMBASSADOR'S APARTMENTS...
...SUCH AS THEY ARE.
THE VIRGIN MOTHER SAVE ME FROM FRENCH DÉCOR, WHICH SO *OBVIOUSLY* TENDS TOWARD THE GROTESQUE.
YOU WON'T BE STAYING IN *THESE* CHAMBERS, OF COURSE, UNLESS THE DON WISHES IT.
SOME ARRANGEM WILL HAVE BE MADE
AND WHERE IS THE AMBASSADOR?
HERE SOMEWHERE, I'M SURE.
DEFEND YOURSELF.

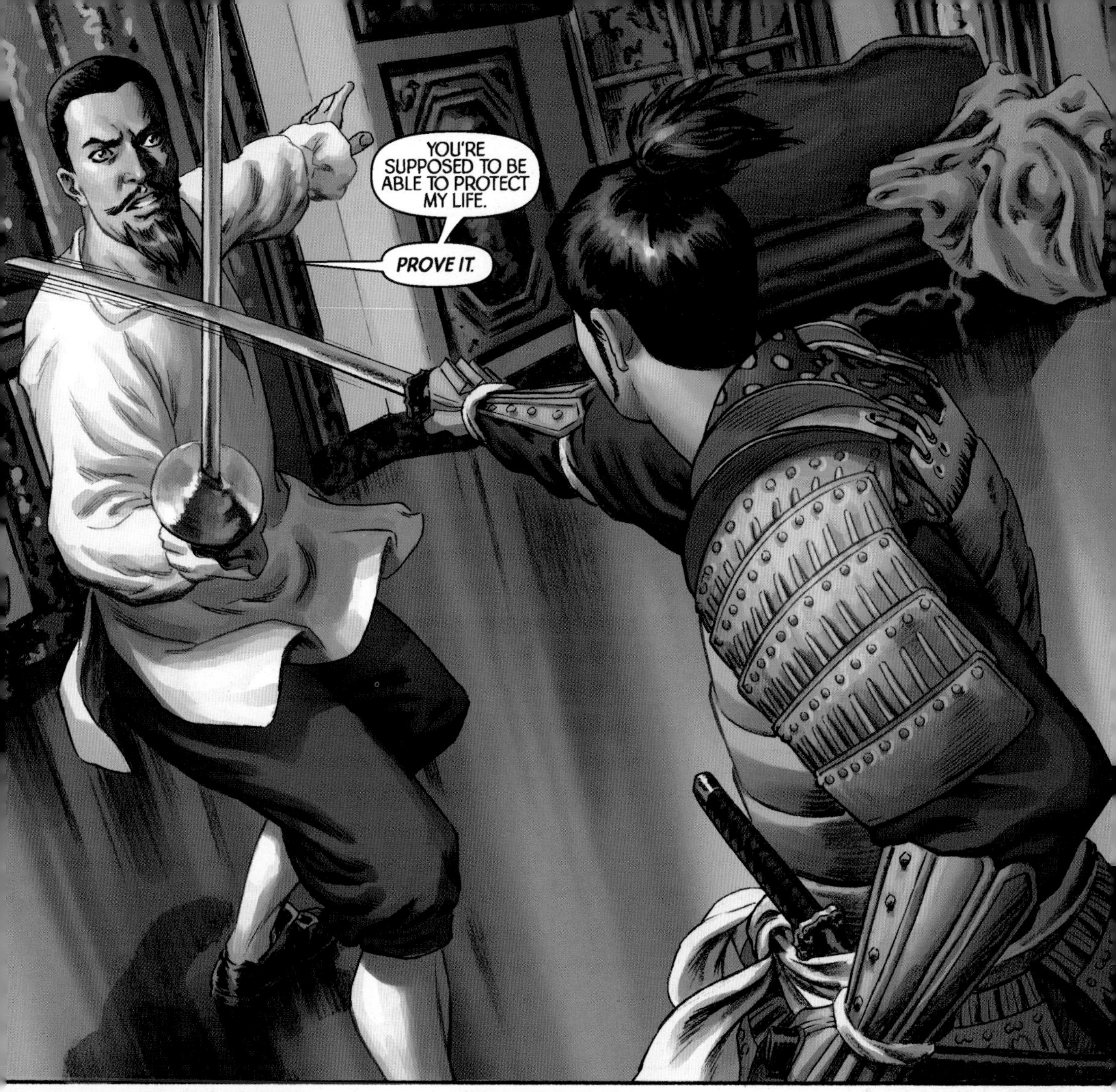
YOU'RE SUPPOSED TO BE ABLE TO PROTECT MY LIFE.
PROVE IT.

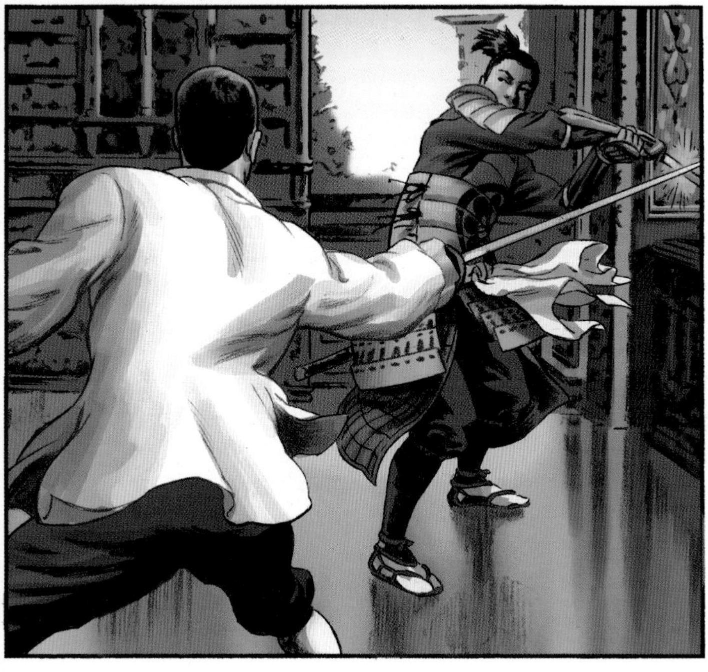

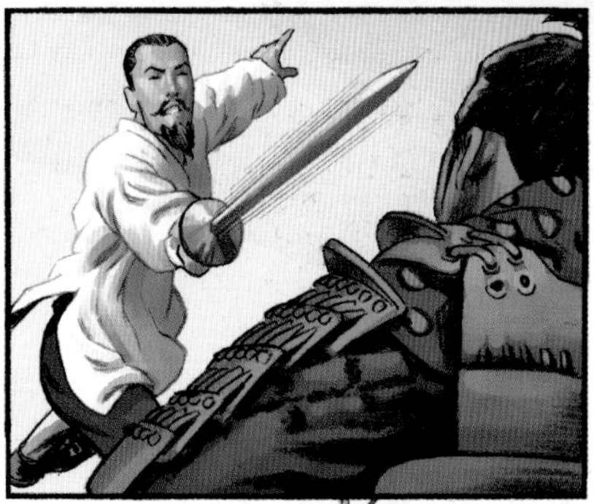

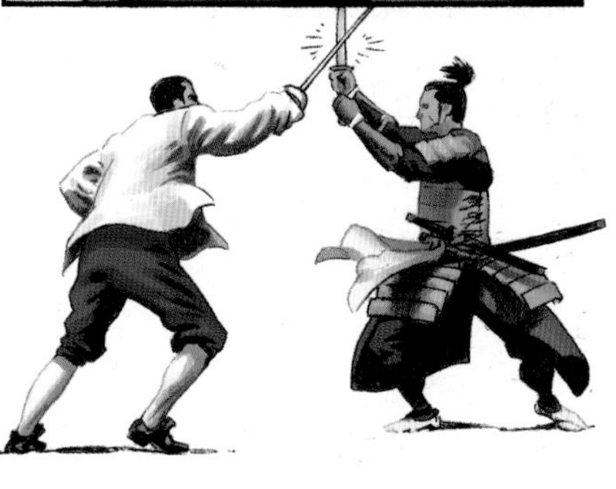

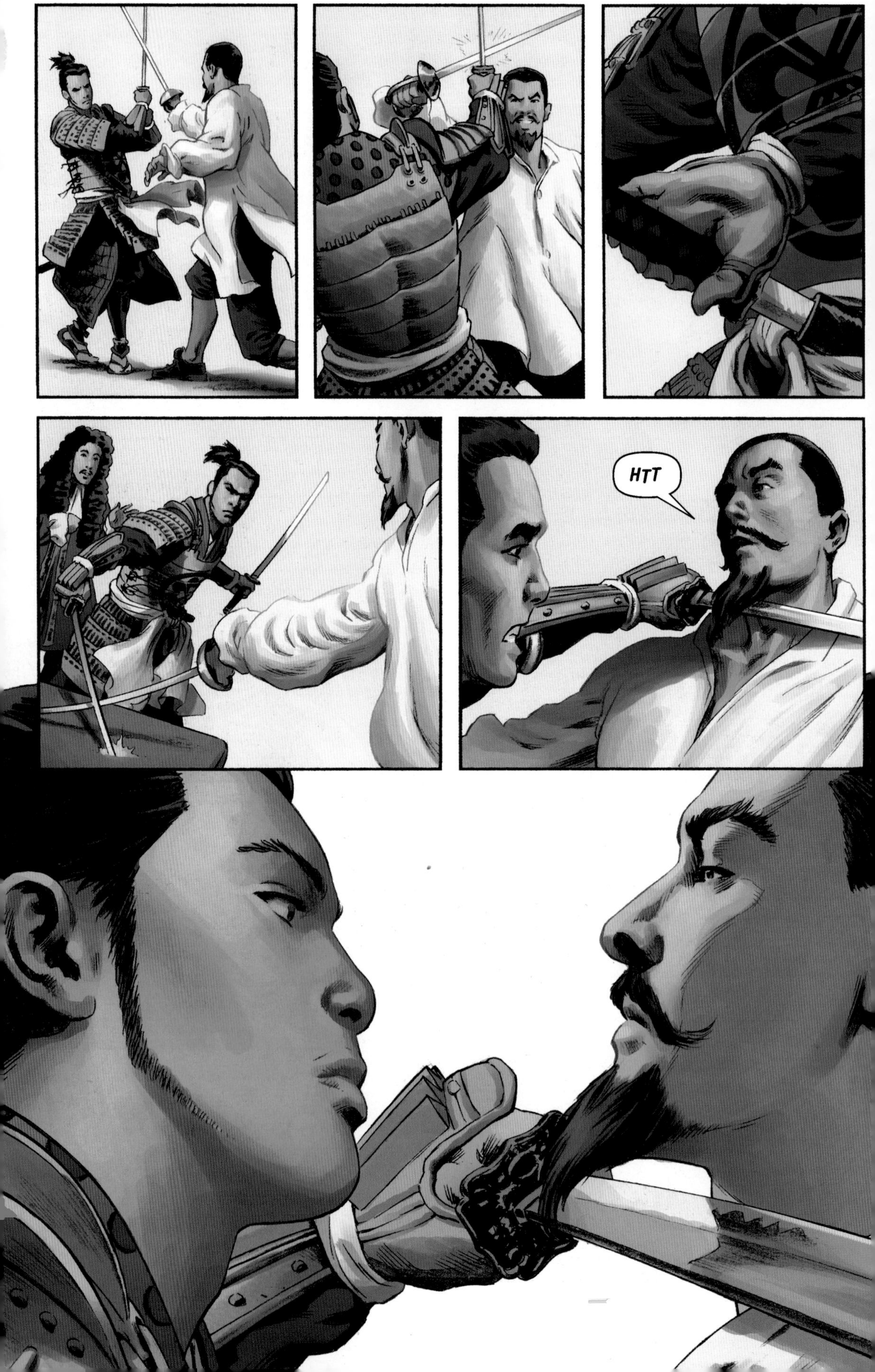
HTT

I SEE I'VE CHOSEN *WELL*.

DaSILVA HERE WILL SEE TO YOUR NEEDS.

MAKE SURE YOU FETCH HIM SOME *PROPER* CLOTHING.

OF COURSE, AMBASSADOR.

WHAT IS IT YOU EXPECT OF ME? *EXACTLY*.

WHAT I TOLD YOU... *EXACTLY*. YOU WILL *PROTECT* ME.

THERE'S NOTHING THESE FRENCH DEVILS WOULD LIKE BETTER THAN HAVING MY *HEAD* ON A PIKE. LOUIS HIMSELF WOULD GLADLY PARADE IT THROUGH HIS HALL OF MIRRORS.

THERE'S A COSTUME BALL TOMORROW EVENING, A TYPICALLY TEDIOUS COURT AMUSEMENT.

YOU'LL ACCOMPANY ME AND DISCOURAGE ANY *UNFORTUNATE* INCIDENTS.

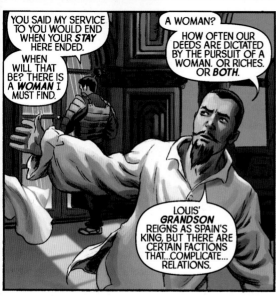

YOU SAID MY SERVICE TO YOU WOULD END WHEN YOUR *STAY* HERE ENDED.

WHEN WILL THAT BE? THERE IS A *WOMAN* I MUST FIND.

A WOMAN? HOW OFTEN OUR DEEDS ARE DICTATED BY THE PURSUIT OF A WOMAN. OR RICHES. OR *BOTH*.

LOUIS' *GRANDSON* REIGNS AS SPAIN'S KING, BUT THERE ARE CERTAIN FACTIONS THAT...COMPLICATE... RELATIONS.

IT WILL LIKELY BE SOME TIME BEFORE MY MISSION HERE IS ACCOMPLISHED...

...PERHAPS *YEARS*.

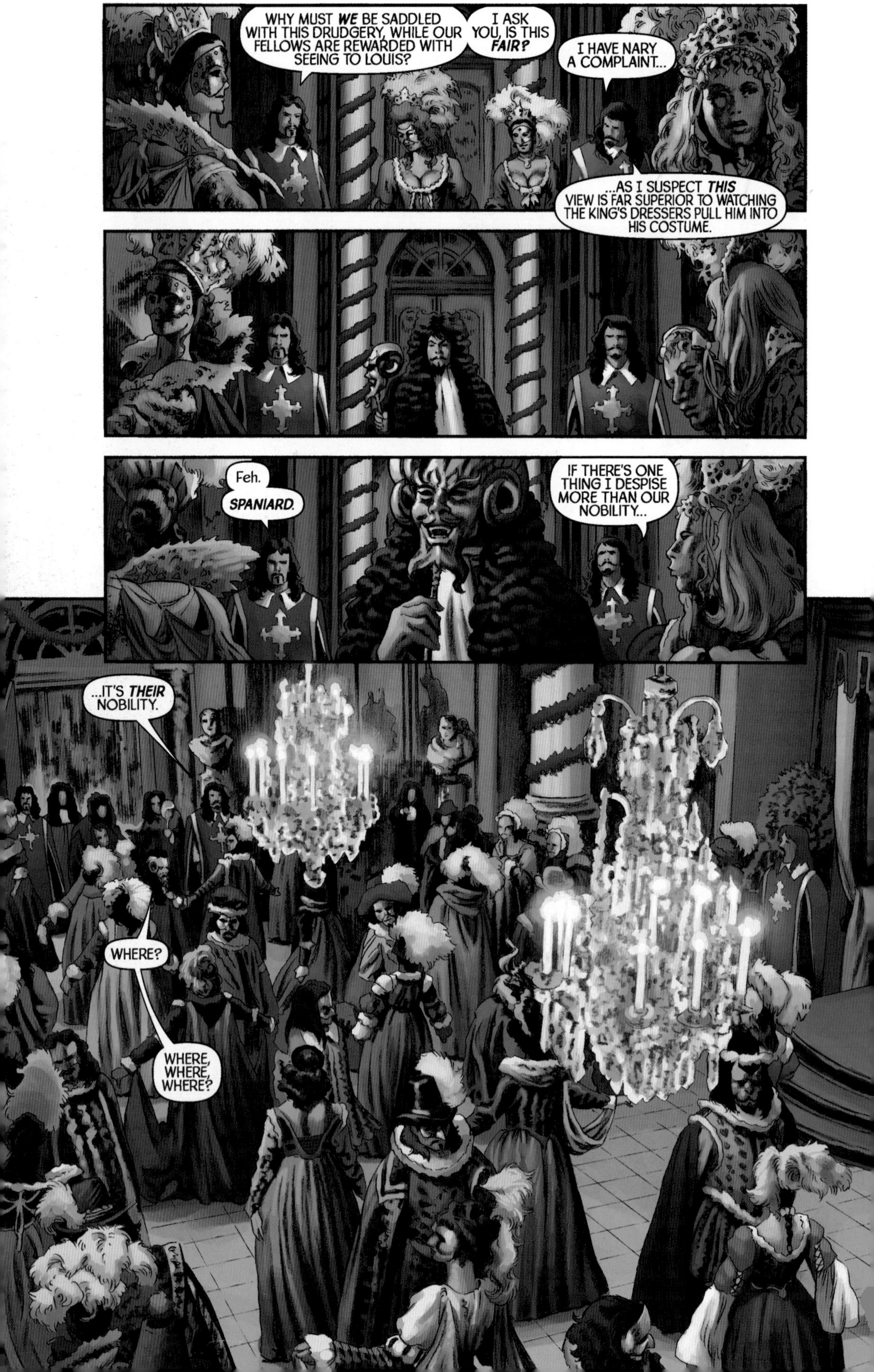
WHY MUST WE BE SADDLED WITH THIS DRUDGERY, WHILE OUR FELLOWS ARE REWARDED WITH SEEING TO LOUIS?
I ASK YOU, IS THIS FAIR?
I HAVE NARY A COMPLAINT...
...AS I SUSPECT THIS VIEW IS FAR SUPERIOR TO WATCHING THE KING'S DRESSERS PULL HIM INTO HIS COSTUME.
Feh.
SPANIARD.
IF THERE'S ONE THING I DESPISE MORE THAN OUR NOBILITY...
...IT'S THEIR NOBILITY.
WHERE?
WHERE, WHERE, WHERE?

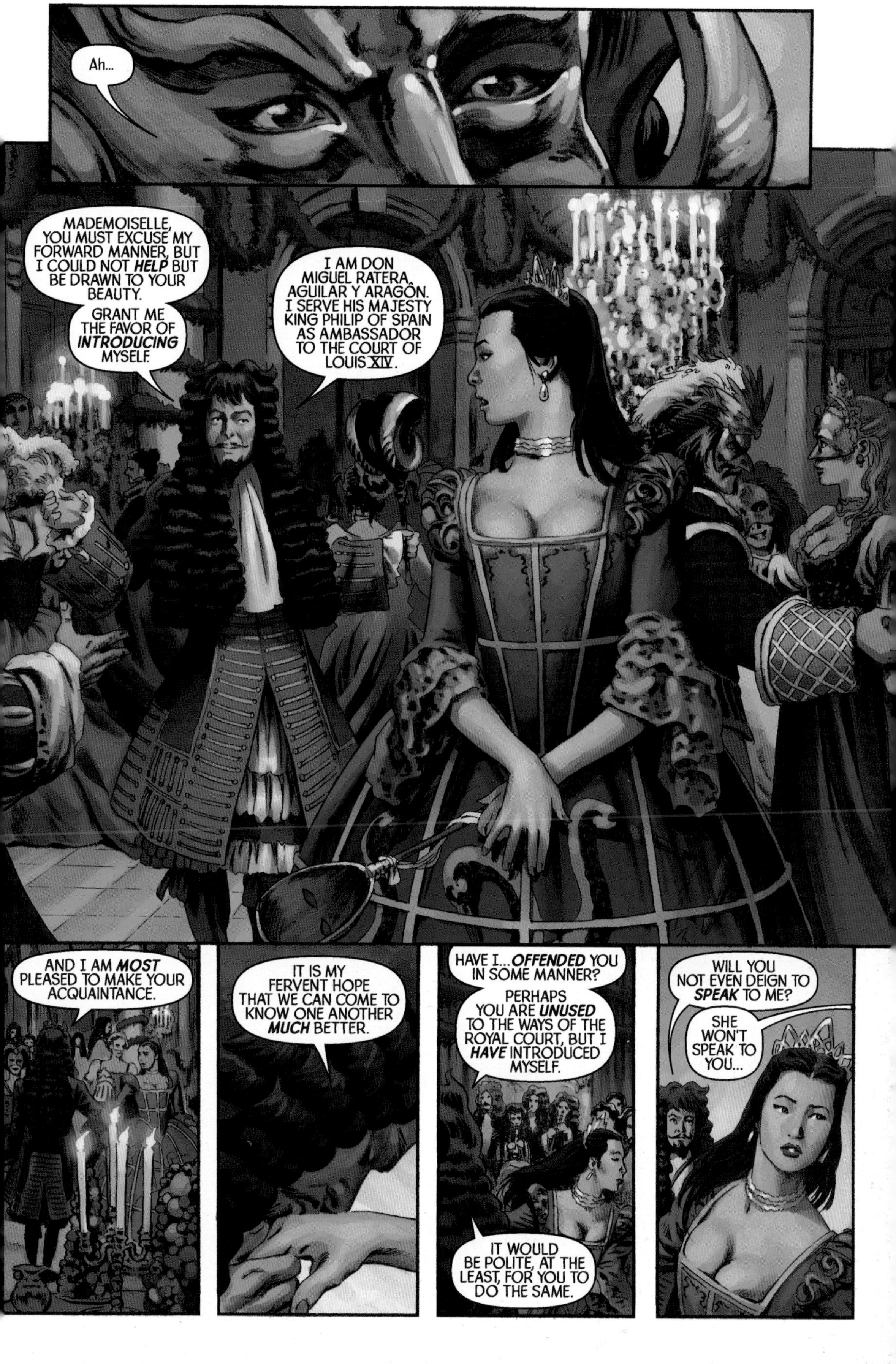

Ah...
MADEMOISELLE, YOU MUST EXCUSE MY FORWARD MANNER, BUT I COULD NOT HELP BUT BE DRAWN TO YOUR BEAUTY.
GRANT ME THE FAVOR OF INTRODUCING MYSELF.
I AM DON MIGUEL RATERA, AGUILAR Y ARAGÔN. I SERVE HIS MAJESTY KING PHILIP OF SPAIN AS AMBASSADOR TO THE COURT OF LOUIS XIV.
AND I AM MOST PLEASED TO MAKE YOUR ACQUAINTANCE.
IT IS MY FERVENT HOPE THAT WE CAN COME TO KNOW ONE ANOTHER MUCH BETTER.
HAVE I...OFFENDED YOU IN SOME MANNER?
PERHAPS YOU ARE UNUSED TO THE WAYS OF THE ROYAL COURT, BUT I HAVE INTRODUCED MYSELF.
IT WOULD BE POLITE, AT THE LEAST, FOR YOU TO DO THE SAME.
WILL YOU NOT EVEN DEIGN TO SPEAK TO ME?
SHE WON'T SPEAK TO YOU...

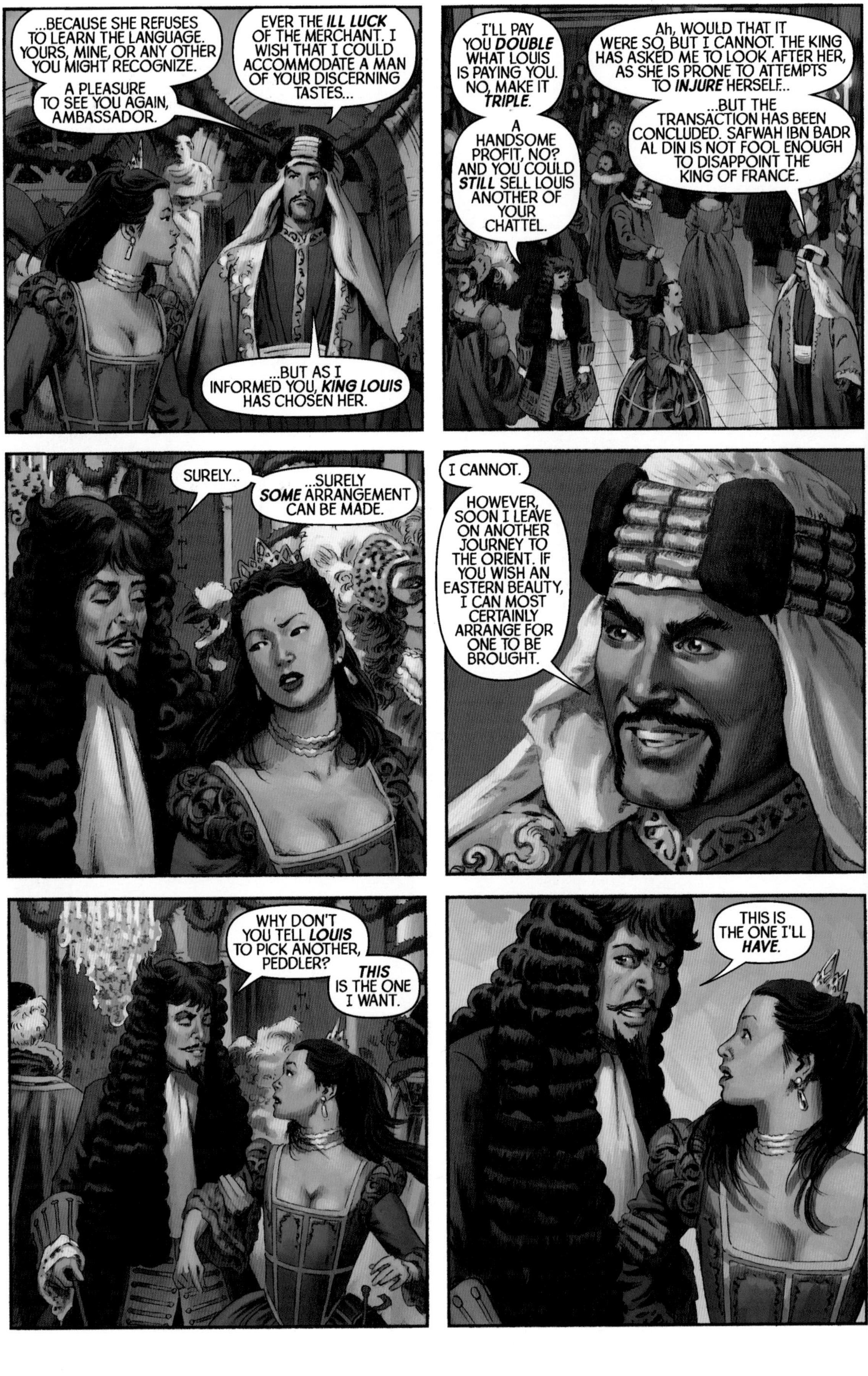
...BECAUSE SHE REFUSES TO LEARN THE LANGUAGE. YOURS, MINE, OR ANY OTHER YOU MIGHT RECOGNIZE.
A PLEASURE TO SEE YOU AGAIN, AMBASSADOR.
EVER THE ILL LUCK OF THE MERCHANT. I WISH THAT I COULD ACCOMMODATE A MAN OF YOUR DISCERNING TASTES...
...BUT AS I INFORMED YOU, KING LOUIS HAS CHOSEN HER.
I'LL PAY YOU DOUBLE WHAT LOUIS IS PAYING YOU. NO, MAKE IT TRIPLE.
A HANDSOME PROFIT, NO? AND YOU COULD STILL SELL LOUIS ANOTHER OF YOUR CHATTEL.
Ah, WOULD THAT IT WERE SO, BUT I CANNOT. THE KING HAS ASKED ME TO LOOK AFTER HER, AS SHE IS PRONE TO ATTEMPTS TO INJURE HERSELF...
...BUT THE TRANSACTION HAS BEEN CONCLUDED. SAFWAH IBN BADR AL DIN IS NOT FOOL ENOUGH TO DISAPPOINT THE KING OF FRANCE.
SURELY...
...SURELY SOME ARRANGEMENT CAN BE MADE.
I CANNOT.
HOWEVER, SOON I LEAVE ON ANOTHER JOURNEY TO THE ORIENT. IF YOU WISH AN EASTERN BEAUTY, I CAN MOST CERTAINLY ARRANGE FOR ONE TO BE BROUGHT.
WHY DON'T YOU TELL LOUIS TO PICK ANOTHER, PEDDLER?
THIS IS THE ONE I WANT.
THIS IS THE ONE I'LL HAVE.

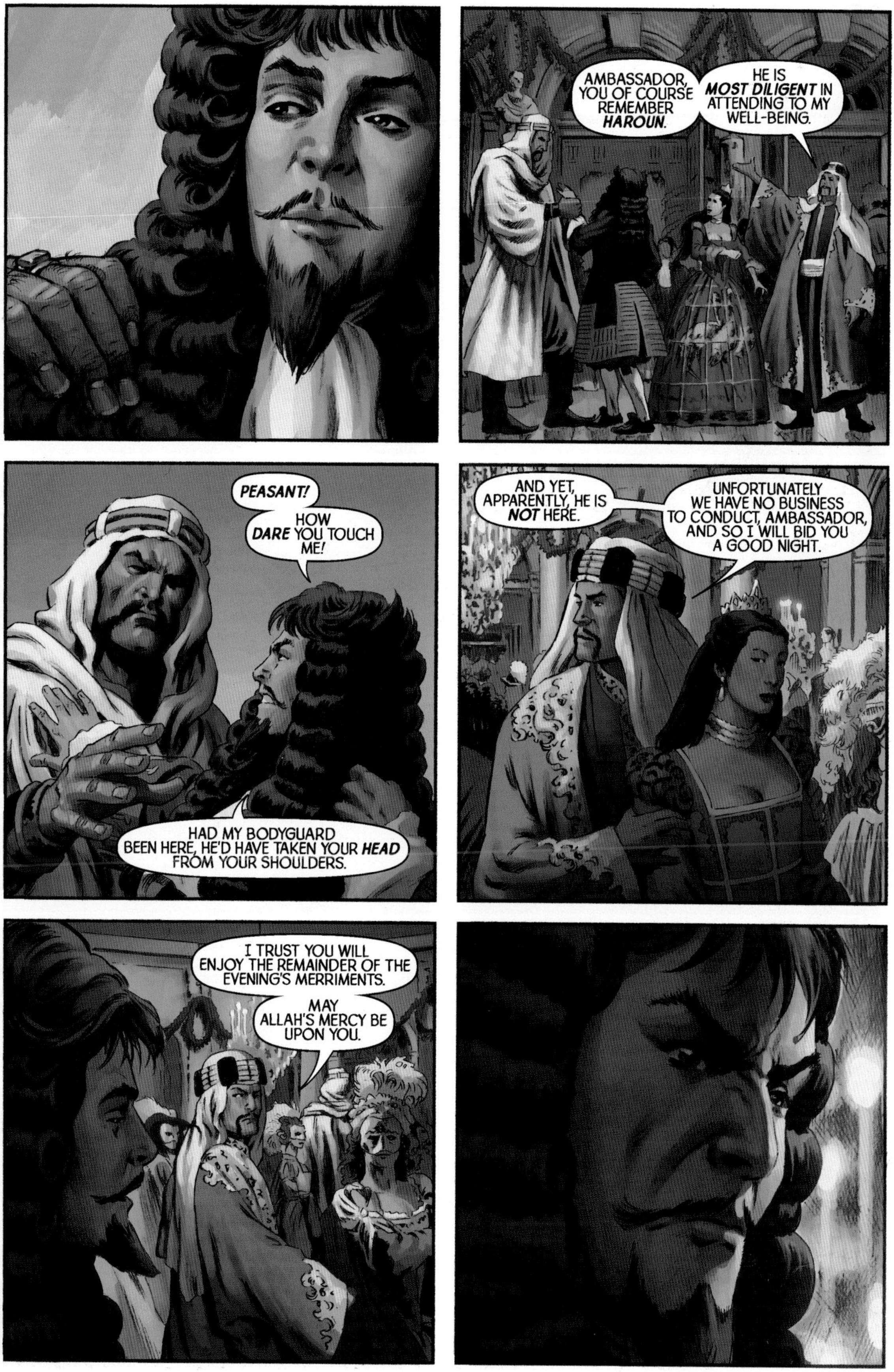
AMBASSADOR, YOU OF COURSE REMEMBER *HAROUN*.
HE IS *MOST DILIGENT* IN ATTENDING TO MY WELL-BEING.
PEASANT!
HOW *DARE* YOU TOUCH ME!
HAD MY BODYGUARD BEEN HERE, HE'D HAVE TAKEN YOUR *HEAD* FROM YOUR SHOULDERS.
AND YET, APPARENTLY, HE IS *NOT* HERE.
UNFORTUNATELY WE HAVE NO BUSINESS TO CONDUCT, AMBASSADOR, AND SO I WILL BID YOU A GOOD NIGHT.
I TRUST YOU WILL ENJOY THE REMAINDER OF THE EVENING'S MERRIMENTS.
MAY ALLAH'S MERCY BE UPON YOU.

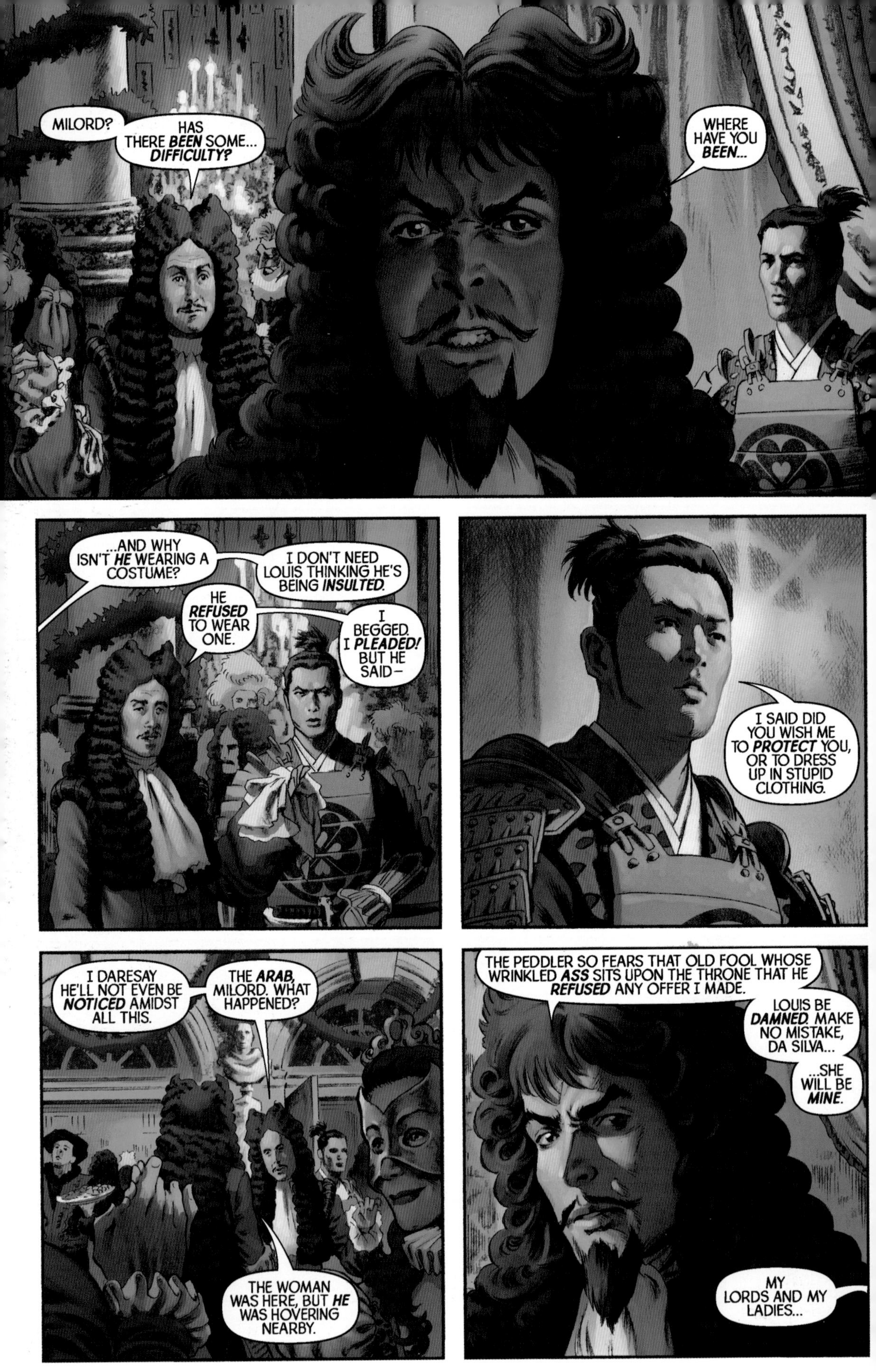
MILORD?
HAS THERE BEEN SOME... DIFFICULTY?
WHERE HAVE YOU BEEN...
...AND WHY ISN'T HE WEARING A COSTUME?
I DON'T NEED LOUIS THINKING HE'S BEING INSULTED.
HE REFUSED TO WEAR ONE.
I BEGGED. I PLEADED! BUT HE SAID—
I SAID DID YOU WISH ME TO PROTECT YOU, OR TO DRESS UP IN STUPID CLOTHING.
I DARESAY HE'LL NOT EVEN BE NOTICED AMIDST ALL THIS.
THE ARAB, MILORD. WHAT HAPPENED?
THE WOMAN WAS HERE, BUT HE WAS HOVERING NEARBY.
THE PEDDLER SO FEARS THAT OLD FOOL WHOSE WRINKLED ASS SITS UPON THE THRONE THAT HE REFUSED ANY OFFER I MADE.
LOUIS BE DAMNED. MAKE NO MISTAKE, DA SILVA...
...SHE WILL BE MINE.
MY LORDS AND MY LADIES...

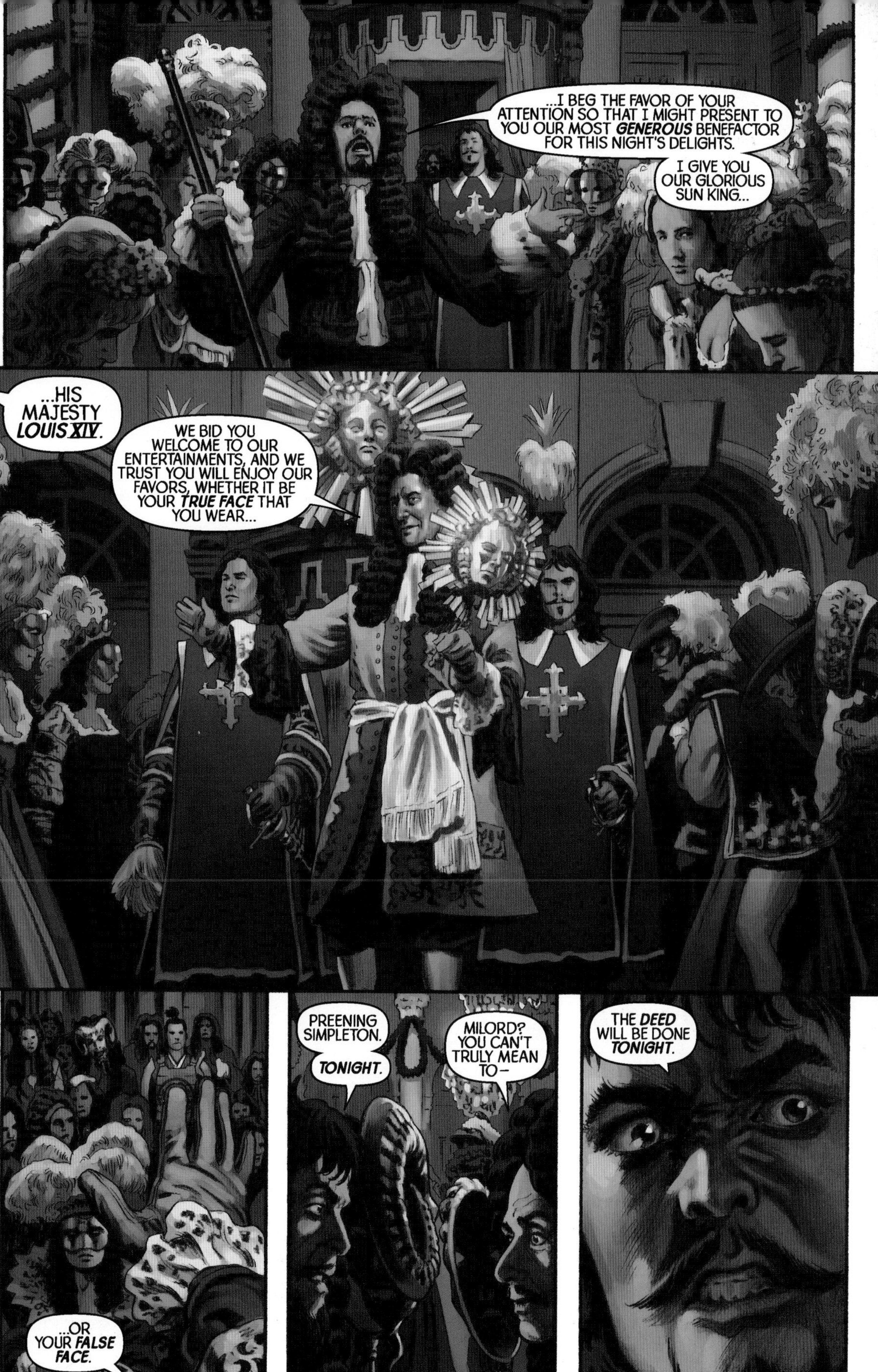
...I BEG THE FAVOR OF YOUR ATTENTION SO THAT I MIGHT PRESENT TO YOU OUR MOST *GENEROUS* BENEFACTOR FOR THIS NIGHT'S DELIGHTS.
I GIVE YOU OUR GLORIOUS SUN KING...
...HIS MAJESTY *LOUIS XIV*.
WE BID YOU WELCOME TO OUR ENTERTAINMENTS, AND WE TRUST YOU WILL ENJOY OUR FAVORS, WHETHER IT BE YOUR *TRUE FACE* THAT YOU WEAR...
...OR YOUR *FALSE FACE*.
PREENING SIMPLETON.
TONIGHT.
MILORD? YOU CAN'T TRULY MEAN TO–
THE *DEED* WILL BE DONE *TONIGHT*.

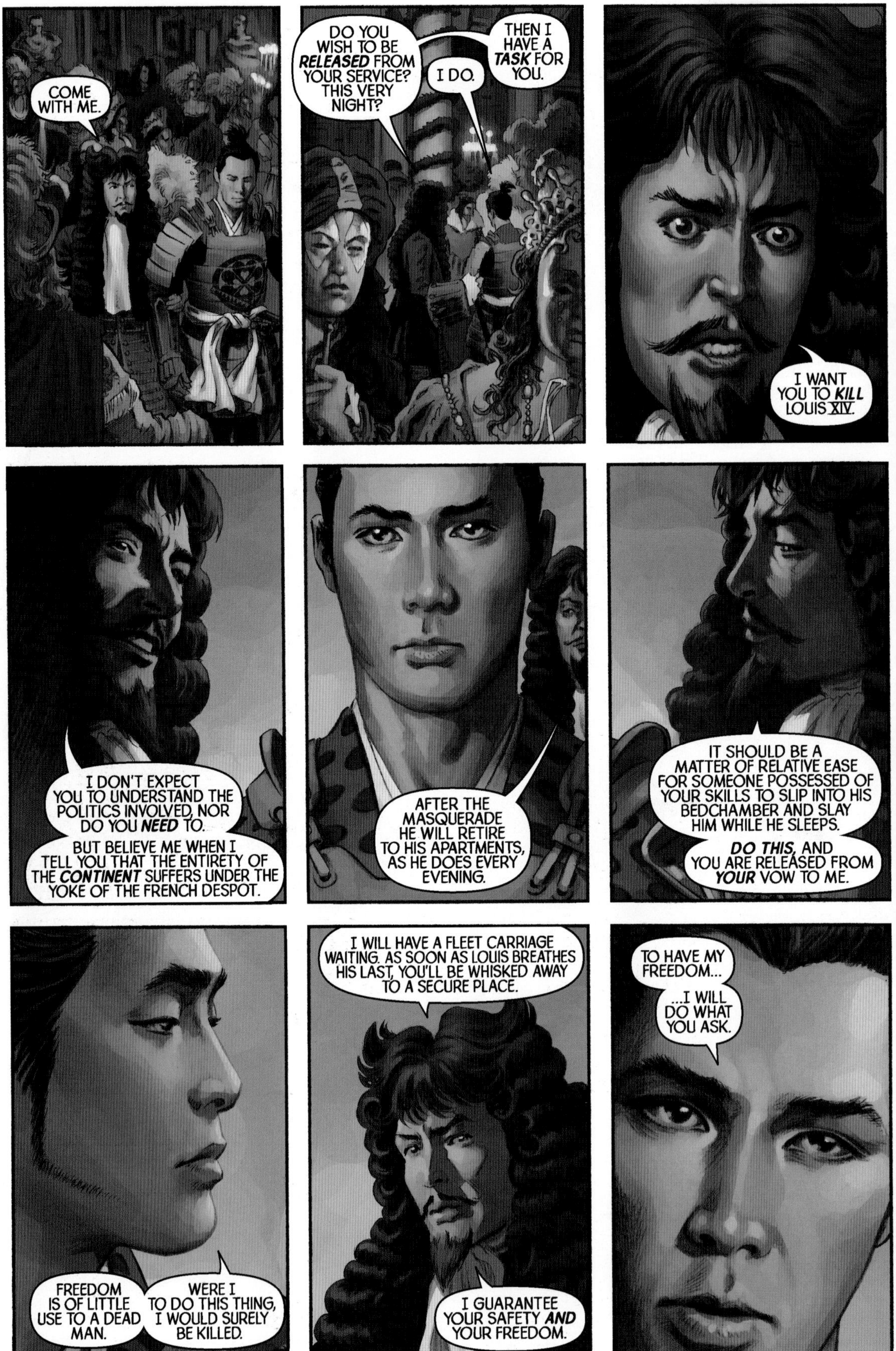
COME WITH ME.
DO YOU WISH TO BE RELEASED FROM YOUR SERVICE? THIS VERY NIGHT?
I DO.
THEN I HAVE A TASK FOR YOU.
I WANT YOU TO KILL LOUIS XIV.
I DON'T EXPECT YOU TO UNDERSTAND THE POLITICS INVOLVED, NOR DO YOU NEED TO.
BUT BELIEVE ME WHEN I TELL YOU THAT THE ENTIRETY OF THE CONTINENT SUFFERS UNDER THE YOKE OF THE FRENCH DESPOT.
AFTER THE MASQUERADE HE WILL RETIRE TO HIS APARTMENTS, AS HE DOES EVERY EVENING.
IT SHOULD BE A MATTER OF RELATIVE EASE FOR SOMEONE POSSESSED OF YOUR SKILLS TO SLIP INTO HIS BEDCHAMBER AND SLAY HIM WHILE HE SLEEPS.
DO THIS, AND YOU ARE RELEASED FROM YOUR VOW TO ME.
FREEDOM IS OF LITTLE USE TO A DEAD MAN.
WERE I TO DO THIS THING, I WOULD SURELY BE KILLED.
I WILL HAVE A FLEET CARRIAGE WAITING. AS SOON AS LOUIS BREATHES HIS LAST, YOU'LL BE WHISKED AWAY TO A SECURE PLACE.
I GUARANTEE YOUR SAFETY AND YOUR FREEDOM.
TO HAVE MY FREEDOM...
...I WILL DO WHAT YOU ASK.

WITH A *SINGLE* BLOW TONIGHT YOU WILL CHANGE THE BALANCE OF POWER IN EUROPE.

I CARE NOT FOR YOUR POLITICS OR YOUR INTRIGUES.

I CARE ONLY THAT I CAN ONCE AGAIN SEEK THE WOMAN WHO WAS STOLEN FROM ME.

DO AS YOU WILL.

YOU UNDERSTAND THE LOCATION OF THE KING'S CHAMBERS?

YES.

KNOW THAT IF YOU *BETRAY* OUR AGREEMENT, I WILL SEE YOU COME TO *REGRET* IT.

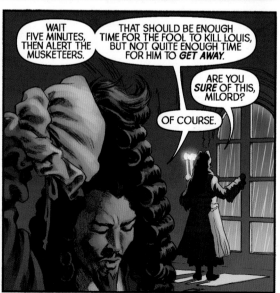

WAIT FIVE MINUTES, THEN ALERT THE MUSKETEERS.

THAT SHOULD BE ENOUGH TIME FOR THE FOOL TO KILL LOUIS, BUT NOT QUITE ENOUGH TIME FOR HIM TO *GET AWAY.*

ARE YOU *SURE* OF THIS, MILORD?

OF COURSE.

WHAT MORE PROOF OF OUR INNOCENCE COULD WE PRESENT THAN ACTUALLY *TURNING* IN THE MURDERER OURSELVES?

THE FRENCH MONARCHY WILL BE IN CHAOS, UNABLE TO PROTECT PHILIP. OUR FRIENDS WILL RISE UP AND *TAKE BACK* THE SPANISH THRONE.

AND I WILL HAVE THE WOMAN BECAUSE LOUIS WILL BE *DEAD...*

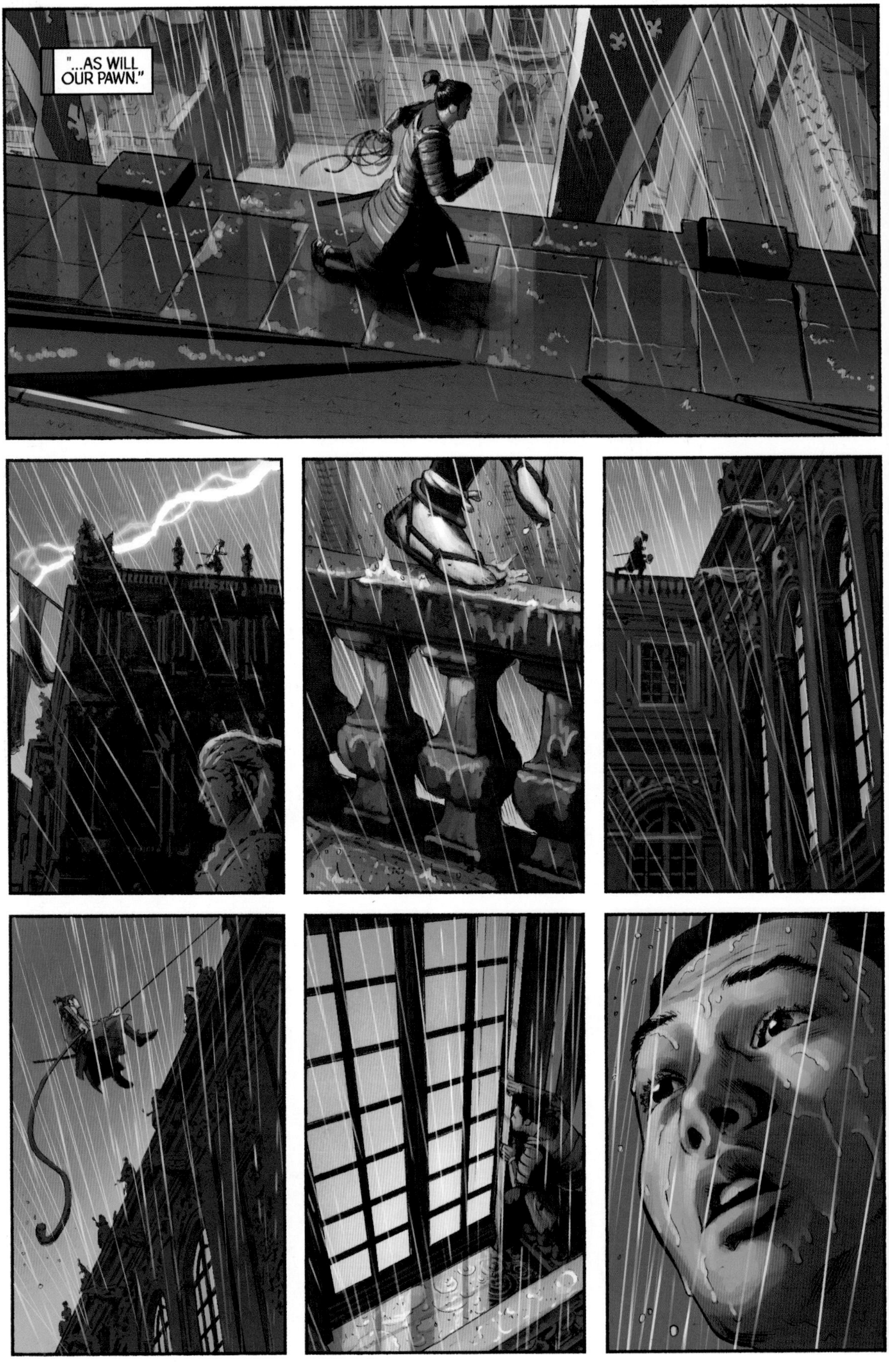
"...AS WILL OUR PAWN."

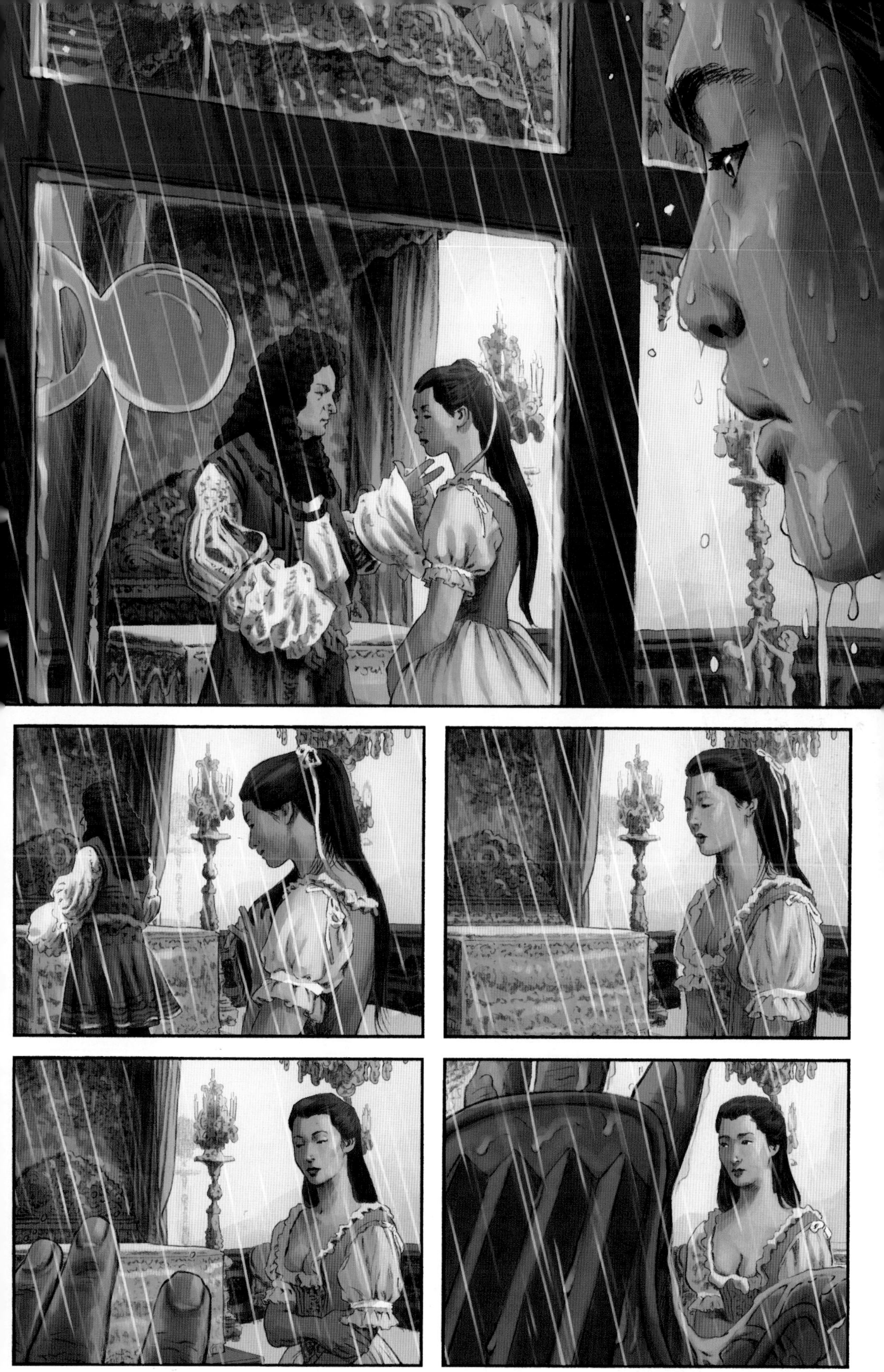

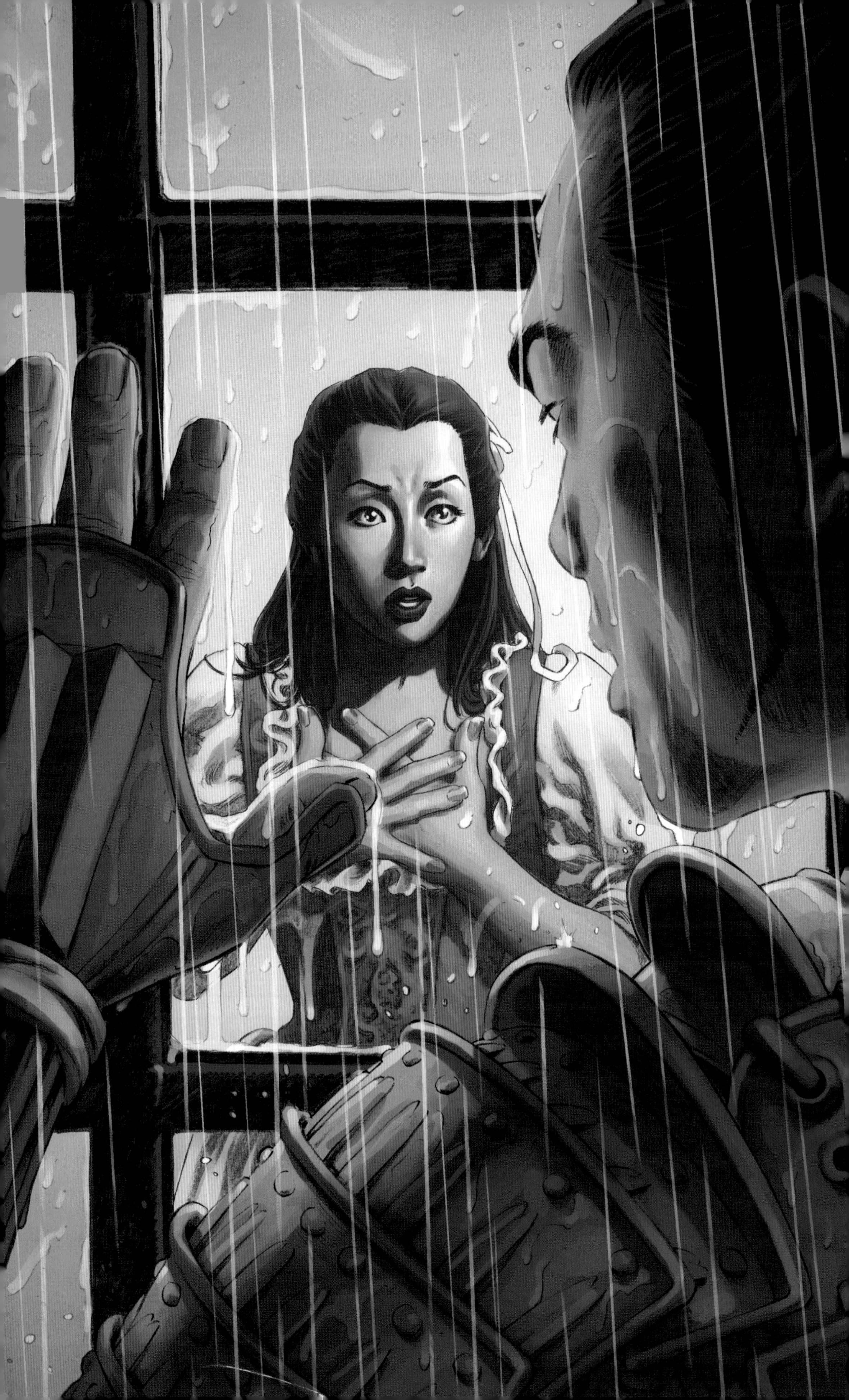

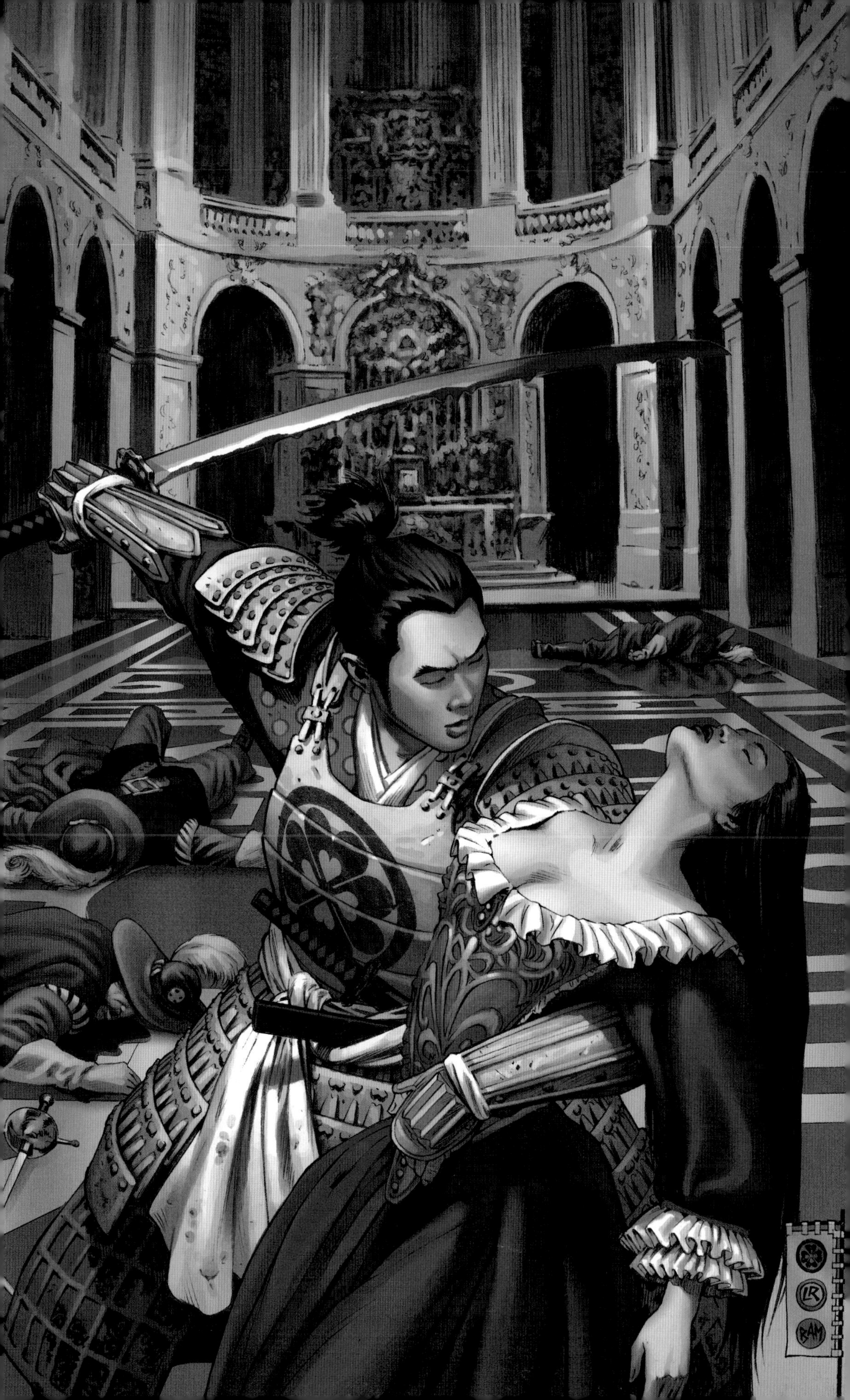
LR
RAM

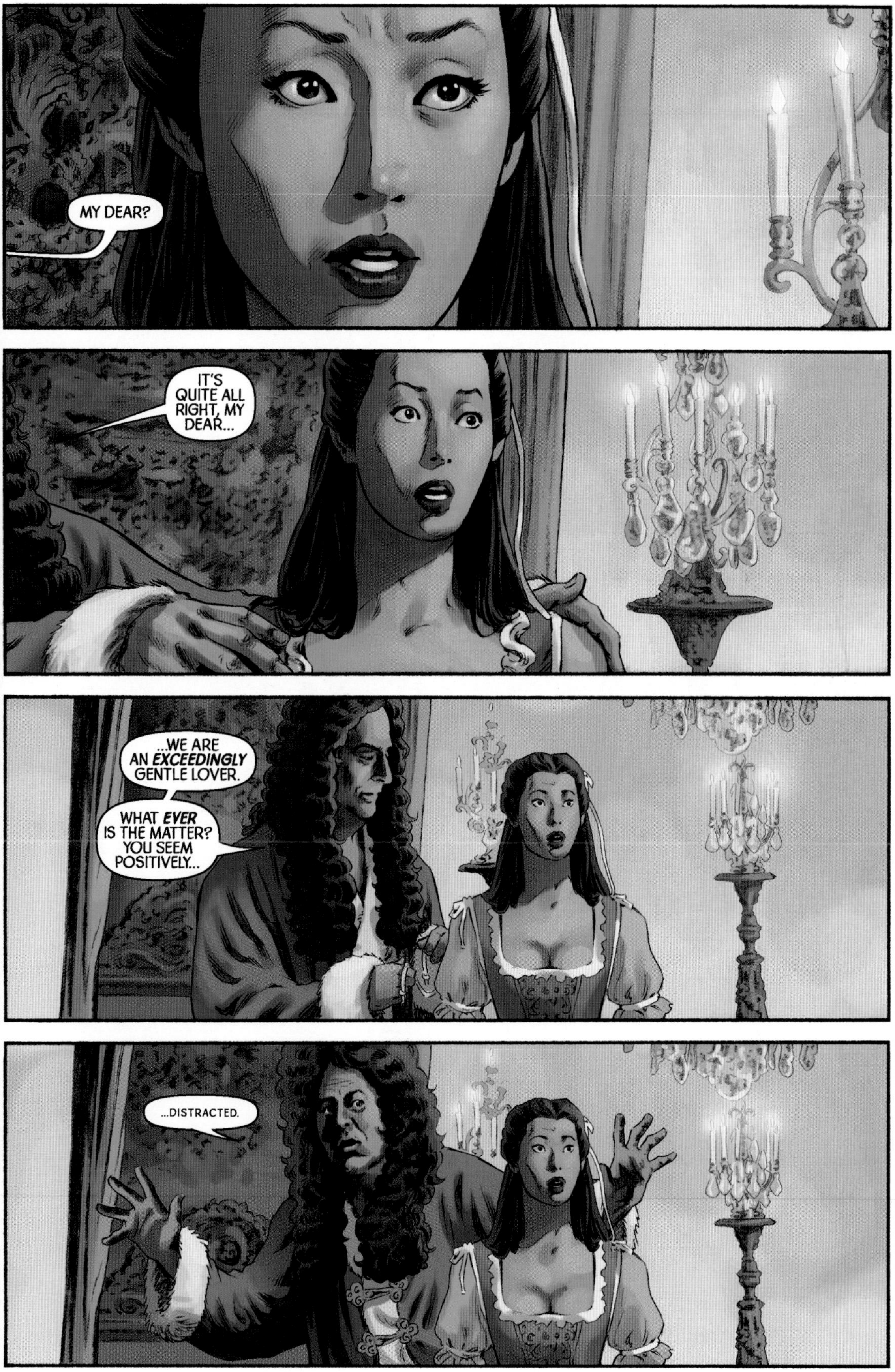
MY DEAR?
IT'S QUITE ALL RIGHT, MY DEAR...
...WE ARE AN *EXCEEDINGLY* GENTLE LOVER.
WHAT *EVER* IS THE MATTER? YOU SEEM POSITIVELY...
...DISTRACTED.

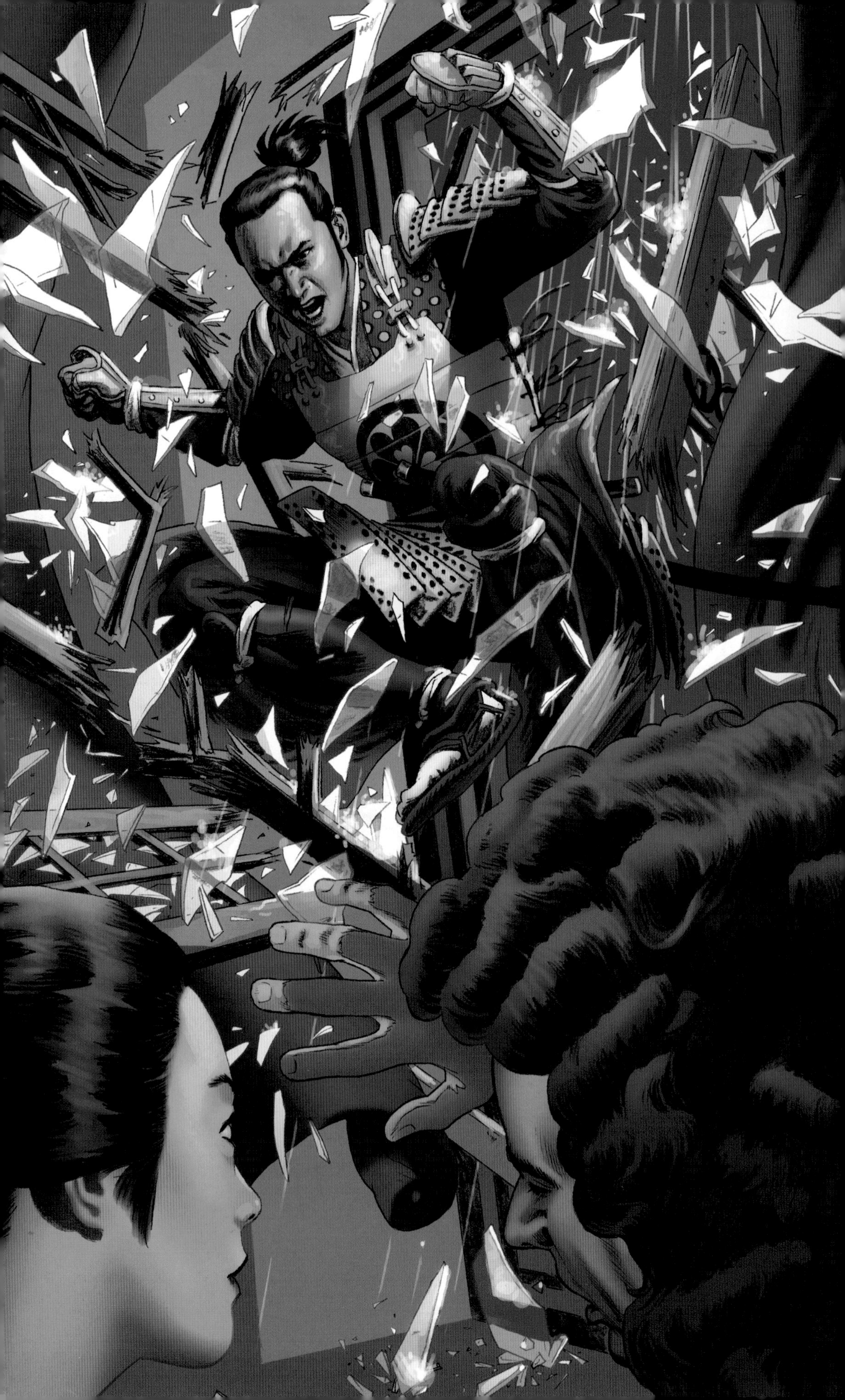

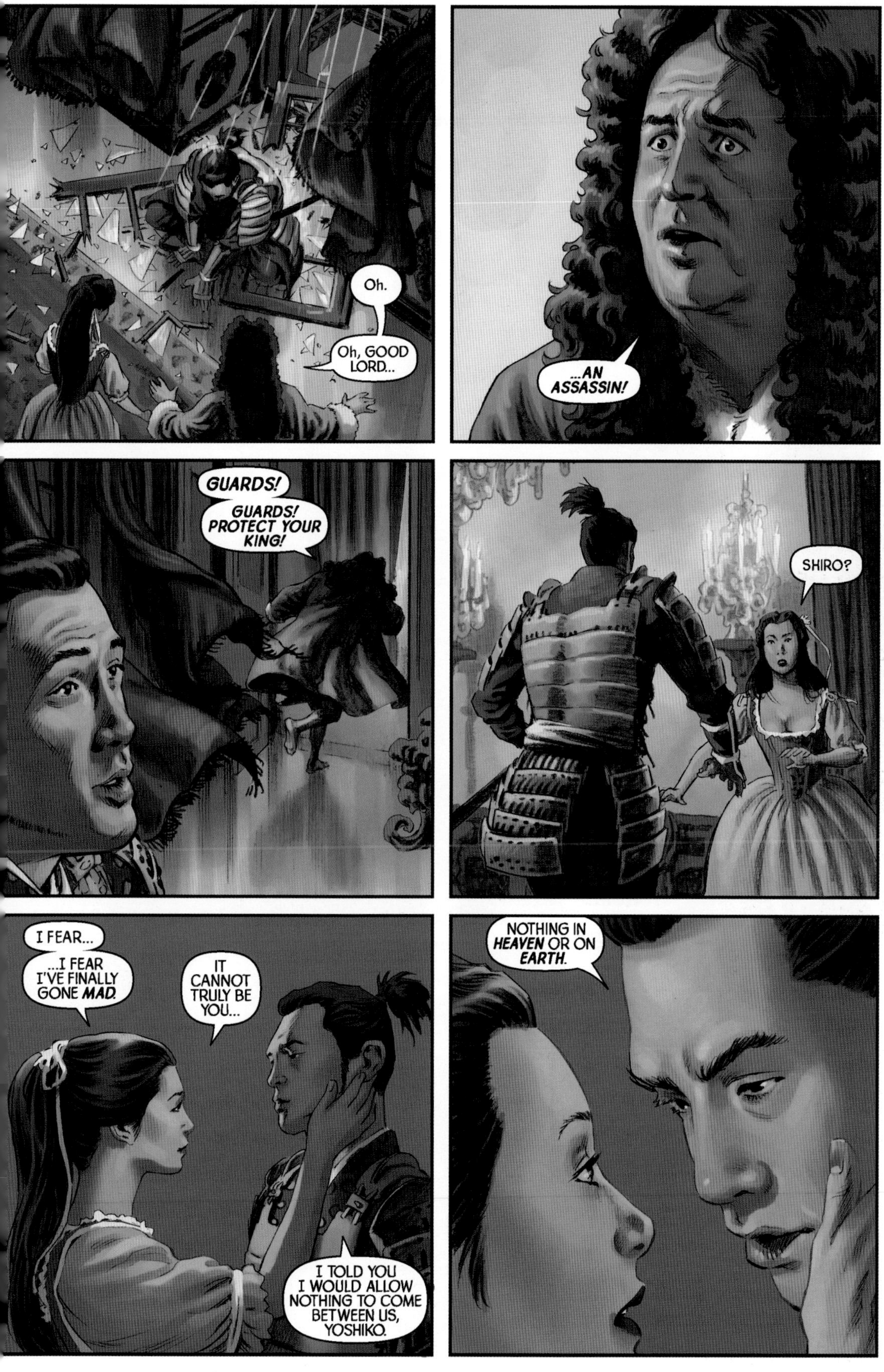
Oh.
Oh, GOOD LORD...
...AN ASSASSIN!
GUARDS!
GUARDS! PROTECT YOUR KING!
SHIRO?
I FEAR...
...I FEAR I'VE FINALLY GONE MAD.
IT CANNOT TRULY BE YOU...
I TOLD YOU I WOULD ALLOW NOTHING TO COME BETWEEN US, YOSHIKO.
NOTHING IN HEAVEN OR ON EARTH.

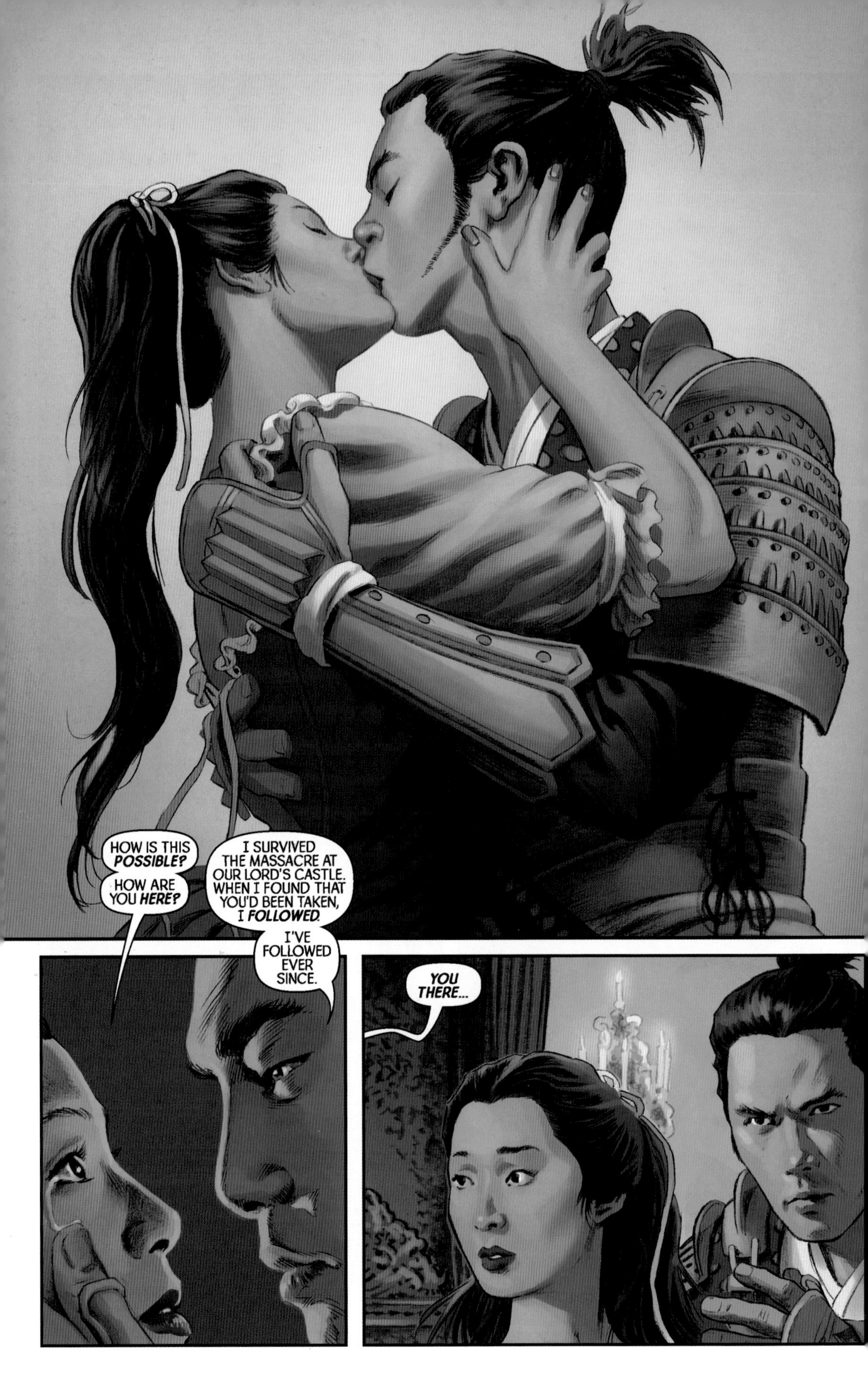
HOW IS THIS *POSSIBLE?*
HOW ARE YOU *HERE?*
I SURVIVED THE MASSACRE AT OUR LORD'S CASTLE. WHEN I FOUND THAT YOU'D BEEN TAKEN, I *FOLLOWED*.
I'VE FOLLOWED EVER SINCE.
YOU THERE...

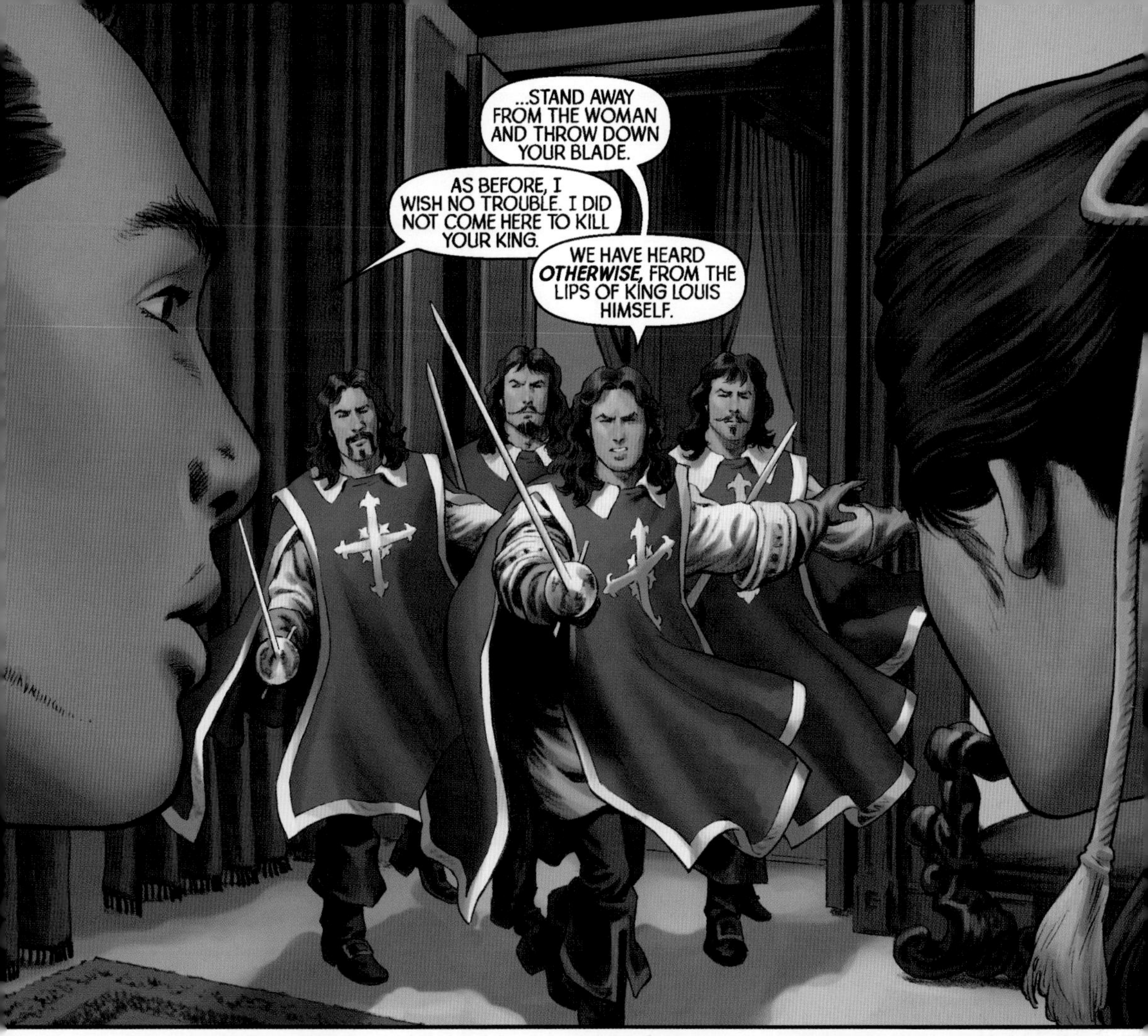
...STAND AWAY FROM THE WOMAN AND THROW DOWN YOUR BLADE.
AS BEFORE, I WISH NO TROUBLE. I DID NOT COME HERE TO KILL YOUR KING.
WE HAVE HEARD *OTHERWISE,* FROM THE LIPS OF KING LOUIS HIMSELF.

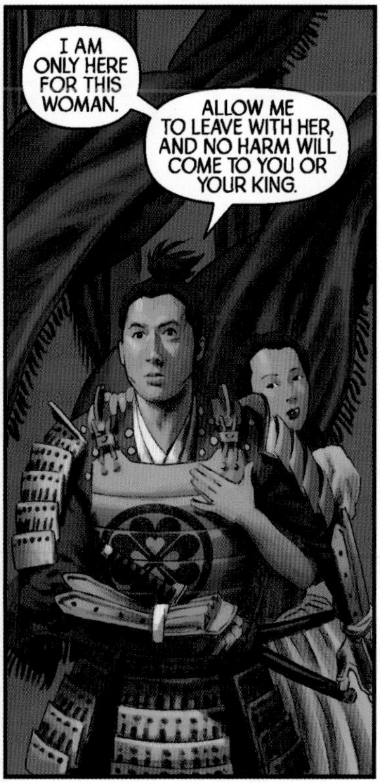
I AM ONLY HERE FOR THIS WOMAN.
ALLOW ME TO LEAVE WITH HER, AND NO HARM WILL COME TO YOU OR YOUR KING.

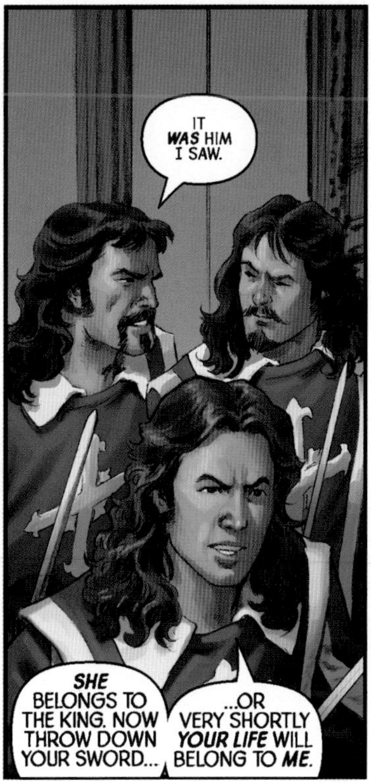
IT *WAS* HIM I SAW.
SHE BELONGS TO THE KING. NOW THROW DOWN YOUR SWORD...
...OR VERY SHORTLY *YOUR LIFE* WILL BELONG TO *ME.*

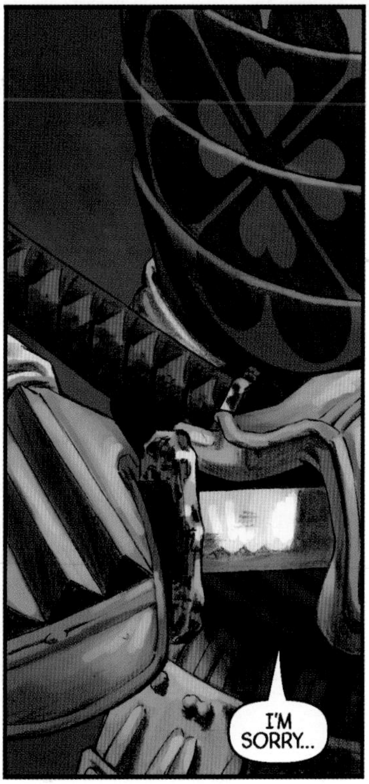
I'M SORRY...

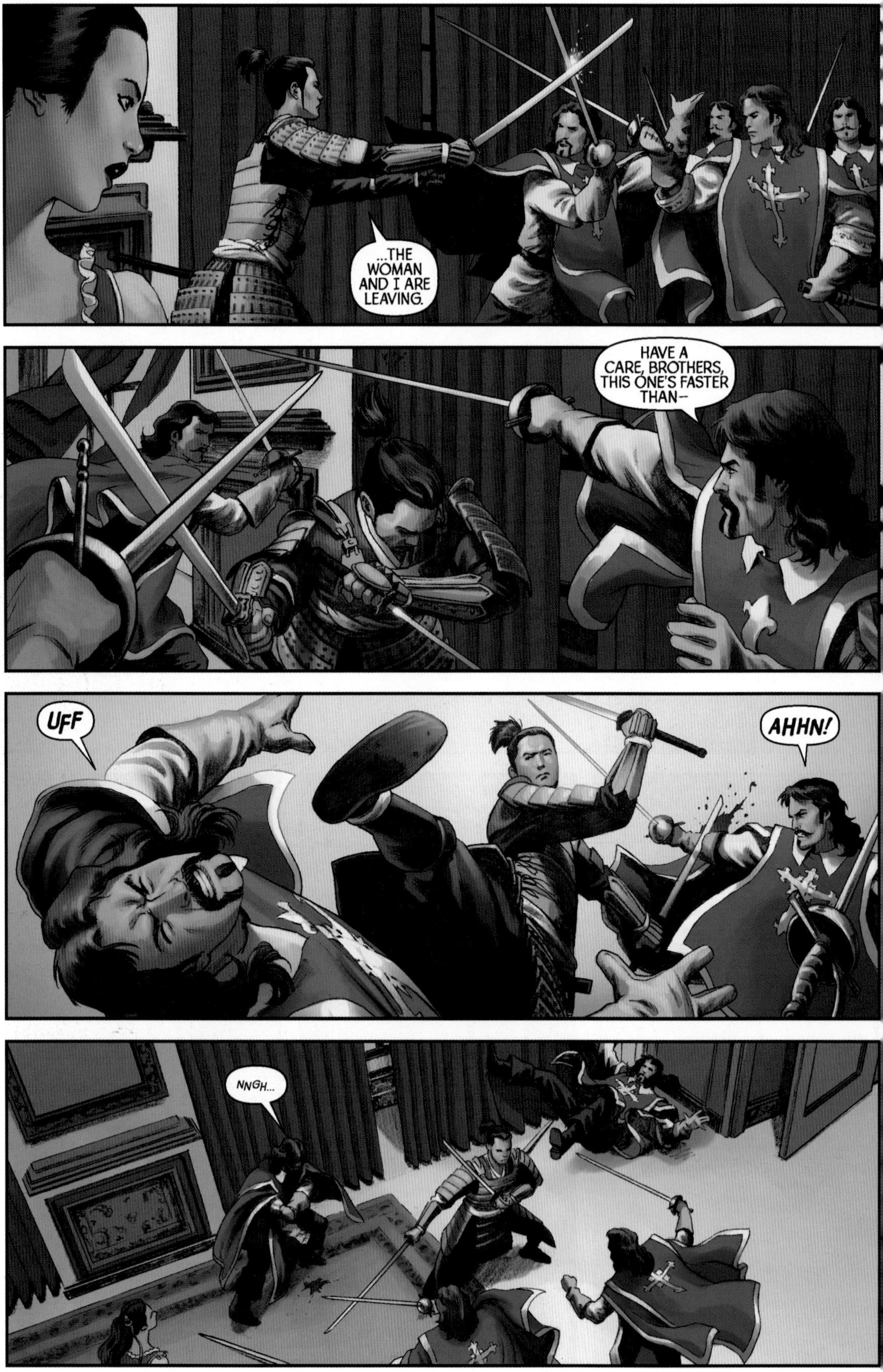
...THE WOMAN AND I ARE LEAVING.
HAVE A CARE, BROTHERS, THIS ONE'S FASTER THAN—
UFF
AHHN!
NNGH...

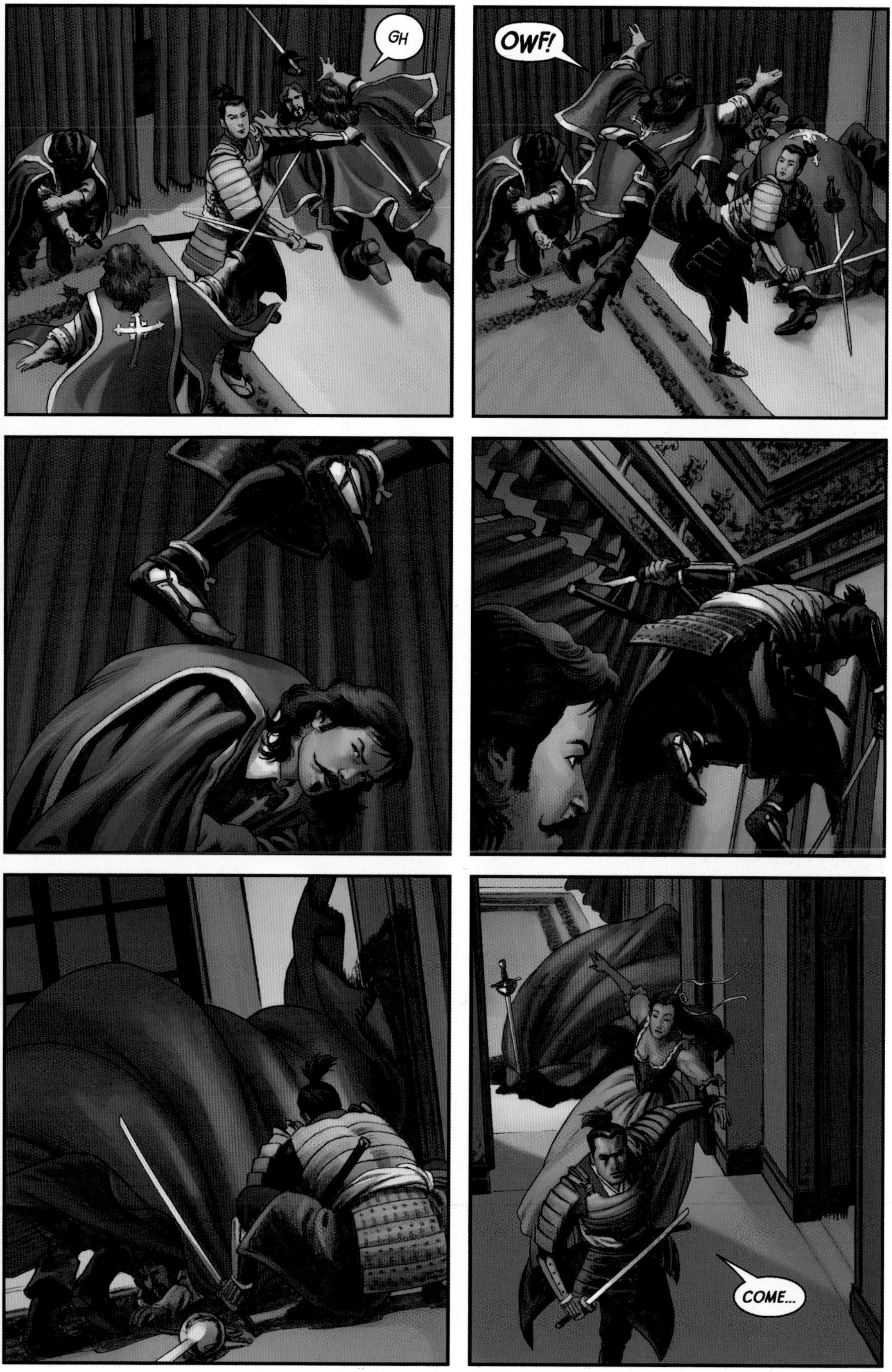
GH
OWF!
COME...

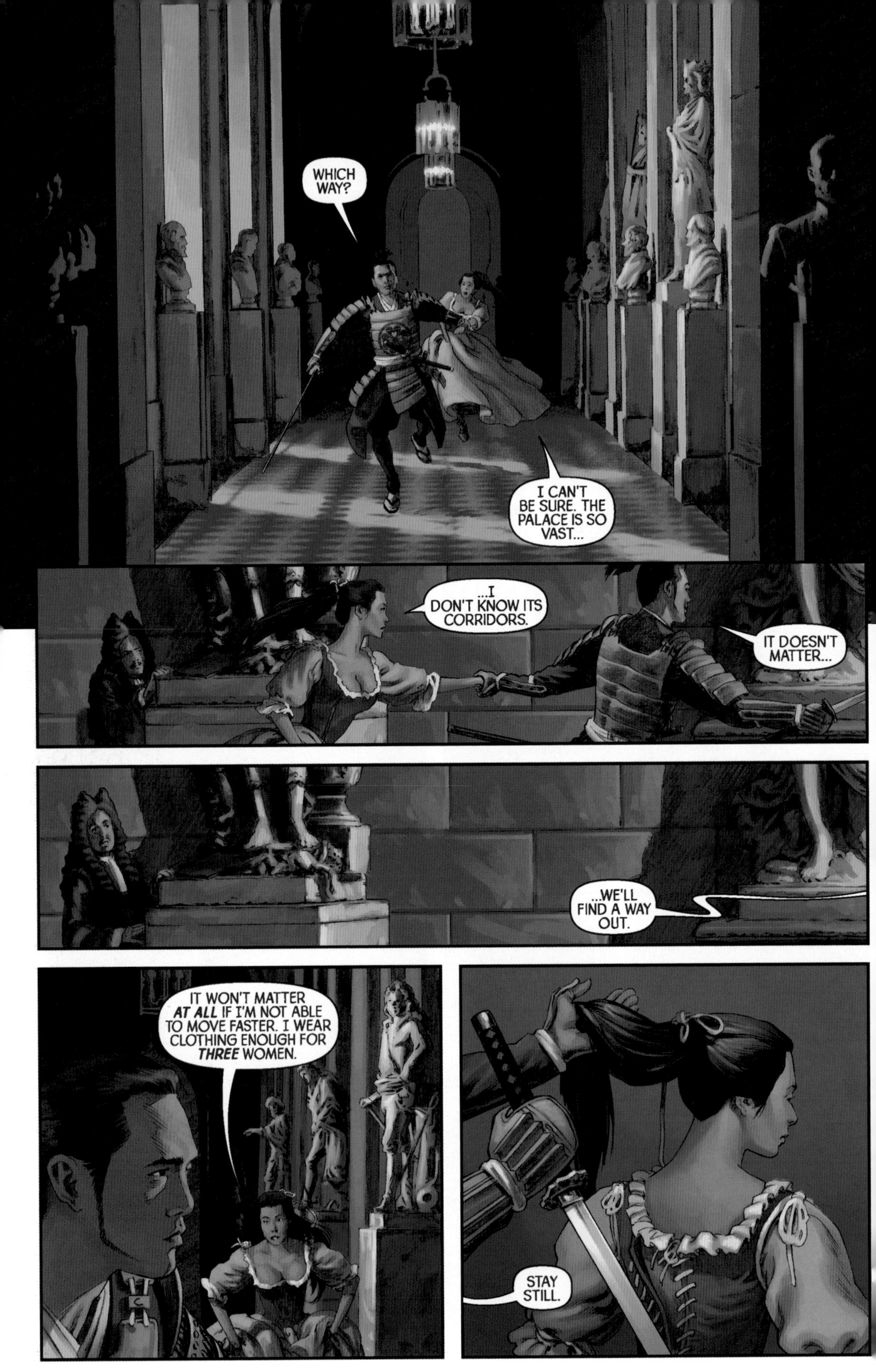
WHICH WAY?
I CAN'T BE SURE. THE PALACE IS SO VAST...
...I DON'T KNOW ITS CORRIDORS.
IT DOESN'T MATTER...
...WE'LL FIND A WAY OUT.
IT WON'T MATTER *AT ALL* IF I'M NOT ABLE TO MOVE FASTER. I WEAR CLOTHING ENOUGH FOR *THREE* WOMEN.
STAY STILL.

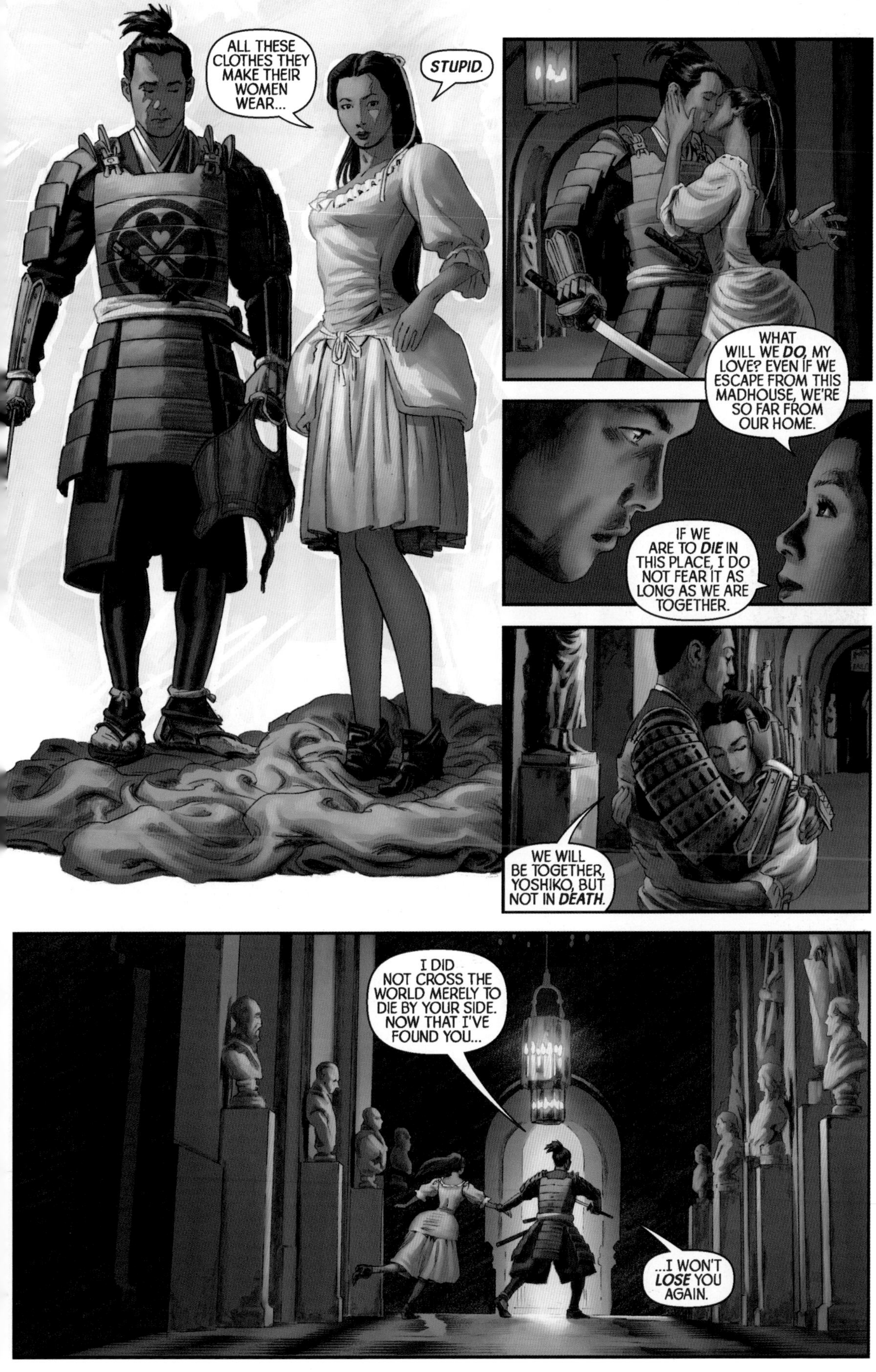
ALL THESE CLOTHES THEY MAKE THEIR WOMEN WEAR...
STUPID.
WHAT WILL WE DO, MY LOVE? EVEN IF WE ESCAPE FROM THIS MADHOUSE, WE'RE SO FAR FROM OUR HOME.
IF WE ARE TO DIE IN THIS PLACE, I DO NOT FEAR IT AS LONG AS WE ARE TOGETHER.
WE WILL BE TOGETHER, YOSHIKO, BUT NOT IN DEATH.
I DID NOT CROSS THE WORLD MERELY TO DIE BY YOUR SIDE. NOW THAT I'VE FOUND YOU...
...I WON'T LOSE YOU AGAIN.

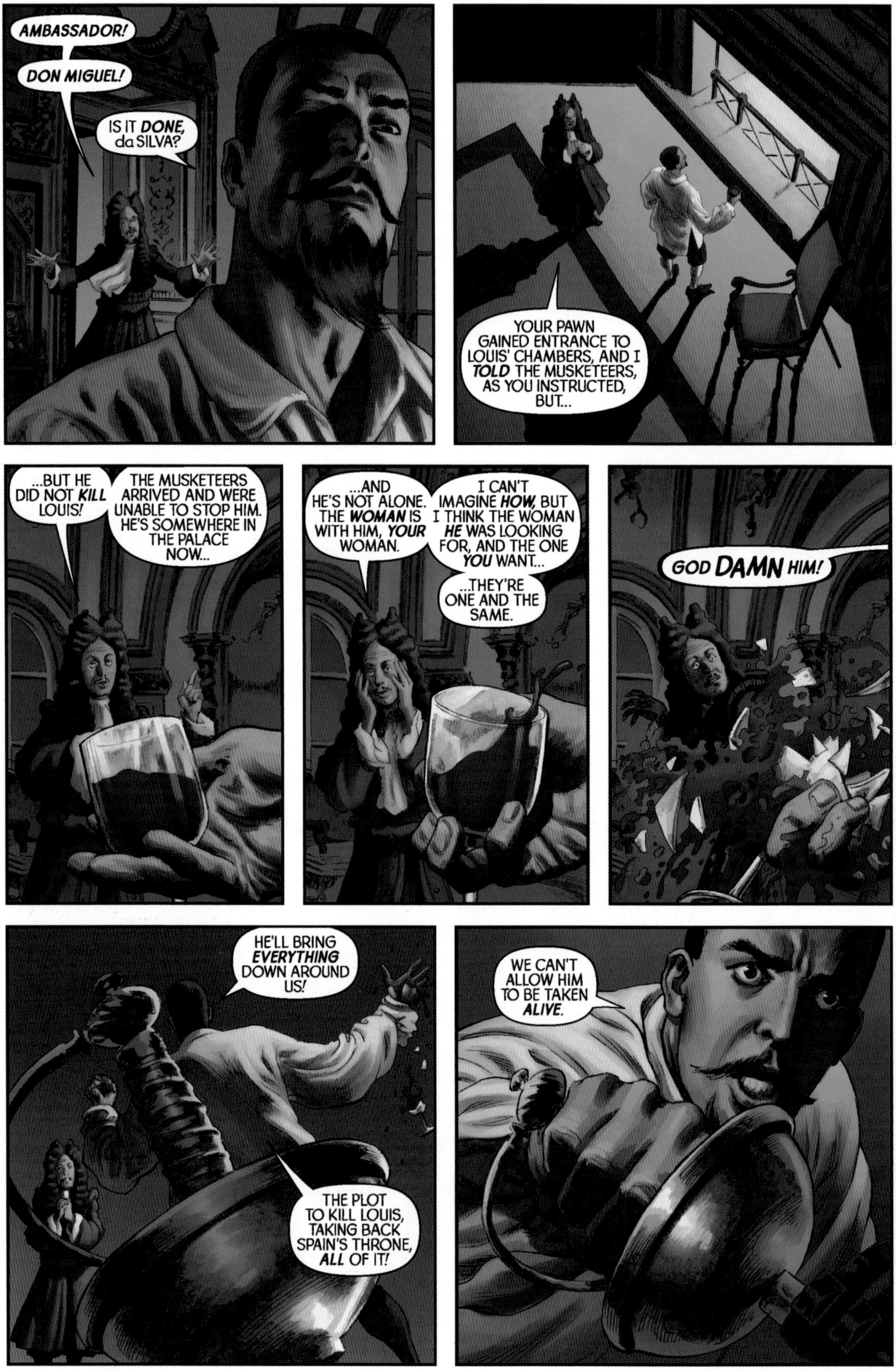
AMBASSADOR!
DON MIGUEL!
IS IT DONE, da SILVA?
YOUR PAWN GAINED ENTRANCE TO LOUIS' CHAMBERS, AND I TOLD THE MUSKETEERS, AS YOU INSTRUCTED, BUT...
...BUT HE DID NOT KILL LOUIS!
THE MUSKETEERS ARRIVED AND WERE UNABLE TO STOP HIM. HE'S SOMEWHERE IN THE PALACE NOW...
...AND HE'S NOT ALONE. THE WOMAN IS WITH HIM, YOUR WOMAN.
I CAN'T IMAGINE HOW, BUT I THINK THE WOMAN HE WAS LOOKING FOR, AND THE ONE YOU WANT...
...THEY'RE ONE AND THE SAME.
GOD DAMN HIM!
HE'LL BRING EVERYTHING DOWN AROUND US!
THE PLOT TO KILL LOUIS, TAKING BACK SPAIN'S THRONE, ALL OF IT!
WE CAN'T ALLOW HIM TO BE TAKEN ALIVE.

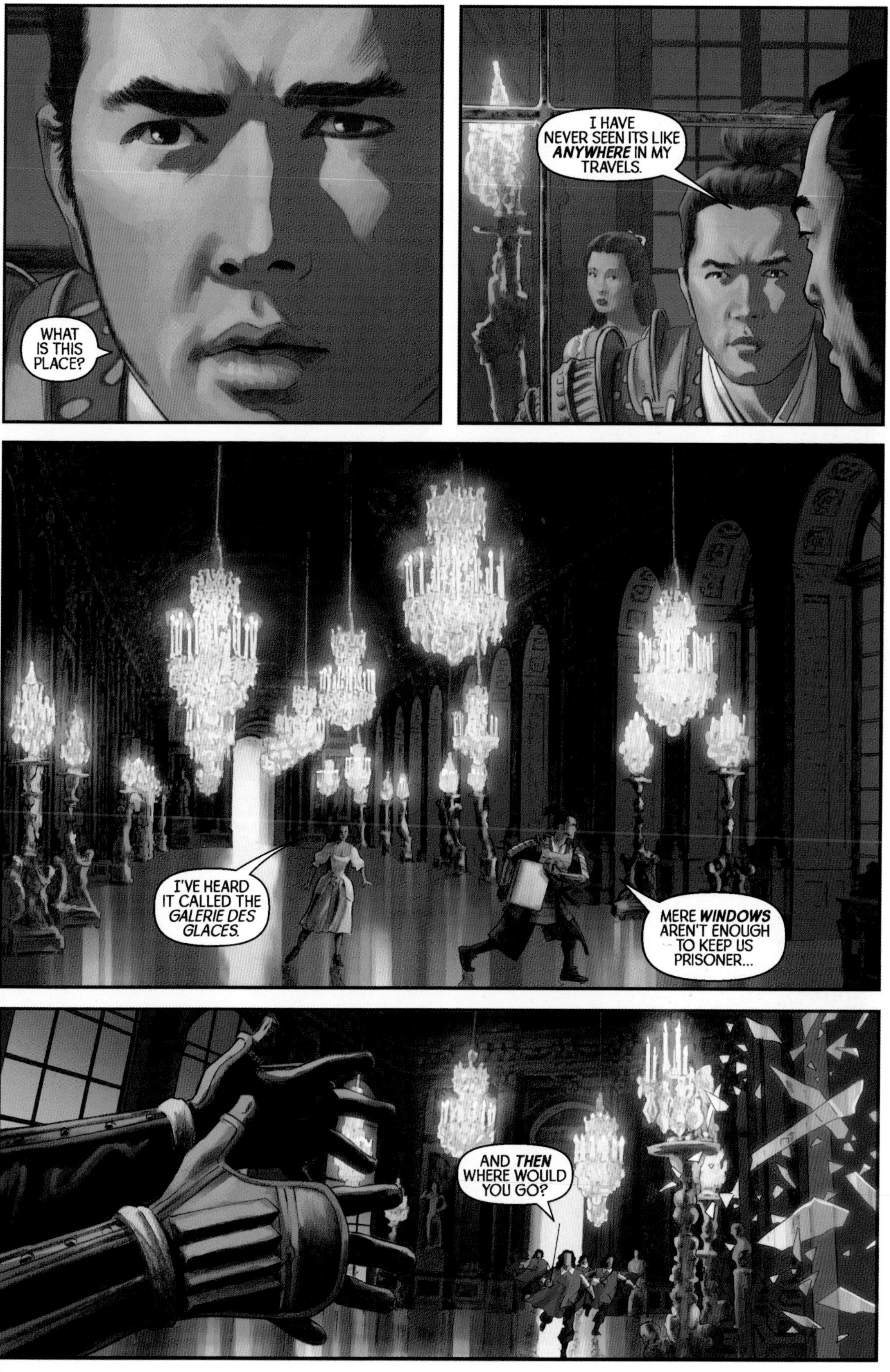
WHAT IS THIS PLACE?
I HAVE NEVER SEEN ITS LIKE *ANYWHERE* IN MY TRAVELS.
I'VE HEARD IT CALLED THE *GALERIE DES GLACES.*
MERE ***WINDOWS*** AREN'T ENOUGH TO KEEP US PRISONER...
AND *THEN* WHERE WOULD YOU GO?

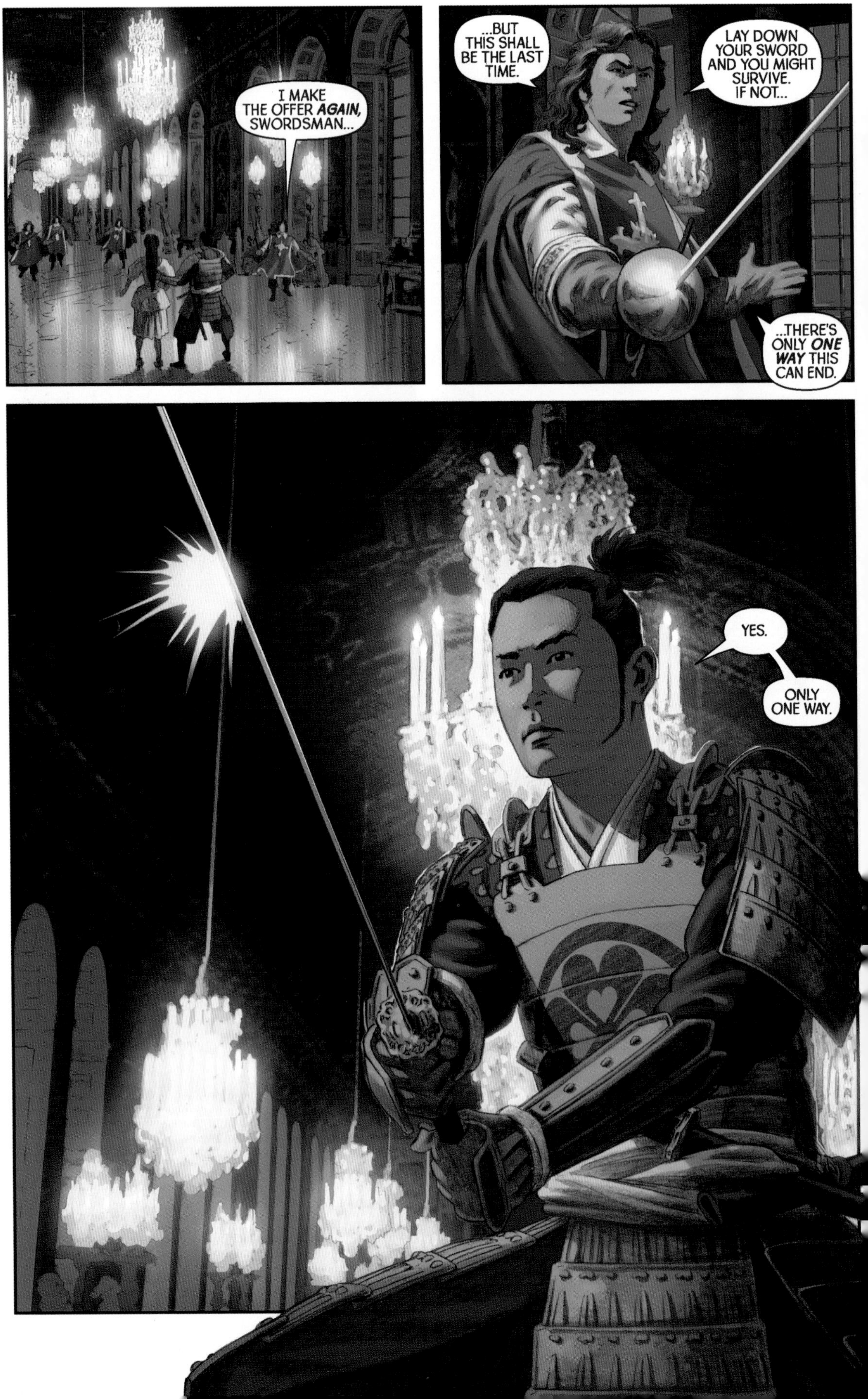
I MAKE THE OFFER *AGAIN,* SWORDSMAN...
...BUT THIS SHALL BE THE LAST TIME.
LAY DOWN YOUR SWORD AND YOU MIGHT SURVIVE. IF NOT...
...THERE'S ONLY *ONE WAY* THIS CAN END.
YES.
ONLY ONE WAY.

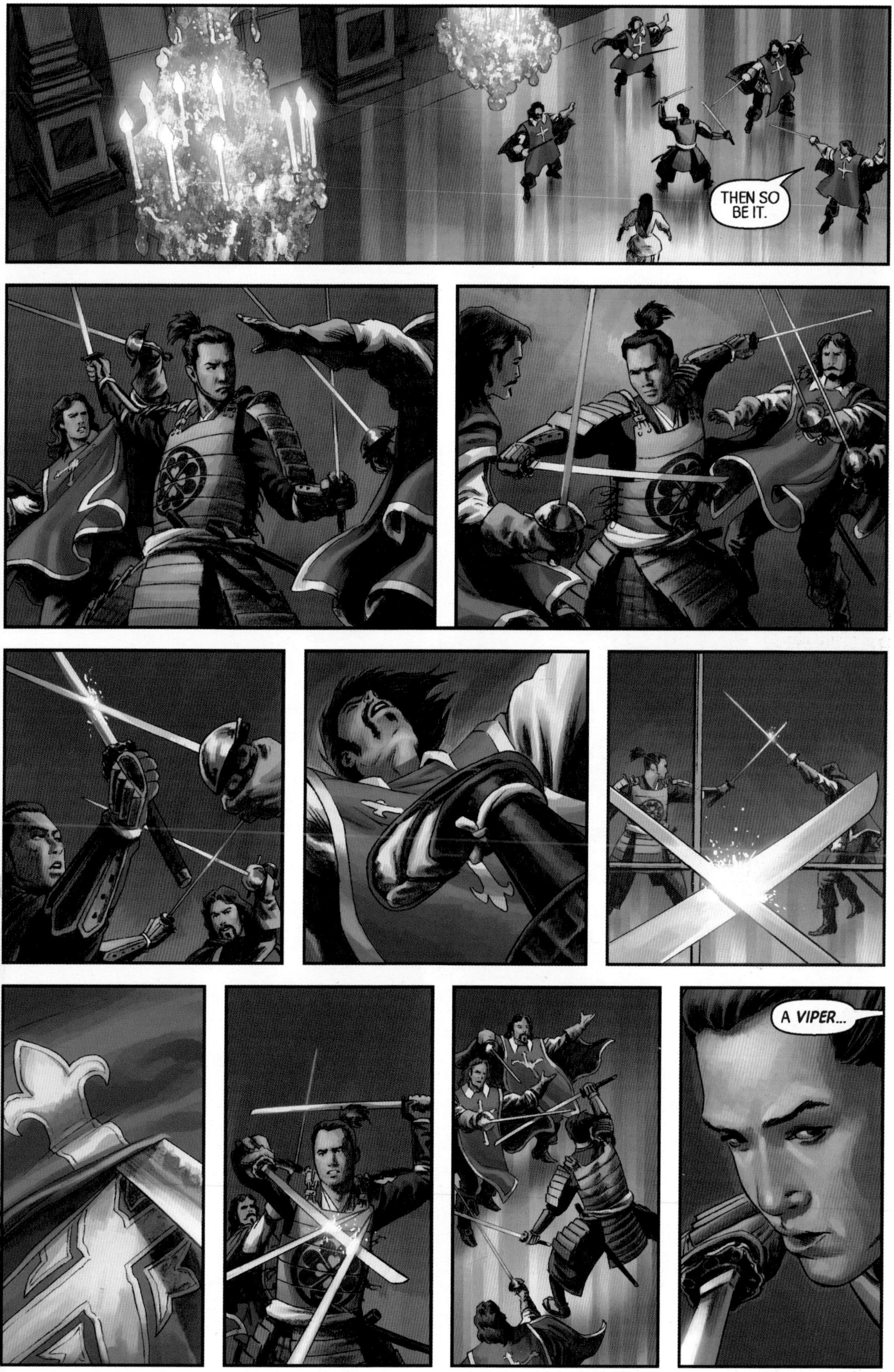
THEN SO BE IT.
A VIPER...

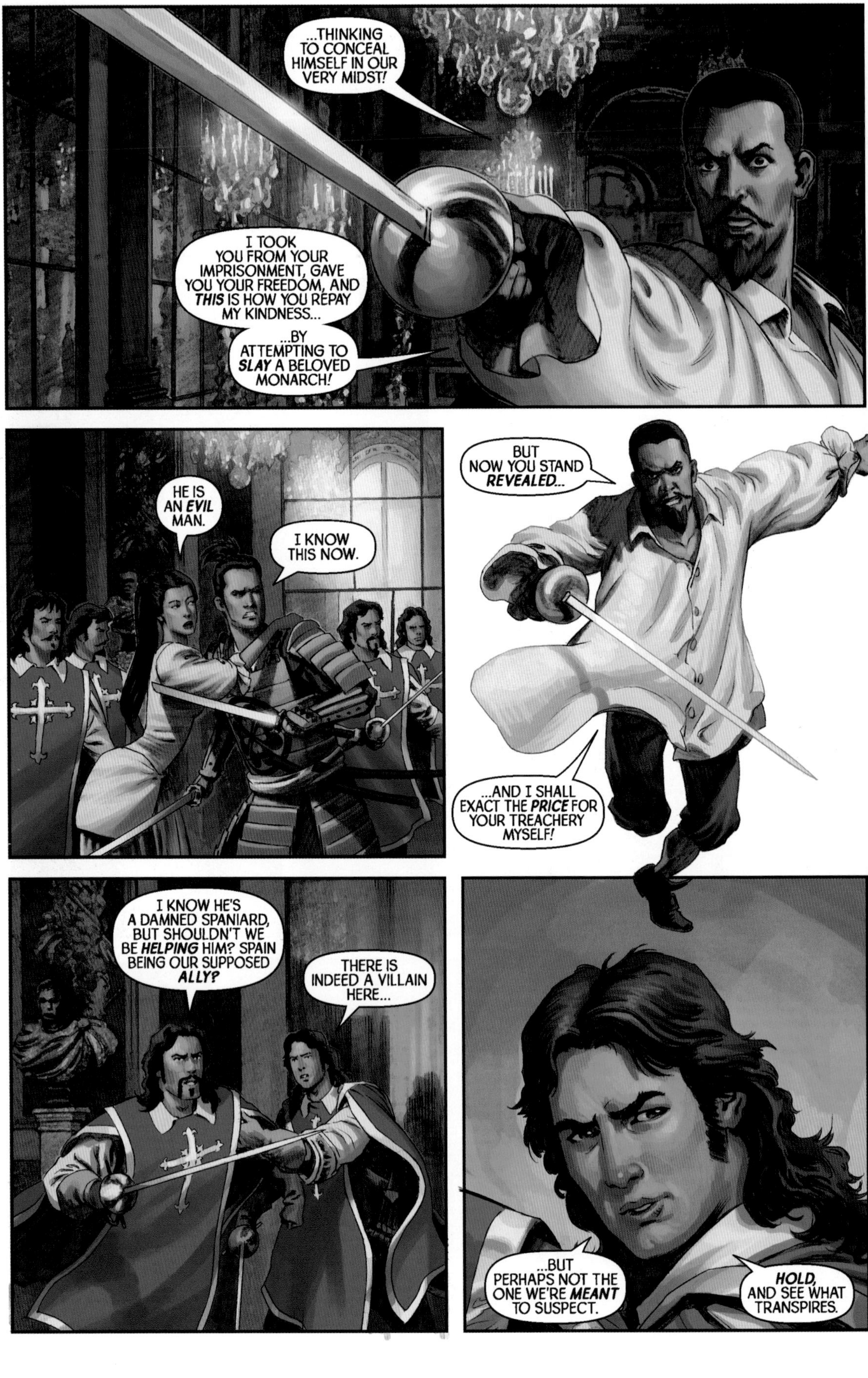
...THINKING TO CONCEAL HIMSELF IN OUR VERY MIDST!
I TOOK YOU FROM YOUR IMPRISONMENT, GAVE YOU YOUR FREEDOM, AND *THIS* IS HOW YOU REPAY MY KINDNESS...
...BY ATTEMPTING TO *SLAY* A BELOVED MONARCH!
HE IS AN *EVIL* MAN.
I KNOW THIS NOW.
BUT NOW YOU STAND *REVEALED*...
...AND I SHALL EXACT THE *PRICE* FOR YOUR TREACHERY MYSELF!
I KNOW HE'S A DAMNED SPANIARD, BUT SHOULDN'T WE BE *HELPING* HIM? SPAIN BEING OUR SUPPOSED *ALLY?*
THERE IS INDEED A VILLAIN HERE...
...BUT PERHAPS NOT THE ONE WE'RE *MEANT* TO SUSPECT.
HOLD, AND SEE WHAT TRANSPIRES.

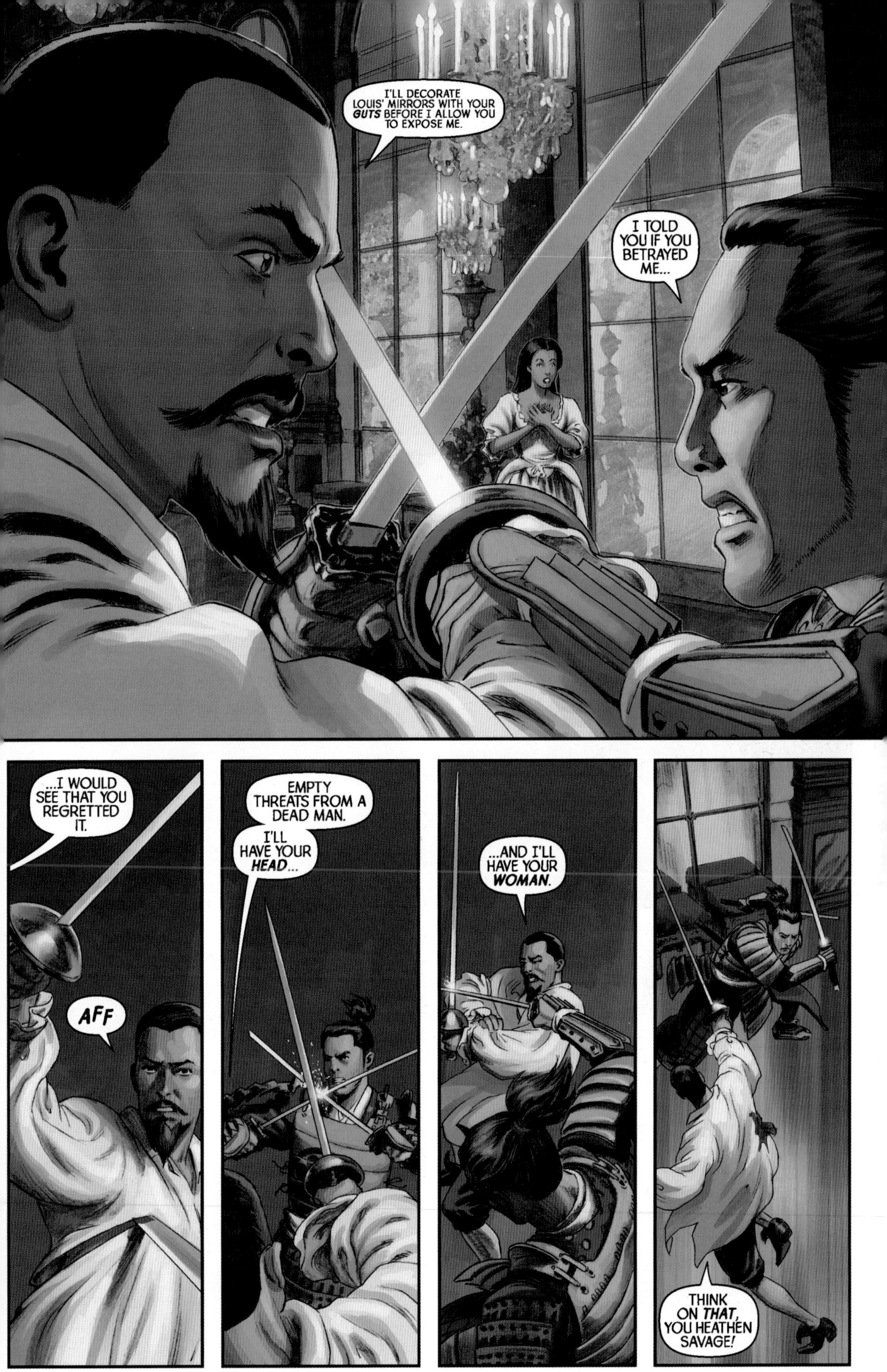
I'LL DECORATE LOUIS' MIRRORS WITH YOUR GUTS BEFORE I ALLOW YOU TO EXPOSE ME.
I TOLD YOU IF YOU BETRAYED ME...
...I WOULD SEE THAT YOU REGRETTED IT.
AFF
EMPTY THREATS FROM A DEAD MAN.
I'LL HAVE YOUR HEAD...
...AND I'LL HAVE YOUR WOMAN.
THINK ON THAT, YOU HEATHEN SAVAGE!

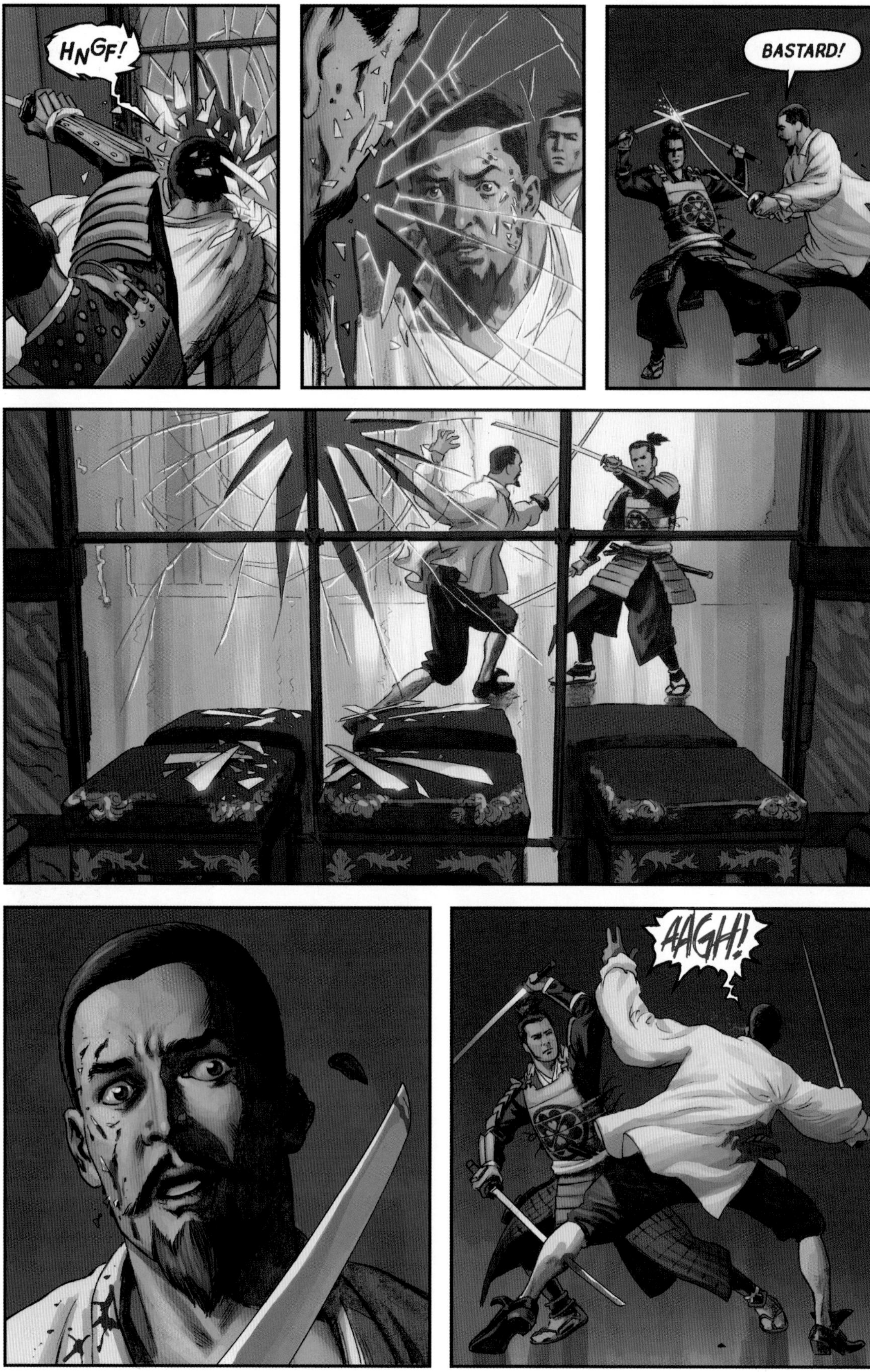
HNGF!
BASTARD!
AAGH!

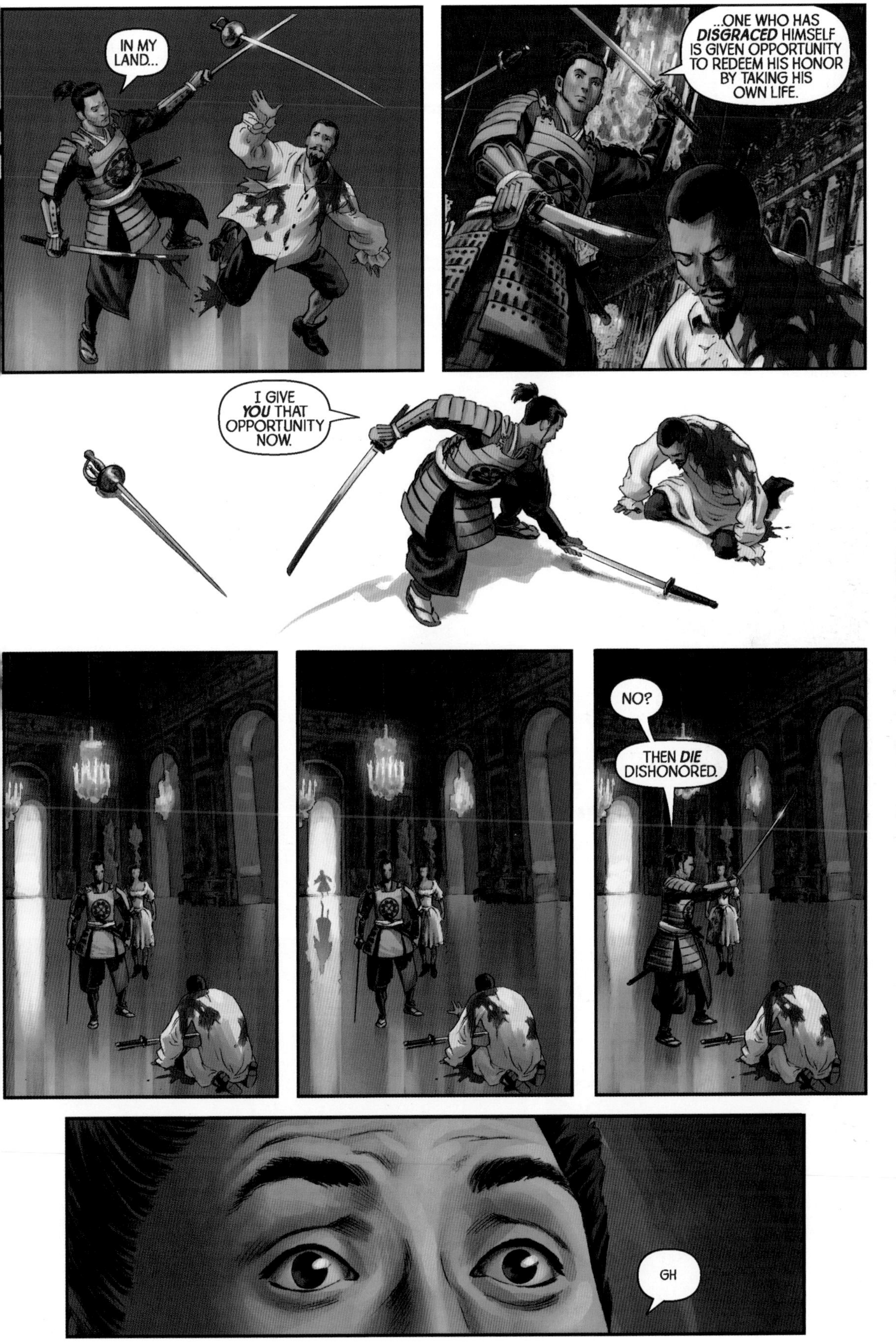
IN MY LAND...
...ONE WHO HAS DISGRACED HIMSELF IS GIVEN OPPORTUNITY TO REDEEM HIS HONOR BY TAKING HIS OWN LIFE.
I GIVE YOU THAT OPPORTUNITY NOW.
NO?
THEN DIE DISHONORED.
GH

WHY COULDN'T YOU SIMPLY DO AS YOU WERE TOLD?

WHY?

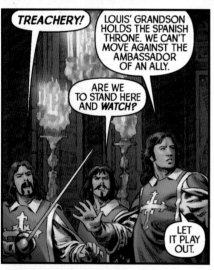

TREACHERY!

LOUIS' GRANDSON HOLDS THE SPANISH THRONE. WE CAN'T MOVE AGAINST THE AMBASSADOR OF AN ALLY.

ARE WE TO STAND HERE AND WATCH?

LET IT PLAY OUT.

YOU SEE? I DID IT FOR YOU, DON MIGUEL, SO THAT WE...

NH

SHE'S MINE...

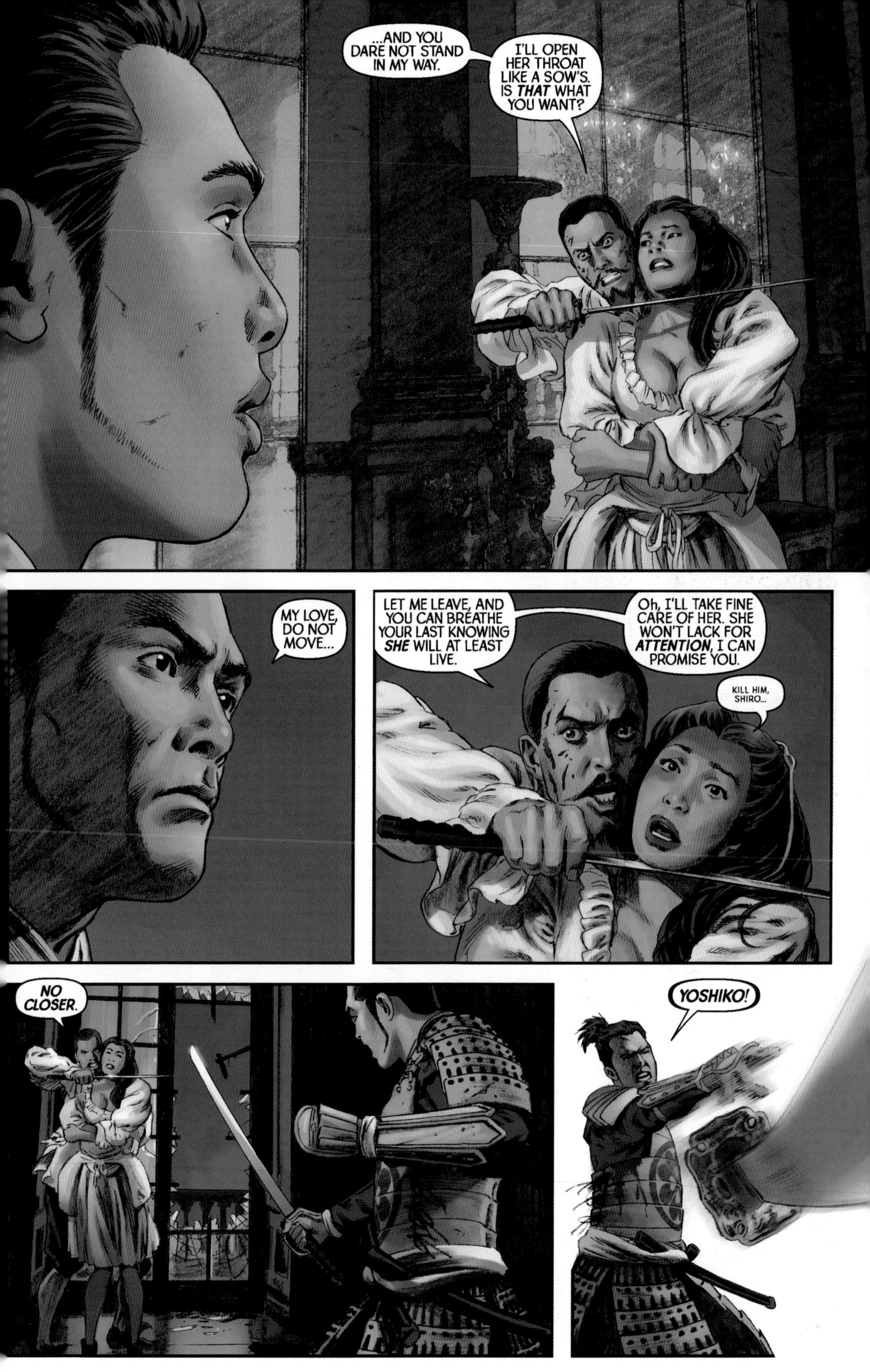
...AND YOU DARE NOT STAND IN MY WAY.
I'LL OPEN HER THROAT LIKE A SOW'S. IS *THAT* WHAT YOU WANT?
MY LOVE, DO NOT MOVE...
LET ME LEAVE, AND YOU CAN BREATHE YOUR LAST KNOWING *SHE* WILL AT LEAST LIVE.
Oh, I'LL TAKE FINE CARE OF HER. SHE WON'T LACK FOR *ATTENTION*, I CAN PROMISE YOU.
KILL HIM, SHIRO...
NO CLOSER.
YOSHIKO!

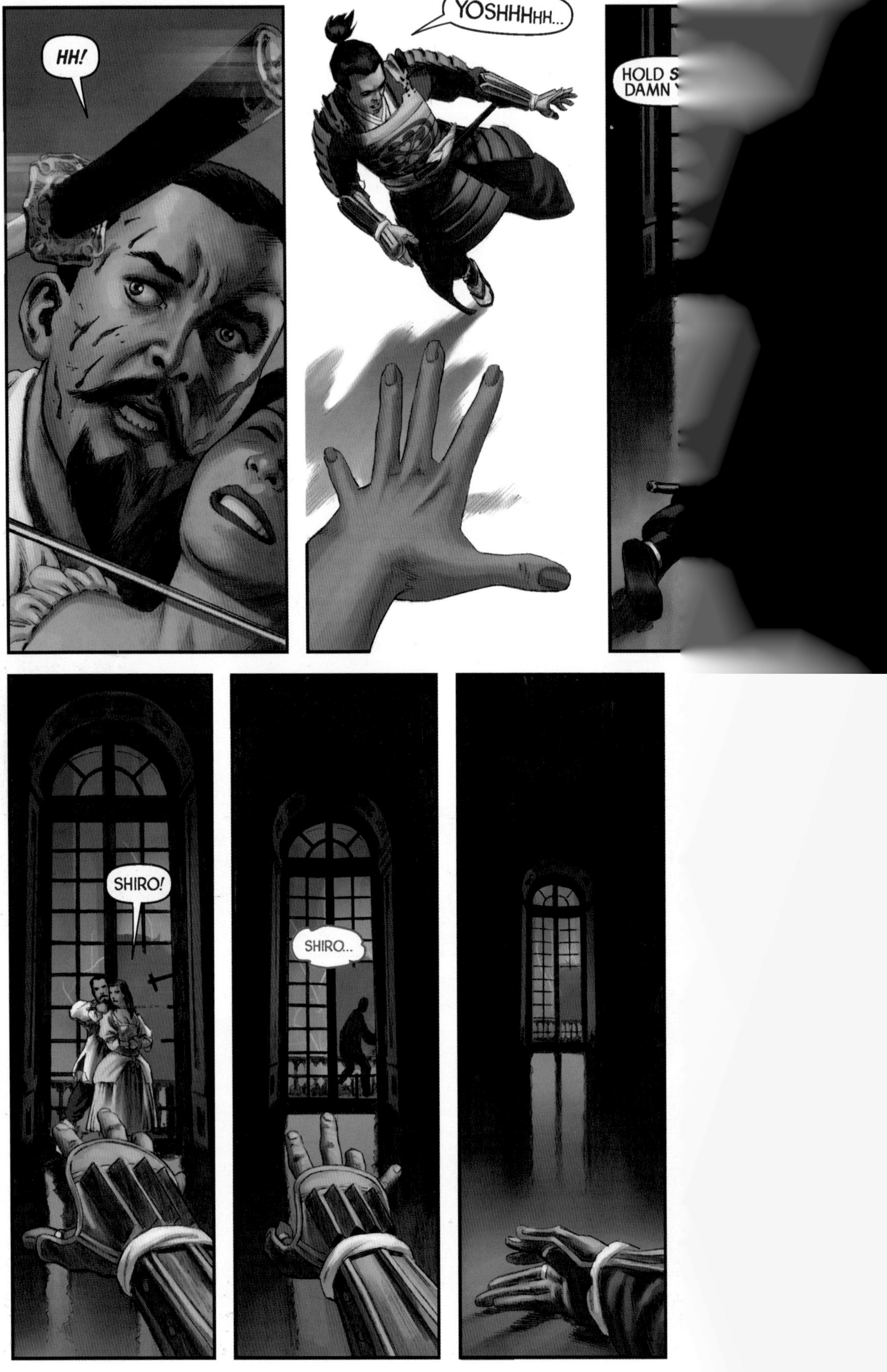
HH!
YOSHHHHH...
HOLD S DAMN
SHIRO!
SHIRO...

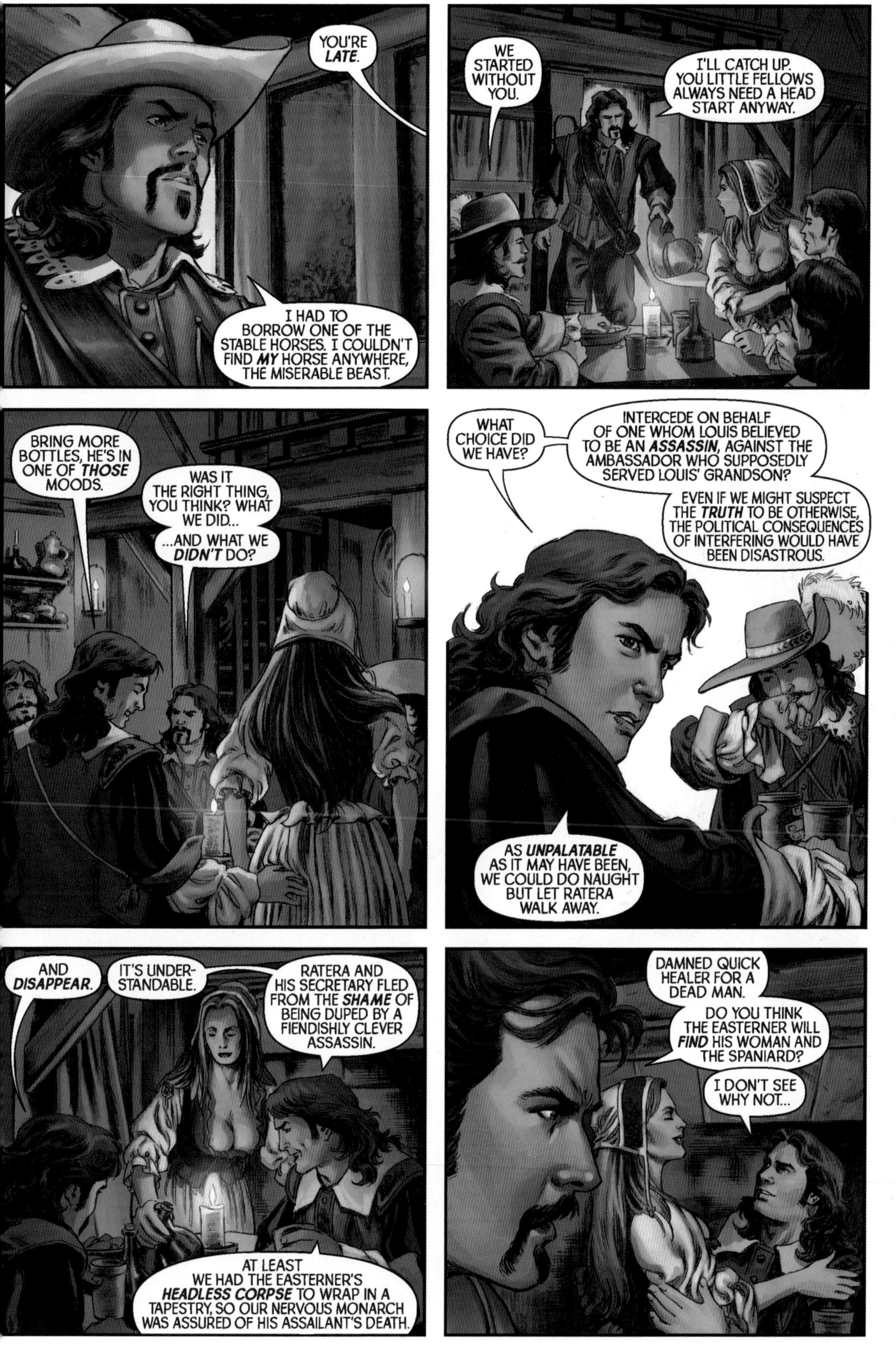
YOU'RE *LATE*.
I HAD TO BORROW ONE OF THE STABLE HORSES. I COULDN'T FIND *MY* HORSE ANYWHERE, THE MISERABLE BEAST.
WE STARTED WITHOUT YOU.
I'LL CATCH UP. YOU LITTLE FELLOWS ALWAYS NEED A HEAD START ANYWAY.
BRING MORE BOTTLES, HE'S IN ONE OF *THOSE* MOODS.
WAS IT THE RIGHT THING, YOU THINK? WHAT WE DID...
...AND WHAT WE *DIDN'T* DO?
WHAT CHOICE DID WE HAVE?
INTERCEDE ON BEHALF OF ONE WHOM LOUIS BELIEVED TO BE AN *ASSASSIN*, AGAINST THE AMBASSADOR WHO SUPPOSEDLY SERVED LOUIS' GRANDSON?
EVEN IF WE MIGHT SUSPECT THE *TRUTH* TO BE OTHERWISE, THE POLITICAL CONSEQUENCES OF INTERFERING WOULD HAVE BEEN DISASTROUS.
AS *UNPALATABLE* AS IT MAY HAVE BEEN, WE COULD DO NAUGHT BUT LET RATERA WALK AWAY.
AND *DISAPPEAR*.
IT'S UNDER-STANDABLE.
RATERA AND HIS SECRETARY FLED FROM THE *SHAME* OF BEING DUPED BY A FIENDISHLY CLEVER ASSASSIN.
AT LEAST WE HAD THE EASTERNER'S *HEADLESS CORPSE* TO WRAP IN A TAPESTRY, SO OUR NERVOUS MONARCH WAS ASSURED OF HIS ASSAILANT'S DEATH.
DAMNED QUICK HEALER FOR A DEAD MAN.
DO YOU THINK THE EASTERNER WILL *FIND* HIS WOMAN AND THE SPANIARD?
I DON'T SEE WHY NOT...

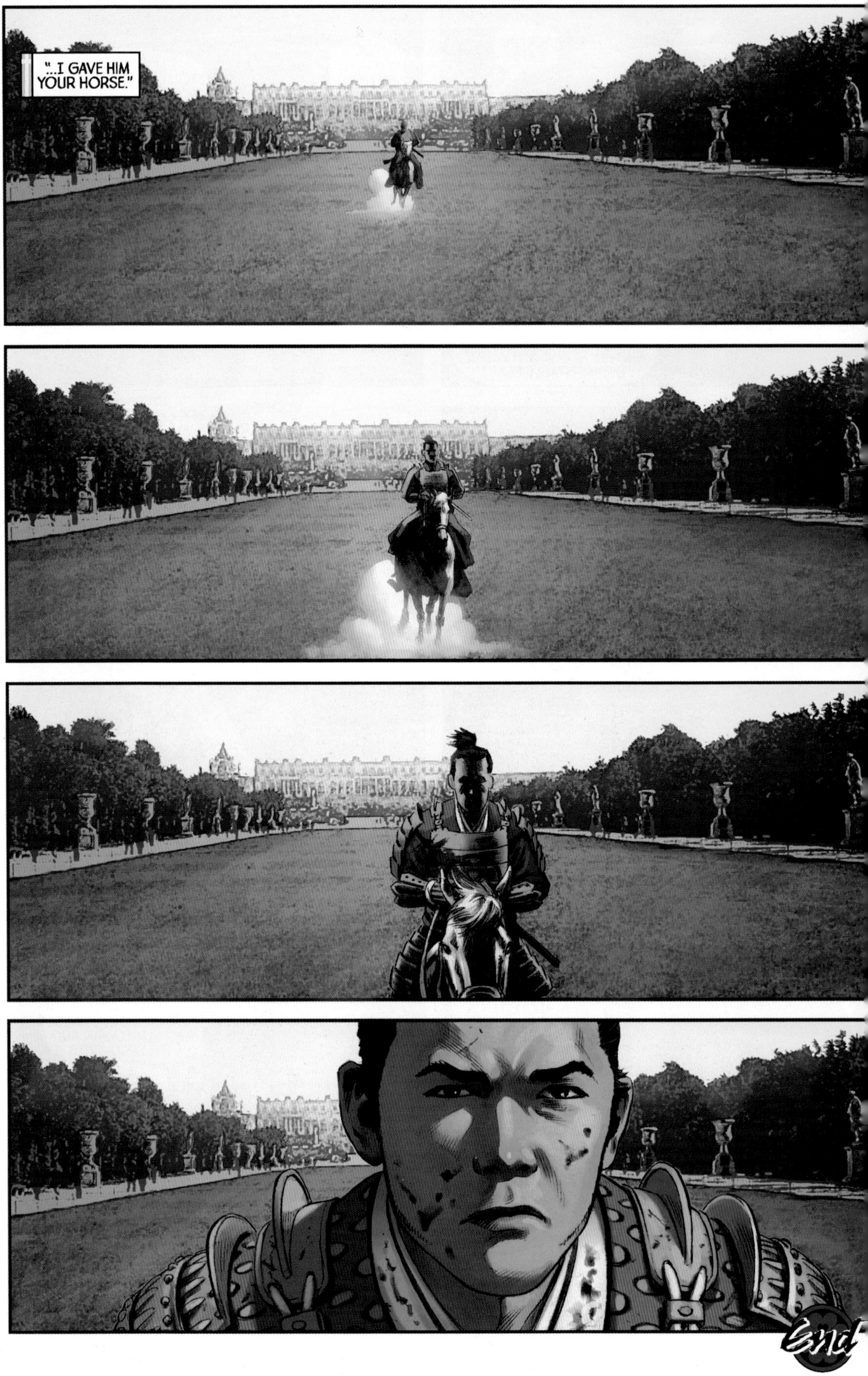
"...I GAVE HIM YOUR HORSE."
End

Samurai: Heaven & Earth
Sketchbook
Art by Luke Ross

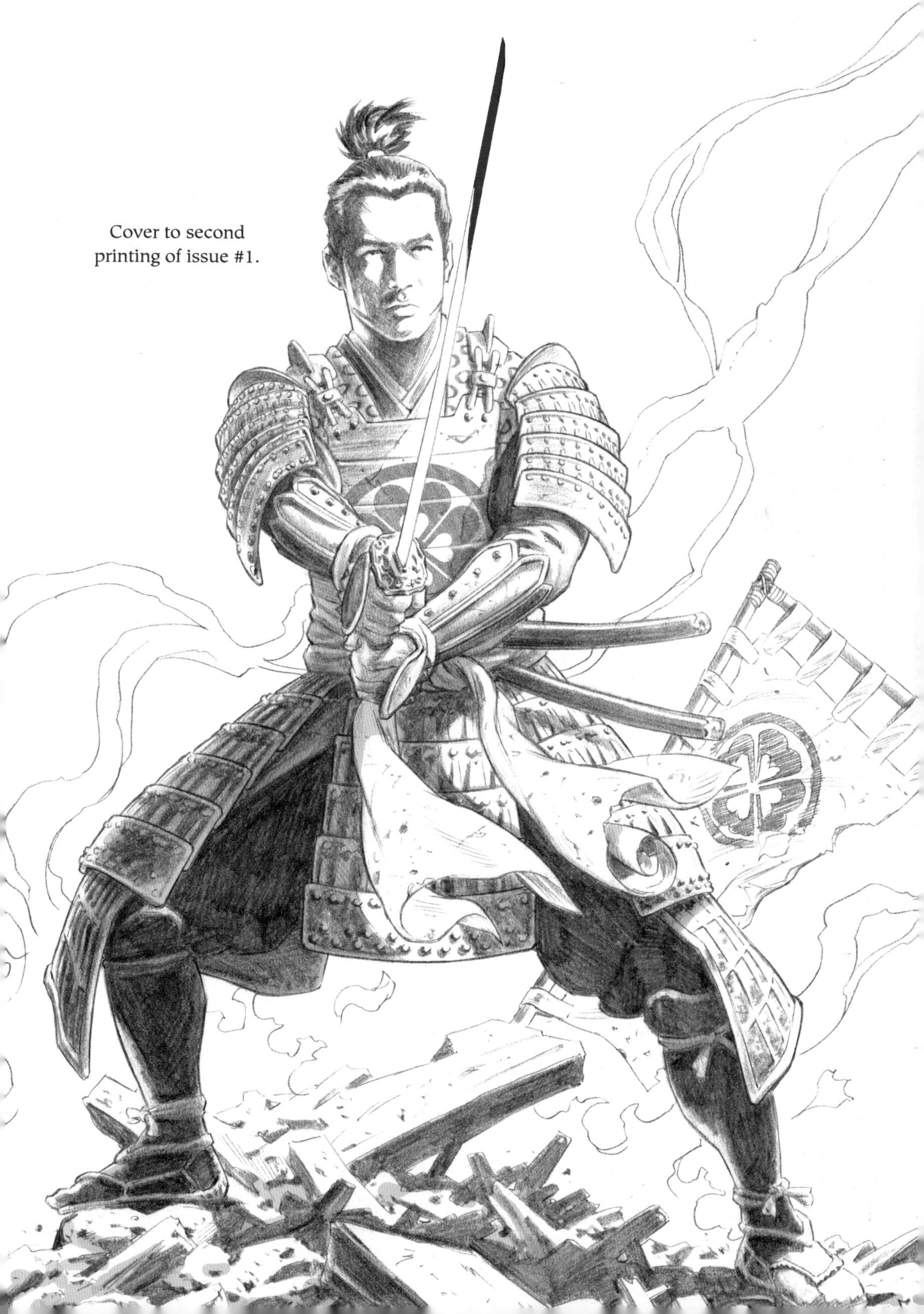

Cover to second printing of issue #1.

Initial character designs. Yoshiko's name was originally to have been Aiko.

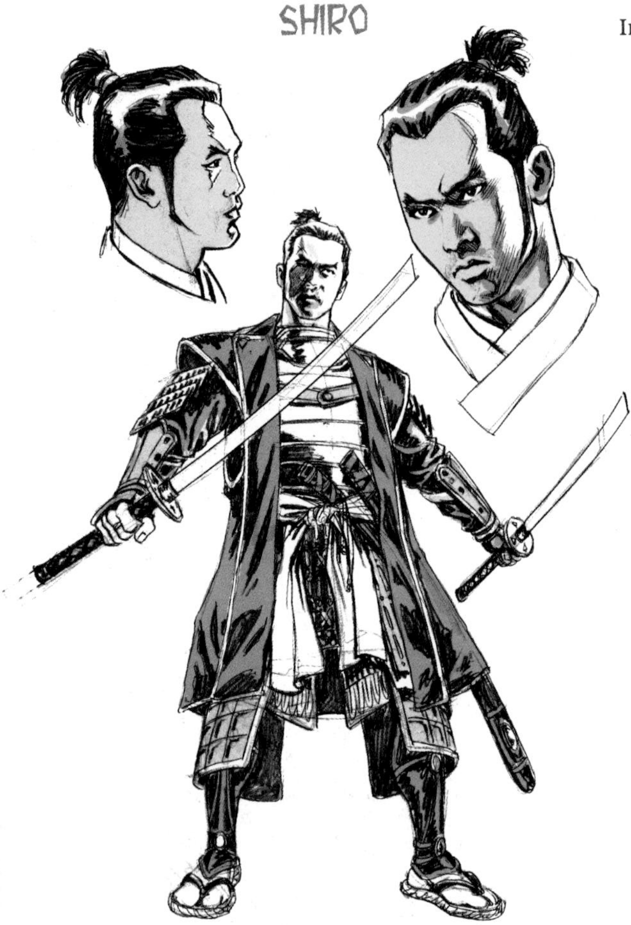
SHIRO

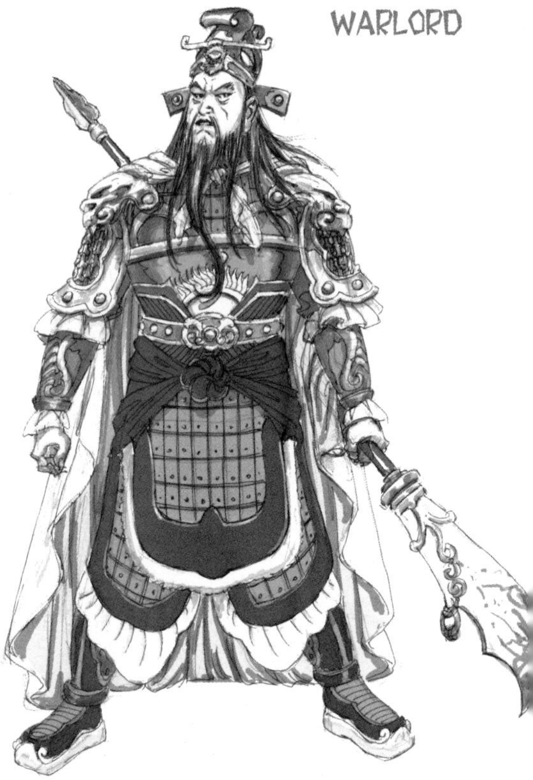
WARLORD

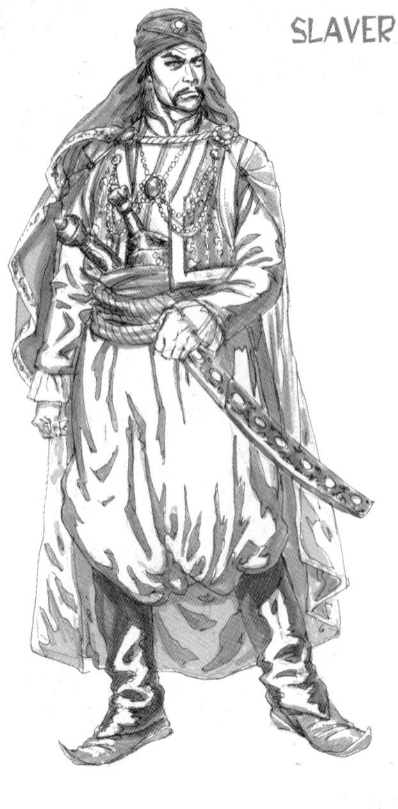
SLAVER

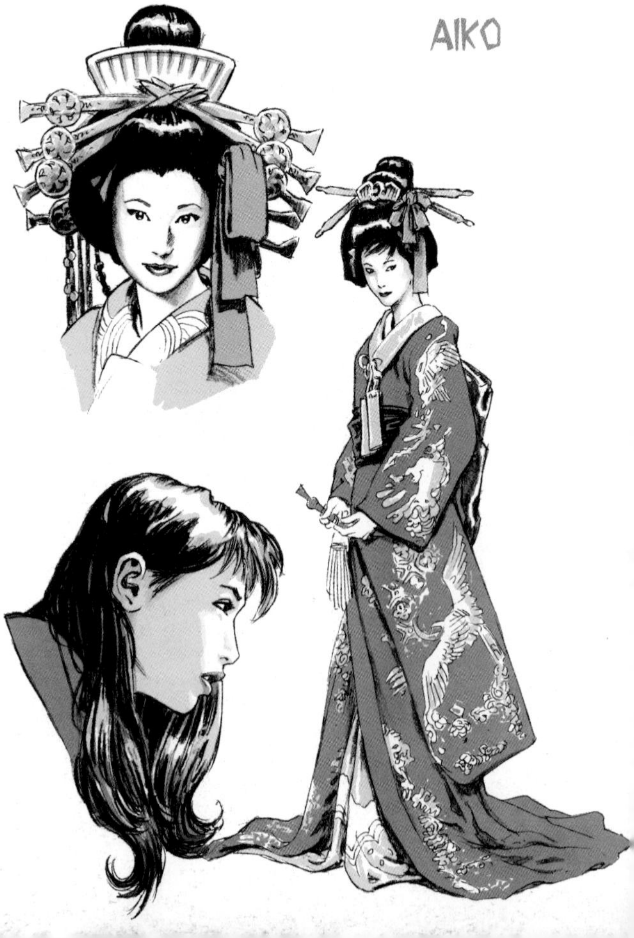
AIKO

Shiro studies and layouts

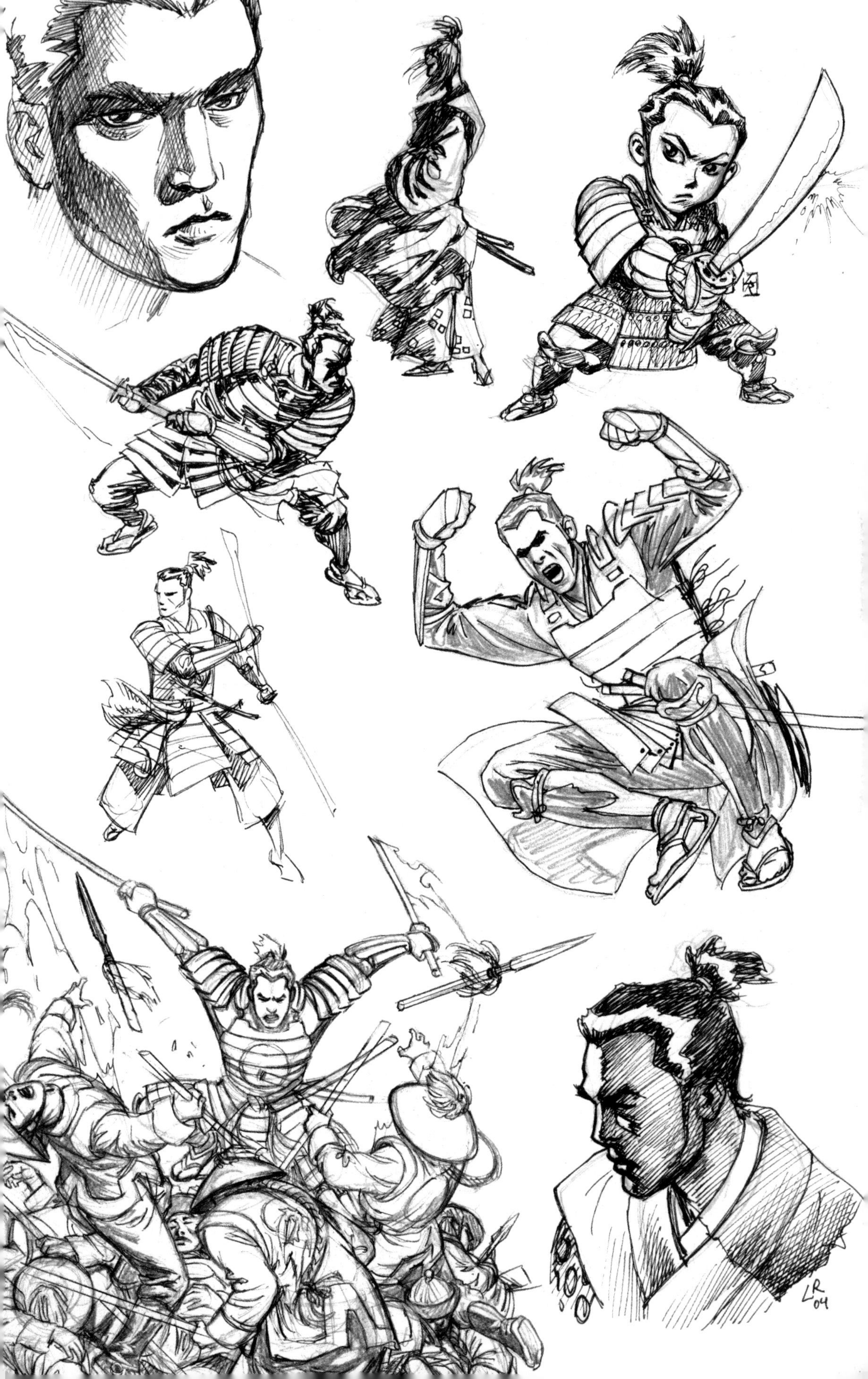

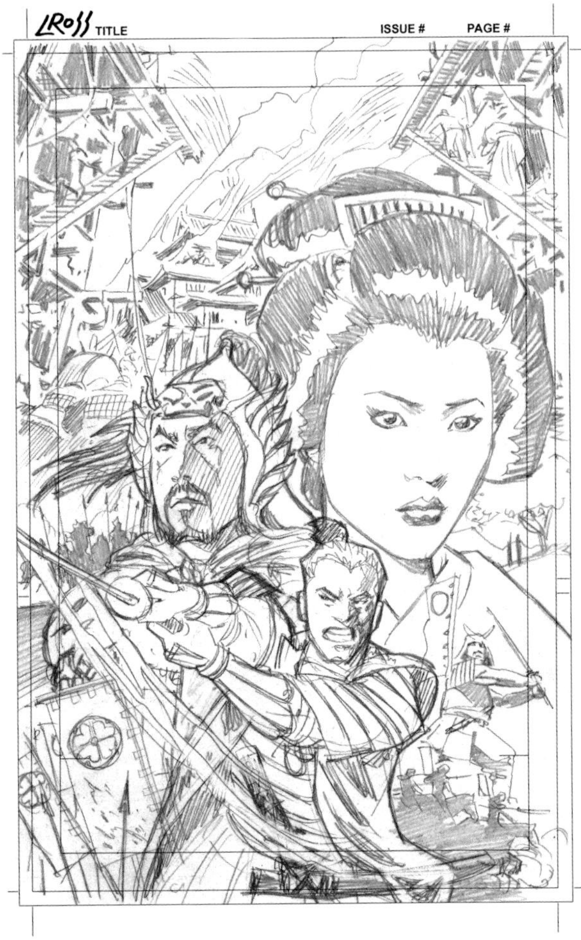
LRoss TITLE
ISSUE #
PAGE #

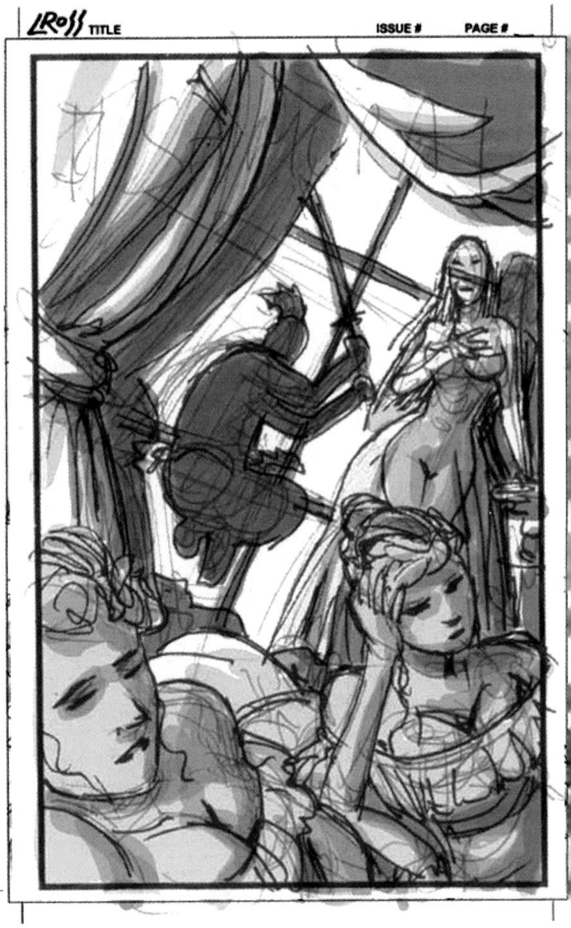
LRoss TITLE
ISSUE #
PAGE #

Unused cover designs

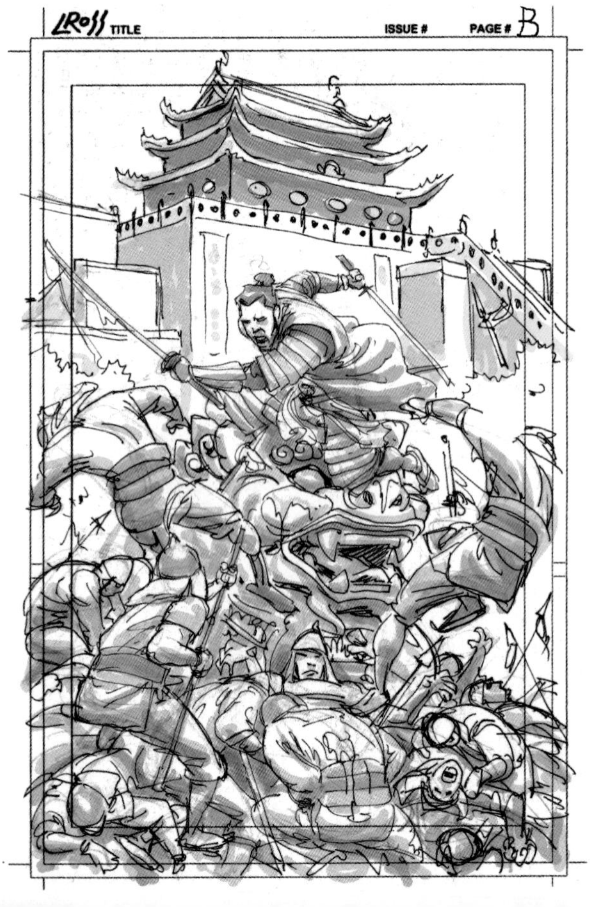
LRoss TITLE
ISSUE #
PAGE # B

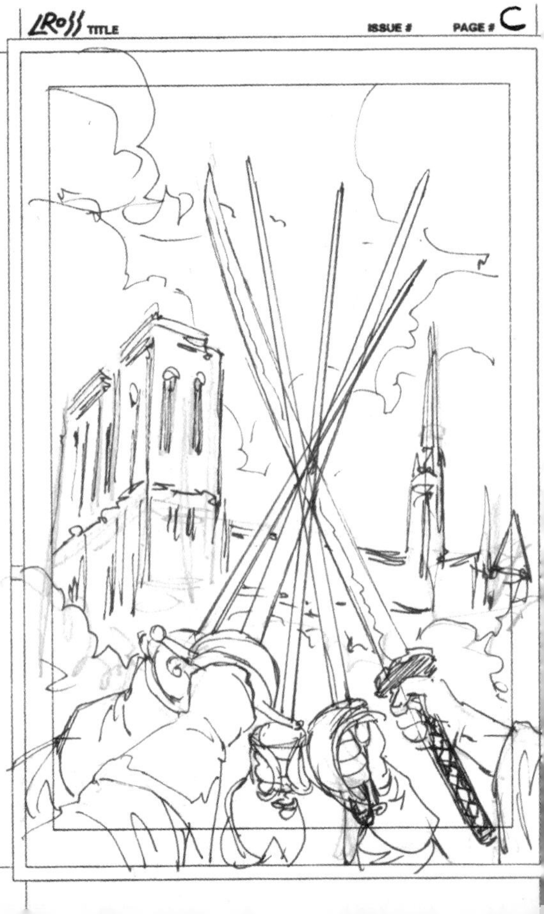
LRoss TITLE
ISSUE #
PAGE # C

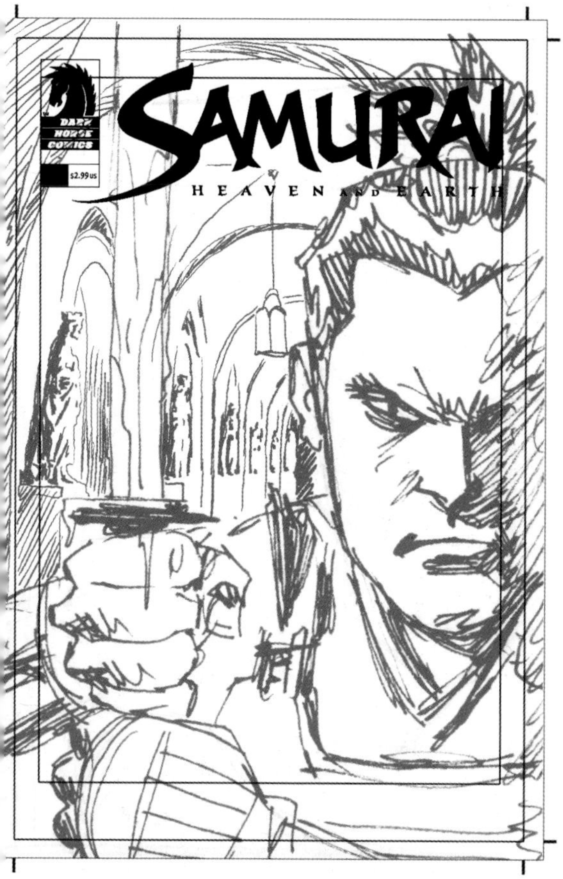
DARK HORSE COMICS
$2.99 US
SAMURAI
HEAVEN AND EARTH

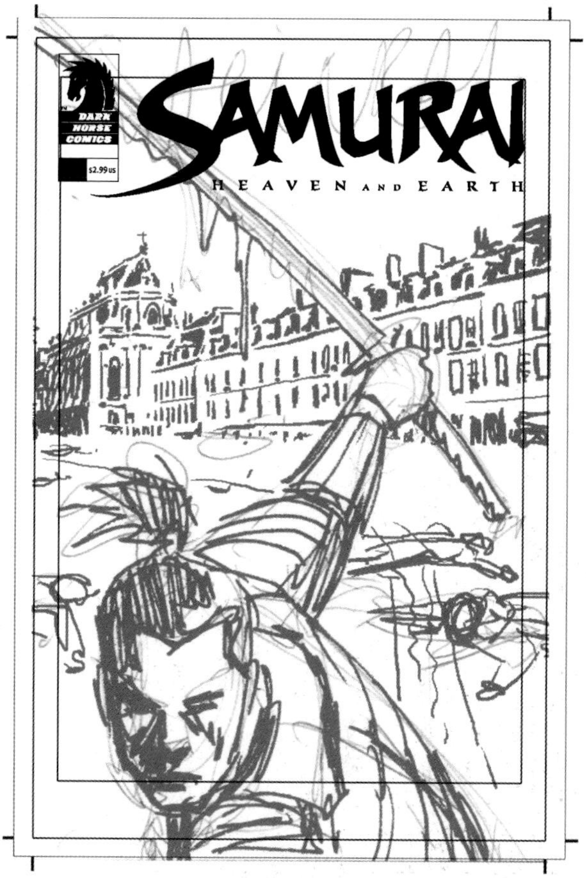
DARK HORSE COMICS
$2.99 US
SAMURAI
HEAVEN AND EARTH

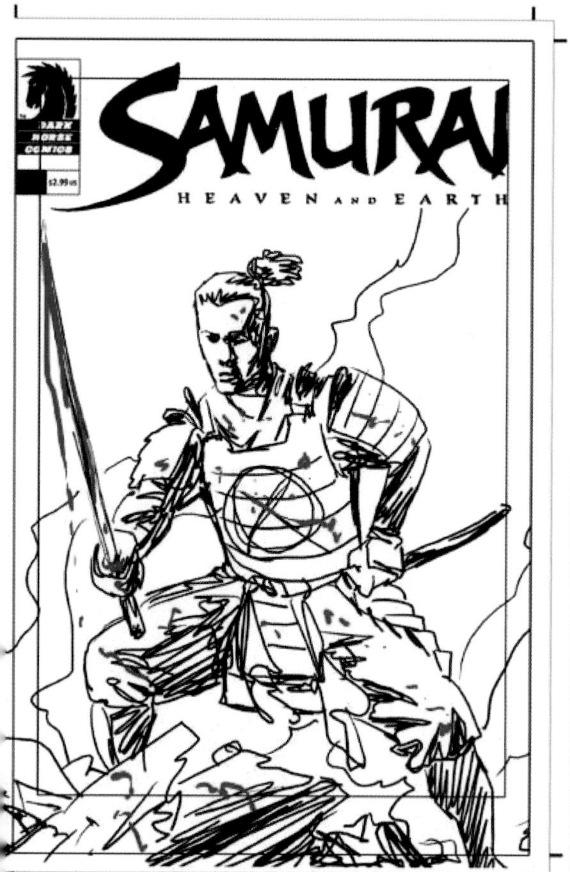
DARK HORSE COMICS
$2.99 US
SAMURAI
HEAVEN AND EARTH

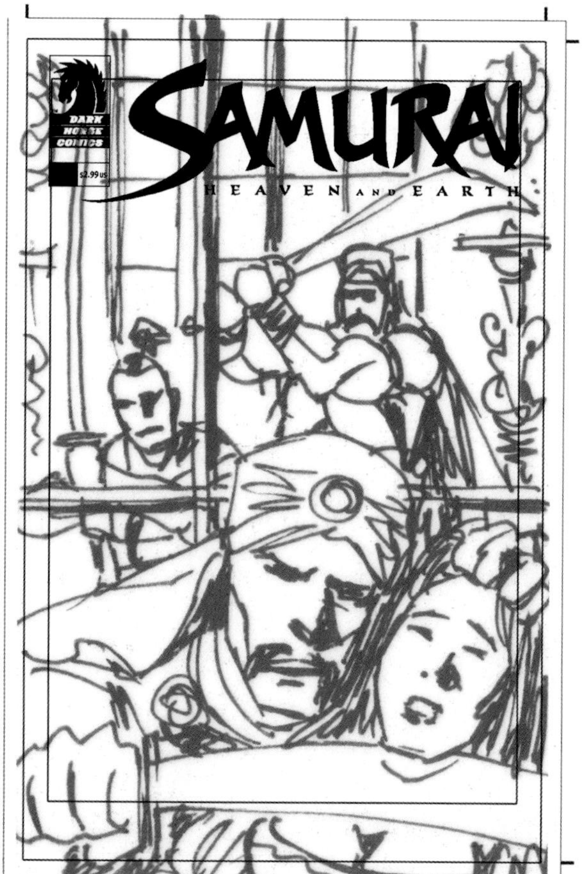
DARK HORSE COMICS
$2.99 US
SAMURAI
HEAVEN AND EARTH

SAMURAI™
HEAVEN AND EARTH

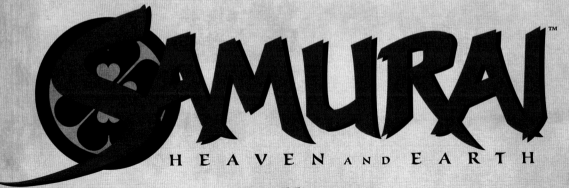

Gallery

Featuring artwork by

Keu Cha

Jim Starlin

Jack Lawrence

Dub and Pierre-Andre Dery

Adriana Melo
with Jason Keith

Lee Moder
with Jason Keith

Kevin Ferrara

Fabio Laguna
with Jason Keith

Rafael Kayanan

and Cully Hamner
with Jason Keith

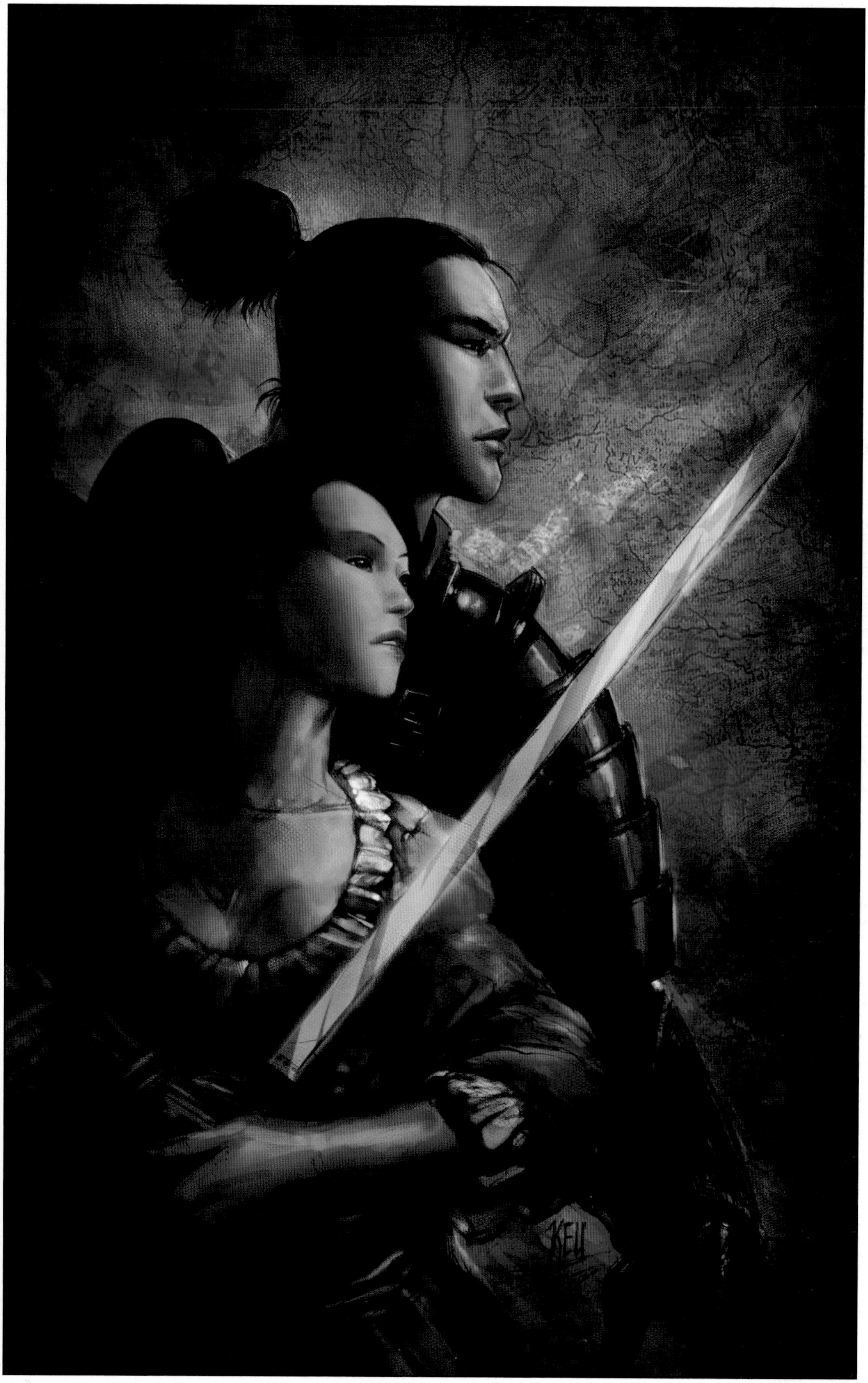
KEU

KEU CHA

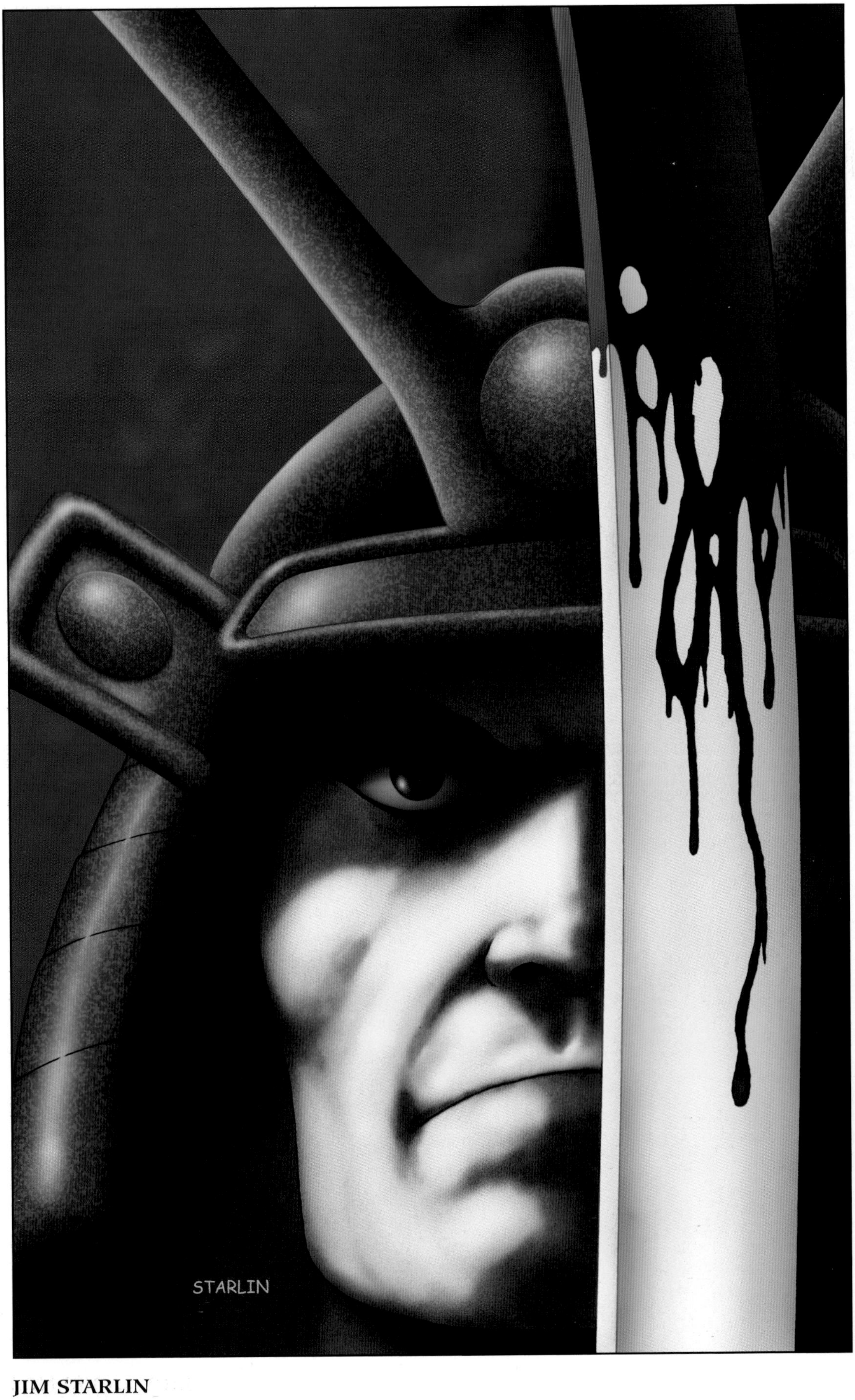
STARLIN

JIM STARLIN

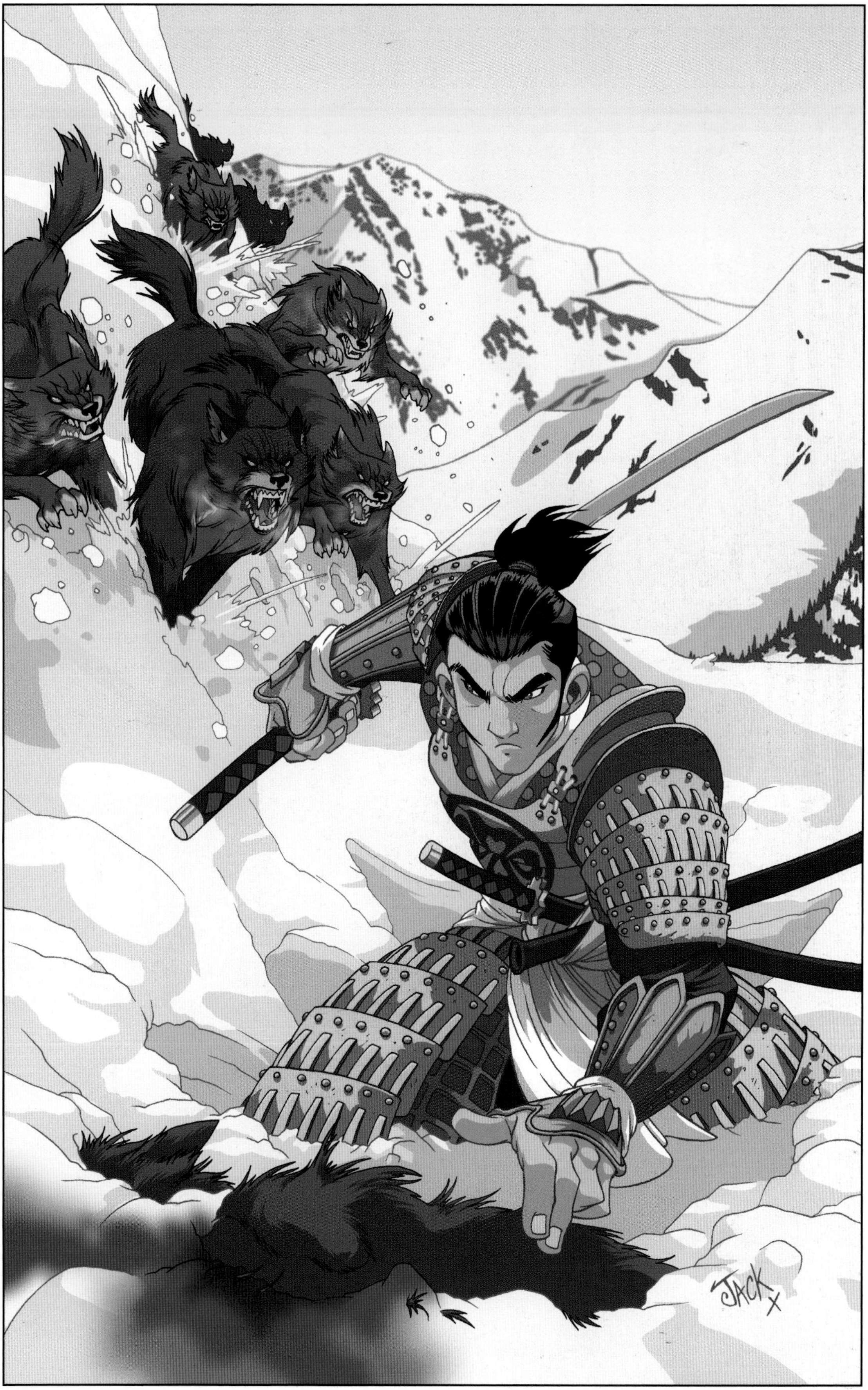
JACK

JACK LAWRENCE

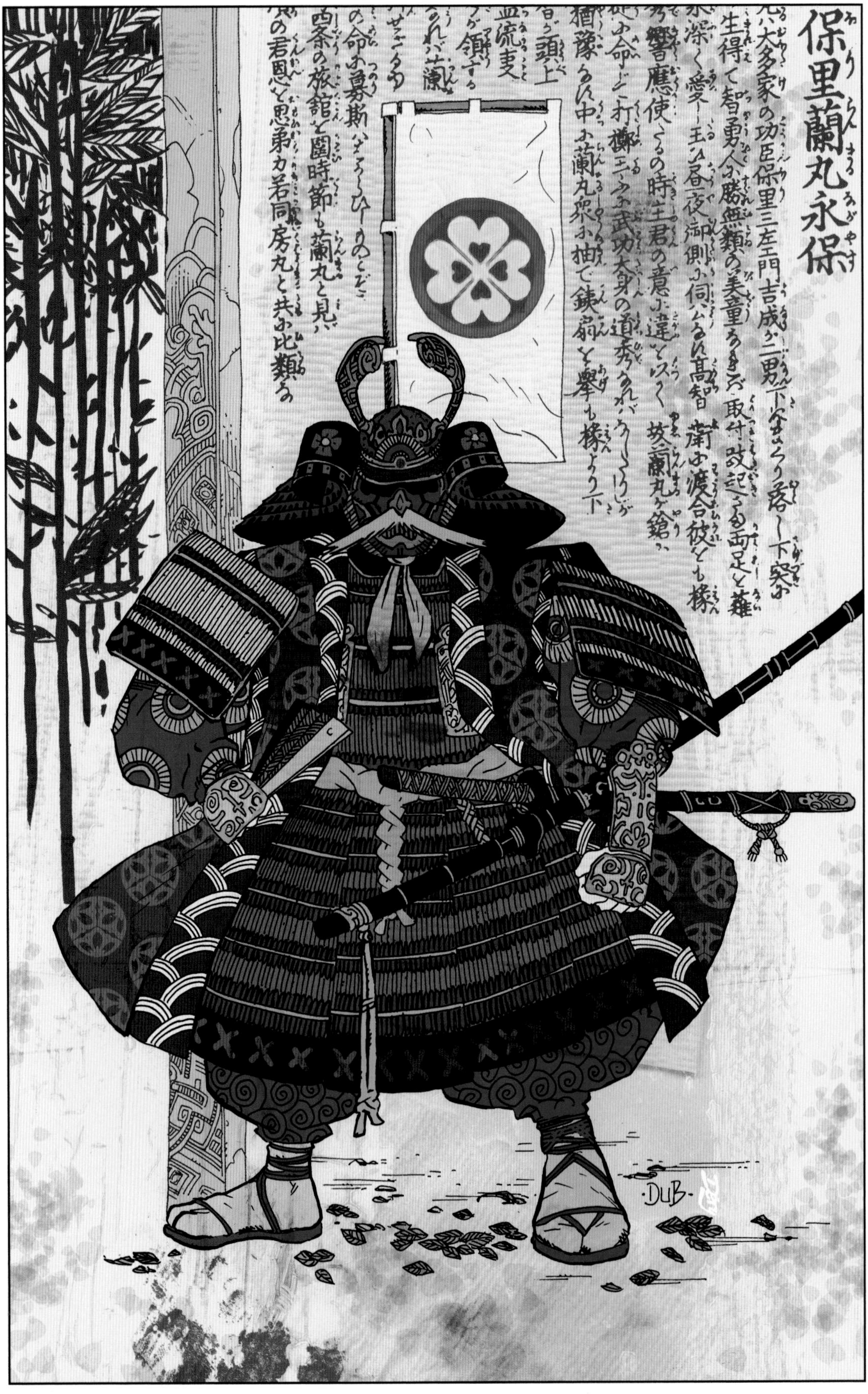
保里蘭丸永保
DUB

DUB and PIERRE-ANDRE DERY

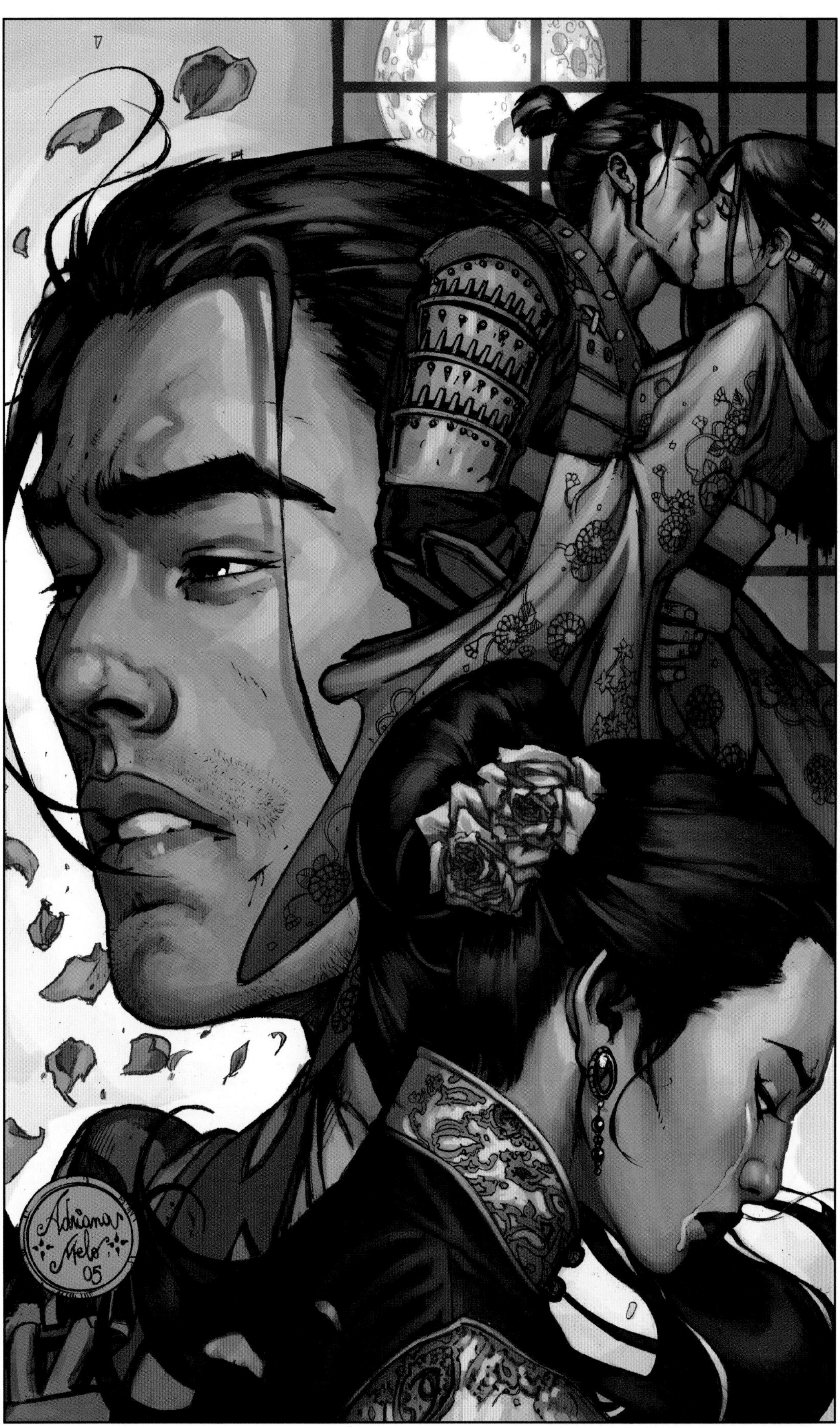
Adriana Melo 05

ADRIANA MELO with JASON KEITH

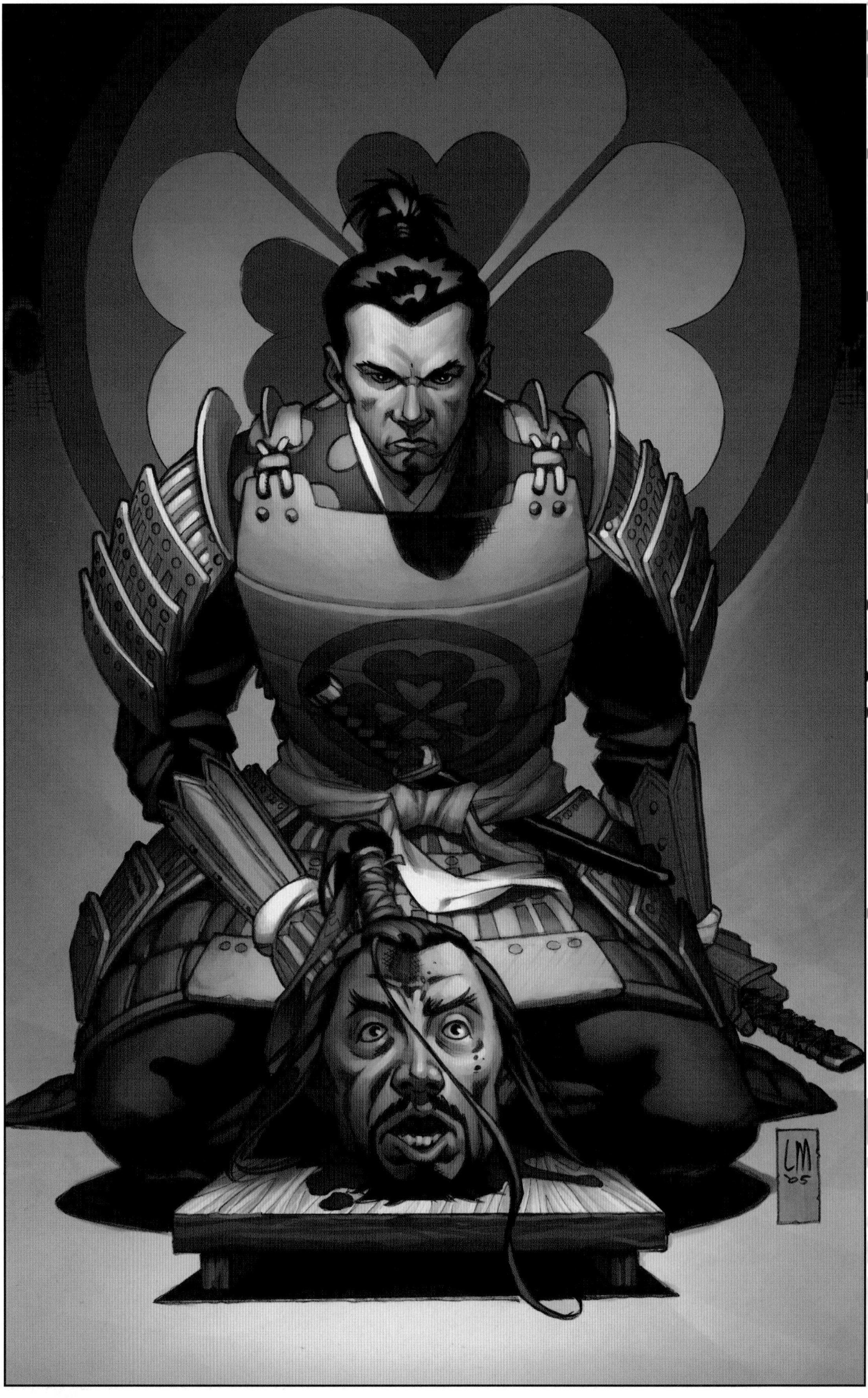
LM
'05

LEE MODER with JASON KEITH

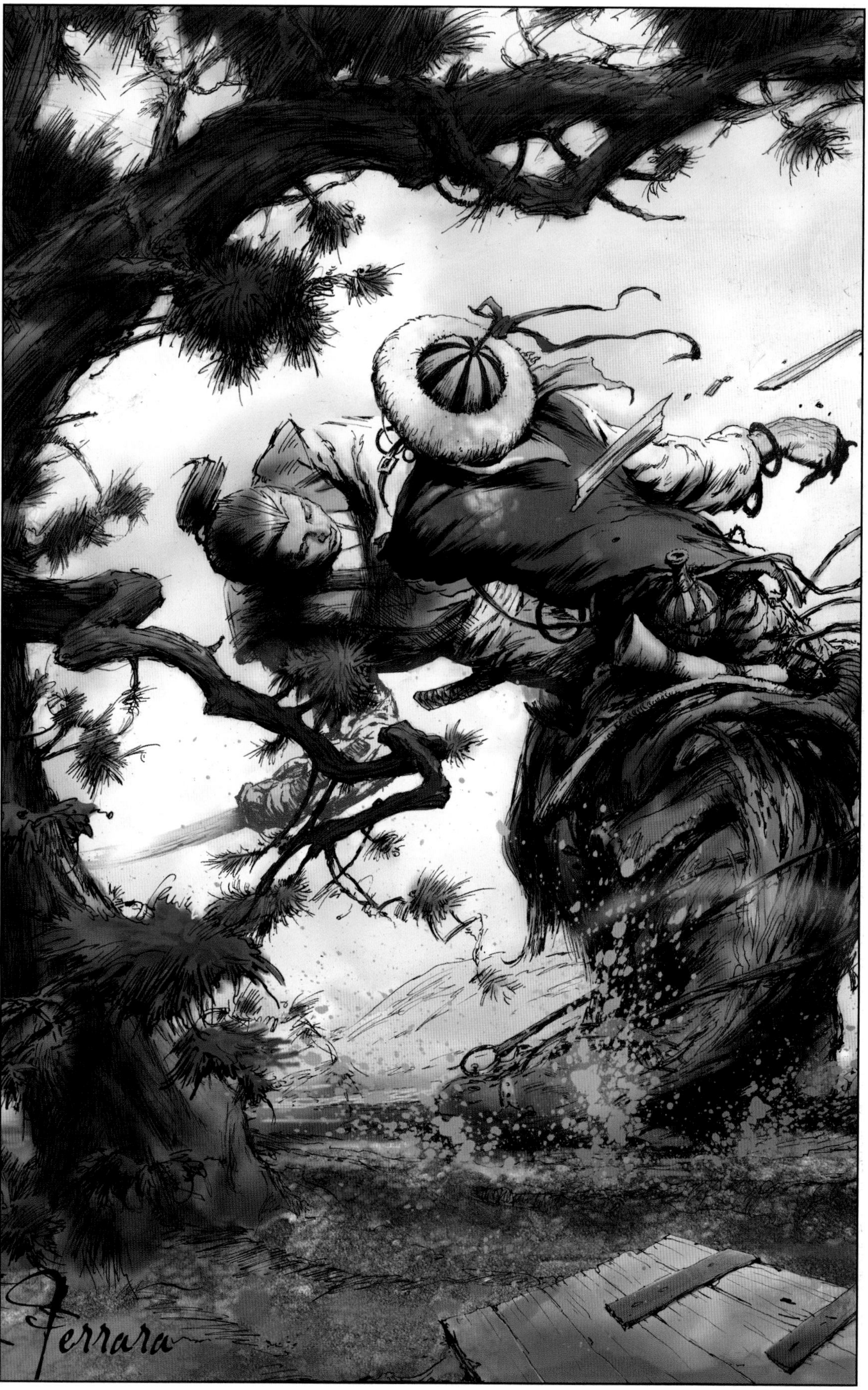
Ferrara

KEVIN FERRARA

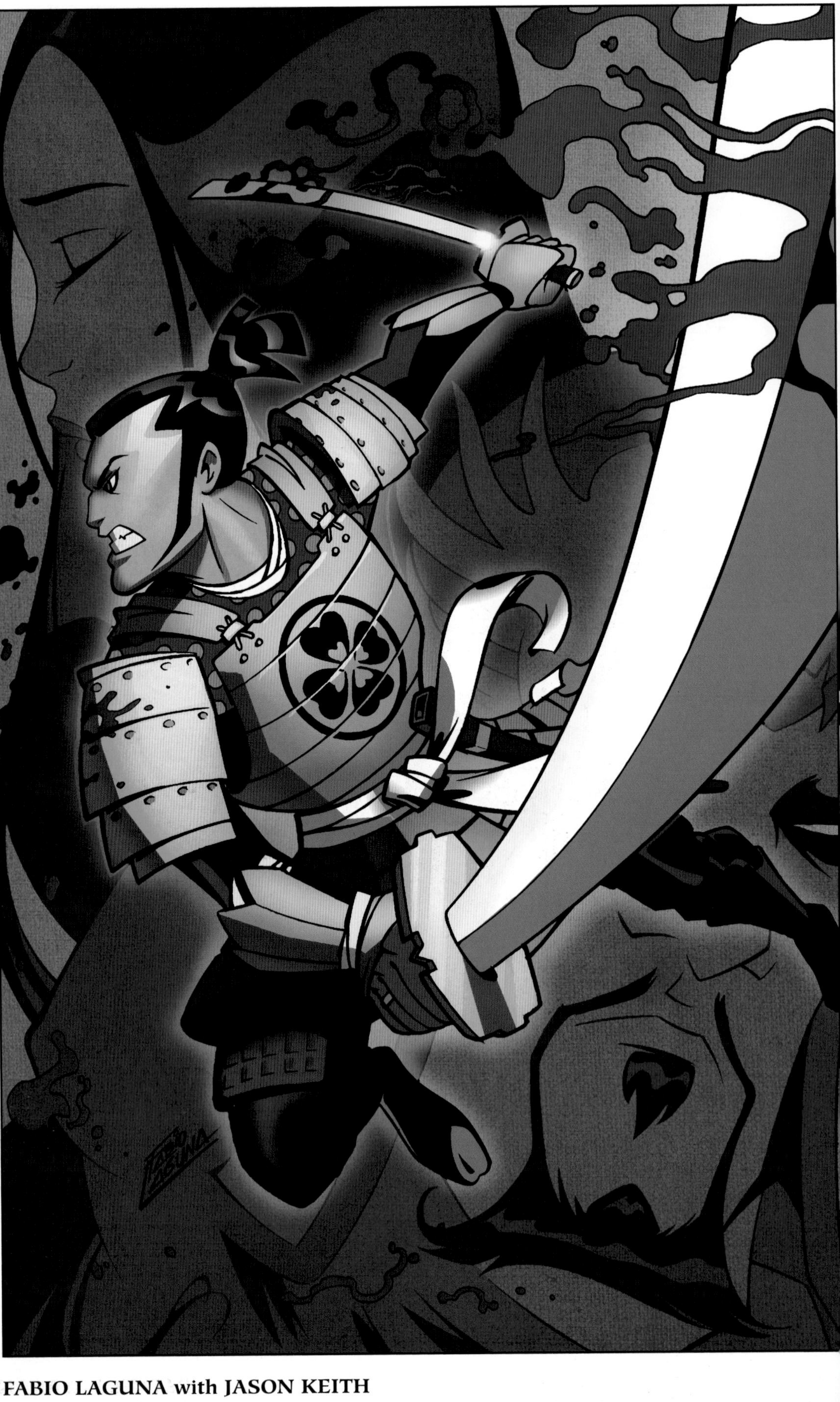

FABIO LAGUNA with JASON KEITH

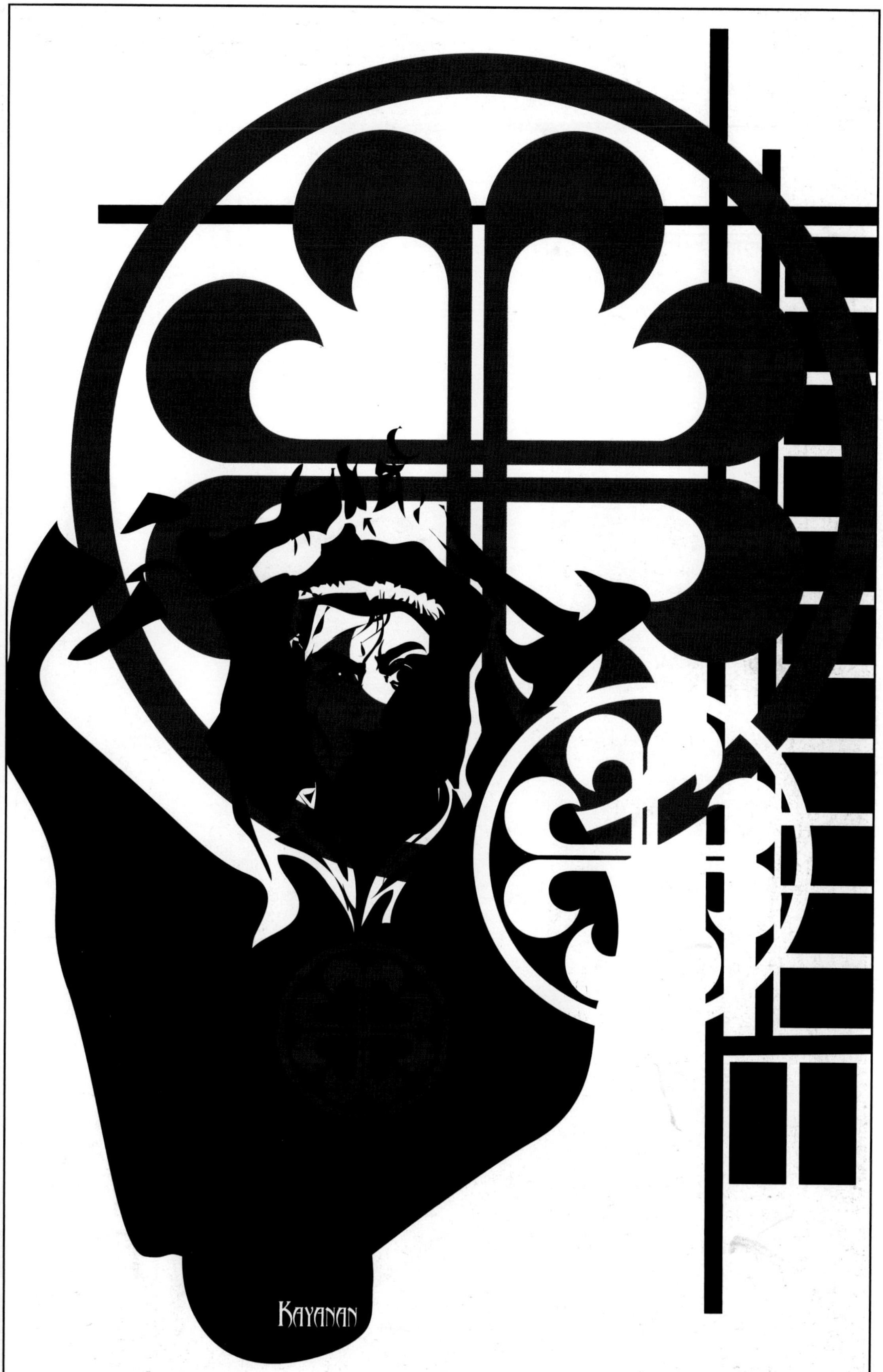
KAYANAN

RAFAEL KAYANAN

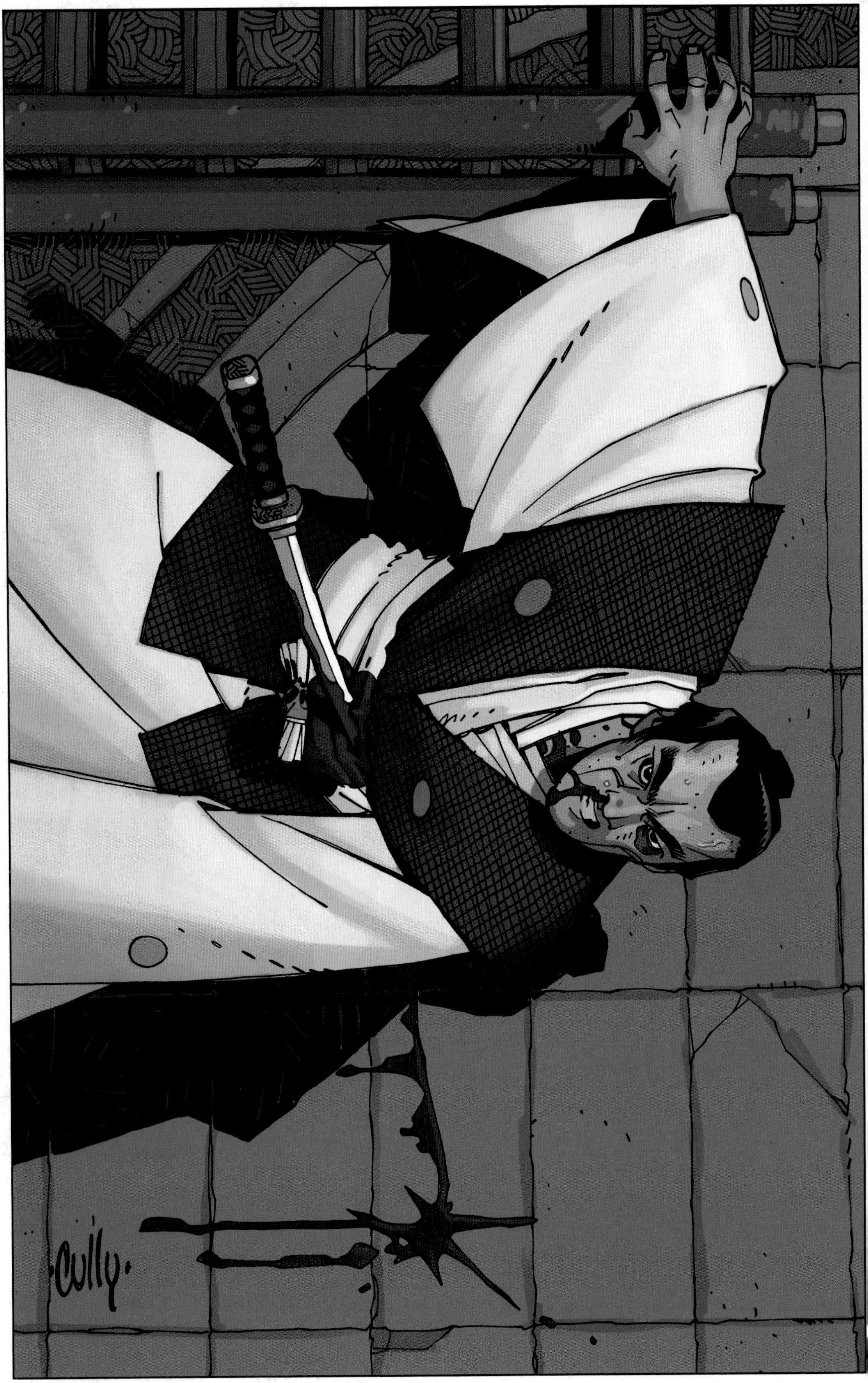

CULLY HAMNER with JASON KEITH